Simulation Analysis of Urban Economy

Tomoru Hiramatsu

Kwansei Gakuin University Press

Simulation Analysis of Urban Economy

Tomoru Hiramatsu

Kwansei Gakuin University Press

Simulation Analysis of Urban Economy

Copyright @ 2012 by Tomoru Hiramatsu

All right reserved.

No part of this book may be reproduced in any form or by any means without permission in writing from the author.

Kwansei Gakuin University Press
1-1-155 Uegahara, Nishinomiya, Hyogo, 662-0891, Japan
ISBN: 978-4-86283-122-4

Table of Contents

Preface i

Chapter 1. Introduction 1

Chapter 2. The Structure of the RELU-TRAN2 Model 11
   2.1 RELU and RELU2 12
      2.1.1 Consumers/Potential Workers 15
      2.1.2 Producers 27
      2.1.3 Landlords 30
      2.1.4 Developers 31
      2.1.5 General equilibrium of RELU2 36
   2.2 TRAN2 42
      2.2.1 Mode Choice 44
      2.2.2 Traffic Flow 45
      2.2.3 Time, Monetary Cost and Generalized Cost 47
      2.2.4 Route Choice Probability 51
      2.2.5 One-Way Trip 52
      2.2.6 Mode Choice Probabilities 53
      2.2.7 Composite Trip Travel Times and Costs 54
   2.3 Post-equilibrium calculations 54
      2.3.1 Basic calculations 54
      2.3.2 The calculations related to gasoline consumption 56
   Appendix 2. Measurement of Welfare 60
      A2.1 Measurement of Social Welfare 61
      A2.2 Alternative Measurement of Welfare 61
         A2.2.1 Welfare Measurement by Consumer's Surplus (CS) 62
         A2.2.2 Measurement by Compensative Variation (CV) 62
      A2.3 Revenue Utilization 64

A2.3.1 Revenue Distribution 65
A2.3.2 Invest in Public Good 65

Chapter 3. The Short- and Long-Run Price Elasticity and Fuel Economy Elasticity of Gasoline Consumption and CO_2 Emission: Calibration and Application of the RELU-TRAN2 Model 67

3.1 Introduction 67
3.2 Data 72
    3.2.1 Target data from RTAMS 73
    3.2.2 Target data from the Illinois Travel Statistics. 75
3.3 Calibration 77
    3.3.1 Key Elasticities of the Mode 77
    3.3.2 Comparison with the literature 85
3.4 The price elasticity of gasoline consumption 90
    3.4.1 Impact of fuel price increase 92
    3.4.2 Review of Small and Van Dender (2007a, b) 100
3.5 Fuel economy elasticity of gasoline consumption 103

Chapter 4. Comparative Statics 109

4.1 Impact on variables related to transportation 110
    4.1.1 Impact of fuel economy 111
    4.1.2 Impact of the Monetary Cost of Public Transportation (MCPT) 112
    4.1.3 Impact of road capacity 112
    4.1.4 Impact of the fuel price 113
    4.1.5 Impact of the construction elasticity 113
4.2 Impact on urban sprawl (jobs and residential population distribution, and vacant land) 114
    4.2.1 Impact of Fuel Economy 116
    4.2.2 Impact of the Monetary Cost of Public Transportation (MCPT) Change 117
    4.2.3 Impact of Road Capacity 118
    4.2.4 Impact of the Fuel Price 119
    4.2.5 Impact of the construction elasticity 120
Appendix 4. The impact on stock, rent and value 122

Chapter 5. The Effects of Anti-Congestion Policies on Urban Sprawl, Gasoline Consumption and CO_2 Emissions 125

5.1 Introduction 125

5.2 Anti-congestion policies: congestion tolls, the cordon toll, the fuel tax and the parking tax 129

    5.2.1 The quasi-Pigouvian congestion toll 130

    5.2.2 The fuel tax 132

    5.2.3 The cordon toll 133

    5.2.4 The parking fee 134

5.3 Technical calculation of the anti-congestion policy instruments 134

    5.3.1 The fuel tax 134

    5.3.2 Quasi-Pigouvian tolls 135

    5.3.3 The cordon toll 139

    5.3.4 The parking fee 139

5.4 Differences and similarities among the policies according to their expected impacts 140

    5.4.1 The CBD cordon toll versus the CBD parking fee 140

    5.4.2 The quasi-Pigouvian toll and the fuel tax 142

    5.4.3 The quasi-Pigouvian toll on all roads versus the limited quasi-Pigouvian toll 143

    5.4.4 The difference between the limited quasi-Pigouvian toll and the cordon Toll 144

    5.4.5 Mode changes 144

5.5 Simulating the impacts of the policies 144

    5.5.1 Revenue-neutral comparison of the policies 145

    5.5.2 Population and job shifts caused by the anti-congestion policies 154

    5.5.3 Impact of the policies on fuel consumption and related variables 169

Appendix 5. Short-run simulations (without Stock Conversion) 173

Chapter 6. The Urban Growth Boundary and Congestion Toll as the Energy Saving Policy and Its Side Effects 175

6.1 Introduction 175

6.2 Impacts of the UGB 180

    6.2.1 Impacts of the UGB on jobs and residential location 180

    6.2.2 Impact of the UGB on fuel consumption and related variables 186

    6.2.3. Impact of the UGB on the consumer's utility 187

  6.3 Local growth controls 194

  6.4 Comparing the effects of quasi-Pigouvian congestion tolling and the UGB 199

Chapter 7. Conclusion 207

  7.1 Extension and Conclusion 207

  7.2 Summary 214

Reference 221

Simulation Analysis of Urban Economy

Tomoru Hiramatsu

The State University of New York at Buffalo

Preface

Urban or regional area as an economic zone is the spatial range where the people perform normal daily activities. Thus, it is important to study the urban or regional economy. There are varieties of economic activities in urban area and so as markets. It is difficult and not necessary to include all markets in one model. Hence, extracting some key markets of interests to analyze the relations among markets would be the thought providing to research. Although such complex model might not provide the solution explicitly, it is possible to obtain the fruitful insight by utilizing the numerical solution. Furthermore, the progress in computer takes the potential of numerical simulation analysis to higher level.

RELU-TRAN (Regional Economy and Land Use and Transportation) is a numerically solvable general equilibrium model (Anas and Liu, 2007), which treats in a unified manner the regional economy, urban land use and urban personal transportation sectors. In this book, the model is extended by adding the consumer-workers' choice of private vehicle type according to the vehicle's fuel economy, by treating congestion on local roads as well as on major roads, and by introducing car fuel consumption as a function of congested vehicle speed. By making the extensions, the model becomes more suitable to analyze the fuel consumption and CO_2 emission consequences of urban development. The model is calibrated and simulated for the Chicago metropolitan area.

By adjusting the model to the longer time span gradually, the short- and long-run price elasticities of fuel consumption are examined. As the time span becomes longer, fuel consumption becomes more elastic with respect to gasoline price. When technological improvements in car fuel economy over comparable time spans are introduced exogenously, the elasticity of fuel with respect to gasoline price becomes similar to that estimated in the econometric literature. Comparative statics exercises show that, if travel by auto becomes relatively more attractive in terms of travel time or travel cost than travel by public transit, then the Chicago Metropolitan Statistical Area (MSA) becomes more sprawled in total developed land area, whereas if public transit travel becomes relatively more attractive, then the Chicago MSA becomes more centralized.

To mitigate fuel consumption and CO_2 emissions, relative effectiveness of quasi-Pigouvian congestion tolls, a fuel tax on gasoline, a cordon toll around the downtown and a downtown parking fee are tested. All of these policies successfully reduce the aggregate fuel consumption and CO_2. The urban growth boundary (UGB) is an alternative policy tested by the model. The UGB directly makes the Chicago MSA more centralized by prohibiting the development into urban use of a part of the vacant land in the suburban areas. The UGB also reduces aggregate fuel and CO_2 emissions, but the impact is much smaller than the quasi-Pigouvian toll. Although Chicago MSA is centralized by both the UGB and the quasi-Pigouvian toll, the auto travel is directly discouraged by quasi-Pigouvian toll and but not by the UGB.

This book adds slight necessary modifications to my Ph.D. dissertation, "The Impact of Anti Congestion Policies on Fuel Consumption, CO_2 Emissions and Urban Sprawl: Application of RELU-TRAN2, a CGE Model." Thus I would like to sincerely thank my dissertation supervisor Professor Alex Anas of SUNY at Buffalo. Without his helpful instructions over the years, the dissertation could not have been completed. I would like to thank my committee members, Professor Peter Morgan and Professor Zhen Liu.

Special thanks to Professor Richard Arnott for the constructive discussion in the project to develop the regional economic analysis of L.A. region which I am currently working for.

I appreciate to Professor Akira Kohsaka (currently in Kwansei Gakuin University) and Professor Minoru Suzuki who are advisers for my graduate study in Osaka University and for my undergraduate study in Kwansei Gakuin Univeristy, respectively. Taking this opportunity, I am thankful to Professor Tetsuo Kubota, Professor Norimichi Matsueda, Professor Junichi Nagamine, Professor Ken-Ichi Shimomura, Professor Musubi Tabuchi, Professor Kikuo Takabayashi, Professor Katsutoshi Wakai, Professor Koji Yamazaki and late Professor Norio Anbo who helped me while I was studying in Kwansei Gakuin University, Osaka University and SUNY at Buffalo.

Since November 2007, I had been supported as a research assistant under Dr. Anas' research award RD-83184101-0 from the United States Environmental Protection Agency's Science to Achieve Results (STAR) program of 2004. The purpose of this grant was to extend the RELU-TRAN model developed under Dr. Anas' previous award (1999-2005) from the National Science Foundation award SES9816816 ("Infrastructure and Metropolitan Development"), in order to make the model capable of addressing the environmental impacts of urban land use and transportation policies.

I thank Kwansei Gakuin University Press. Especially Mr. Naoya Tanaka of KGU Press gave me various supports for the publication of this book. And at last, but not least, I am grateful to my family.

Tomoru Hiramatsu
February 1, 2012
at Buffalo, New York

Chapter 1. Introduction

The emergence of environmentally friendly societies may be one of the most important developments of the 21st century. Global warming is one of the central issues among environmental problems. Many people think that it is now the time to take some serious action on global warming. CO_2 emissions from human and natural sources are the main cause of global warming. Until recently the U.S. was the biggest emitter of CO_2 but it is estimated that in 2006 China passed the U.S. which is now in second place, but still in first place on a per capita basis. The U.S. carbon dioxide emissions in 2000 were 5,844 million tons. The sources of these emissions were 1,178 (20.1%) from residential, 1,012 (17.3%) from commercial, 1,783 (30%) from industrial and 1,873 (32%) from transportation[1].

The transportation sector is the main culprit of CO_2 emissions and this is our foremost interest in this study. In particular most of the emissions from transportation are from urban personal transportation, that is from the use of private motorized vehicles or automobiles. As a whole, the individual consumers are surely an important part of all economic activities while the industry and commercial activities are also of great significance. The consumer's environmentally friendly behavior is an important key to improve the burden on the environment. Governments or NGOs could lead consumers to change their lifestyles for achieving a sustainable society through an awareness campaign. But government also could give the right incentives so that utility maximizing consumers behave in an environmentally friendly way. I study several policies that would mitigate CO_2 emissions together with the fuel consumption of consumers in the urban personal transportation sector. The precautionary remark is that such a policy approach could suppress the economic growth and so the business world

---

[1] Source: U.S. Energy Information Administration. http://www.eia.doe.gov/oiaf/1605/flash/flash.html

could face difficulties. But it is important to study how these policies would affect emissions and fuel use, miles traveled, trip patterns, the price of land, the decentralization of jobs and residences and urban sprawl.

Urban sprawl is believed to be intimately related to fuel consumption and CO_2 emissions from urban personal travel. So, in this book, I will study the relationship between urban sprawl and CO_2 emissions. Since traffic congestion is a major negative externality that affects urban areas, it affects directly and indirectly environmental emissions. On the one hand, congestion because it is not properly priced distorts travel causes too much of it. On the other hand, planners and some economists have claimed that the use of automobiles creates too much urban sprawl. I will observe how anti-congestion policies affect the degree of urban sprawl. Urban sprawl itself destroys a part of the natural environment by turning undeveloped land into developed. In addition, it is believed that a sprawled city would require its residents to use vehicles more heavily. Conversely, it might be expected intuitively that to prevent urban sprawl leads to the reduction of vehicle usage. A little thought shows that this is not always true. If a sprawled urban area contains a lot of subcenters and residents could complete most of their daily activities near these, the vehicle usage could be less than it would be in a very compact and high density city with a single center. In the city with a lot of subcenters congestion would be less serious than in the monocentric city. In the model I observe the intuitive result and a hypothetical urban growth boundary that could be placed around suburban Chicago indeed mitigates the fuel consumption and CO_2 emissions from the personal urban transportation in that MSA.

To most experts it may seem that the two issues should be studied in different models, since normally the urban sprawl problem is studied in a land use model and the fuel consumption issue is studied in a transportation model. Actually, most of researches study those two topics separately, but there is a limited number of researches, not surprisingly economists, that can provide the model that combines the capabilities of a land use model with that of a transportation model.

One such model is RELU-TRAN (Regional Economy, Land Use and

Transportation) model, (Anas and Liu, 2007). It exists at the junction of those two different research streams as a computable general equilibrium (CGE) model that combines these two sectors and their interaction. Although this model has the potential to study urban sprawl and CO_2 emissions, it is unfortunate that although Anas and Liu (2007) provided the model and developed a clever algorithm for it, they did not offer an empirical calibration and a full quantitative assessment of their model. That task has fallen on me.

I extend their model so that the model can analyze better and in more detail the issues that are of interest. I simulate the extended RELU-TRAN model numerically to execute some anti-congestion policies in the Chicago MSA the conditions of the year 2000. I will show the impact of those policies on urban sprawl, vehicle miles traveled, gasoline consumption and CO_2 emissions and other variables. Since this model has both the land use and the transportation sectors, the issues that I am concerned with could be studied simultaneously. Furthermore, the model has the potential capacity to research the energy use and CO_2 emissions originating from consumer or industrial behavior not related to transportation, although to do so it requires further modifications that are not within the scope of this book.

There is a trade off between an analytically solvable model and a numerically solvable model. The analytical model approach is usually based on very strong assumptions that serve to simplify the model excessively. The result is almost always explainable very clearly. Models that are solved numerically can be much more complex especially if they are general equilibrium models. The results are not as easily explained fully because of circular causation. But these models are much more appropriate for policy analysis. In the urban economics literature, for example, the monocentric model assumes that there is only one Central Business District (CBD), that is jobs center, in the center of the city and that this CBD does not occupy any space. Such a simple model can only explain a limited number of things about a real urban area. A numerically solvable model would accept more realistic assumptions such as the polycentric nature of urban areas and many other things assumed in RELU-TRAN, and so such a model can be empirically applied to a real urban area.

In chapter 2, I extend the RELU-TRAN model and then I apply it to the Chicago metropolitan area. The main extension includes the introduction of gasoline consumption by cars, and the choice by the consumer-workers of their vehicle fuel economy. I also incorporate into the model the relationship between fuel consumption and the speed of traffic. Using this model, it is possible to seriously analyze the fuel consumption and CO_2 emission processes from personal urban transportation, since the model includes the most important margins: congestion, road capacity, choice of fuel economy, public transit, and local versus major roads.

In RELU, consumers, producers, landlords and developers all maximize their objectives within a general equilibrium model. Consumer's decisions include locations where reside and work, housing type and vehicle fuel economy. It is assumed that the cars that are gasoline inefficient and therefore more expensive to drive have larger bodies and are more comfortable and safer to drive. The most important given information for consumers' decisions is the expected travel time and cost of driving. Those travel time and cost are calculated in TRAN and passed from TRAN to RELU. Given this information, the number of work and non-work trips between and within the zones of the MSA are also included among the consumer's decisions. This number of trips, or more precisely the matrix of trips, is the variable passed to TRAN from RELU. In the model, producers, developers and landlords also maximize their objectives. All their activities equilibrate in the general equilibrium.

In TRAN, travelers (they are consumers in RELU), counting the travel time and cost, will choose the mode of each trip that is whether by transit or by car, and if they decide to travel by auto, they then choose which route to take. Hence the number of cars on each road is decided. If there are too many cars, it will cause congestion. Congestion will increase the travel time and decrease the driving speed. Congested speed results not only in time delay but also in higher fuel cost. Thus I find the travel time and cost between and within zones of the urban area. The expected travel time and cost over the modes are passed to RELU.

In the following chapters, the model is numerically solved. In chapter 3, the data and the model's calibration are explained. Some of the elasticities are calculated and explained how they are close to the econometric estimates obtained by other researches and if are not close, then why are different from the estimates of other researches. Then by simulating different parts of the model, I calculate the price elasticity of fuel for various short- and long-run horizons. As the time horizon becomes longer, the drivers' route choices, the drivers' mode choices, consumer's non-work trips, then the consumer's residence-job-housing-vehicle type choices, and their labor market participation choices are adjusted one by one, the final state being the full general equilibrium. It is found that the price elasticity of fuel is not as elastic compared to other estimates in the literature, such as those of Small and Van Dender (2007a,b). If I adjust the vehicle inefficiency by assuming that exogenous technological progress is occurring, the price elasticity becomes closer to that in the literature. This implies that technological progress is an important factor for mitigating fuel consumption and CO_2 emissions. The elasticity of fuel consumption with respect to vehicle fuel economy is also tested in a similar way. The fuel consumption and the CO_2 emissions are reduced more in the short-run than in the long-run. The reason for this is that there is a rebound effect, that is when the technological progress and the travel cost decrease, the consumers drive more. Since in the long-run consumers can adjust more by increasing their travel miles, the fuel consumption and CO_2 emissions increase.

In chapter 4, comparative statics exercises are performed to see if the model is behaving reasonably. The variables that are changed in these comparative statics exercises are the fuel price, the vehicle inefficiency, the travel cost by public transport, the road capacity and the construction elasticity. The convenience of vehicle travel is an important suburbanization force. When the travel cost by auto becomes relatively cheaper, miles traveled increase and roads become more congested. Thus fuel consumption and CO_2 emissions increase. The accessibility to public transport is an important centralization force. When the travel cost of public transportation becomes relatively cheap, the locations near the center become more popular, because they are easy to access from other zones by public transit. When the construction becomes more elastic, more construction occurs especially in the suburban zones where there is plenty of vacant land. This causes suburbanization. I find the intuitive result that the centralization reduces the fuel consumption and the CO_2 emissions. But it is also mentioned that the suburbanization could also mitigate the fuel consumption and the CO_2 emissions if there are lots of jobs accessible to suburban residents.

In chapter 5, the quasi-Pigouvian toll, the fuel tax, the cordon toll and the parking fee are tested as possible anti-congestion policies. The quasi-Pigouvian toll is designed to remove the externality due to the time delay and the externality fuel consumption. The fuel externality part of the quasi-Pigouvian toll is necessary because the congestion makes the driving speed slower and the slow driving speed is fuel inefficient. On the other hand, if the driving speed is too fast, it is also fuel inefficient. In such a case, by making the road more congested, the fuel consumption can become efficient. This part of the quasi-Pigouvian toll would be negative and it means that it is a subsidy for the drivers. In the simulation, cordon tolls are charged on the link roads that enter the CBD and parking fees are charged only on the drivers whose destination is the CBD. The drivers of the through traffic could be viewed as free riders of the parking fee since the parking fee would reduce the congestion but through traffic does not pay the cost. If I watch closely the job and residence location choices and mode choices, the consumers' behavior becomes clear. As the congestion pricing becomes higher, the consumers who travel by auto decrease and those who travel by the other modes increase. Fuel consumption and CO_2 emissions are smoothly reduced as congestion toll increases. In the comparative statics, an increase in the cost of travel by auto acted as a centralization force causing population to concentrate more in the center of the area, that is the city of Chicago. But in the case of the cordon toll, although the cordon toll increases the travel cost by auto, the MSA is suburbanized when the toll is low. This is because the cordon toll is a fixed charge for all cars crossing the cordon and thus increases the travel cost by auto for those who are located near the CBD by a higher percentage, and thus have lower distance related auto costs.

The parking fee is also a fixed charge that does not vary with distance traveled. But the effect of the parking fee is weaker than that of the cordon toll because fewer people who reside outside the CBD pay the parking. Under the parking fee, the jobs in the CBD decrease but residents in the CBD increase. Residents can move into the CBD but if they work outside the CBD they do not pay the parking fee. Therefore, those residing in the CBD increase.

The quasi-Pigouvian toll charged only on the major roads and the revenue neutral gasoline tax have opposite impacts on jobs location, although the residents are centralized under both policies. Under the quasi-Pigouvian toll, the jobs are suburbanized and residents are centralized because the commuters who reside and work in the same zone are not tolled because they use local roads which are not tolled. Thus, jobs can move to a suburban zone and employ local residents from the same zone. Under the gasoline tax, all commuters by auto are taxed whether they use major roads or local roads. Because the gasoline tax reduces car travel and congestion, while increasing the monetary cost of travel, it impacts high and low income consumers differently. High income consumers have a high value of time and a higher demand for land, so they are attracted by the lowered travel time and become decentralized to suburban areas. Lower income consumers have a low value of time and care more about the monetary transport cost so they respond to the gas tax by switching to transit. In order to be able to switch to transit they locate more in the central city where transit is more available. The reductions of aggregate fuel consumption under the quasi-Pigouvian toll charged only on major roads and under the revenue neutral gasoline tax are 7% and 12.3%, respectively.

When all major and minor roads are tolled by the quasi-Pigouvian toll, both jobs and residents are centralized. The MSA is centralized more under the fuel tax than under the quasi-Pigouvian toll. The quasi-Pigouvian toll is higher where there is more congestion and lower where there is less congestion. Consider, for example, a commuter who resides in the suburbs but works in the CBD. Such a commuter pays more in congestion tolls than another who resides closer to the CBD and also works in the CBD. Under the gas tax, the cost of gasoline increases by the tax rate and those traveling longer distances pay a larger amount of gas tax than those traveling a shorter distance. The income effect of the gas tax on suburban residents who work in the center is larger than the income effect on similar residents who reside closer to their central jobs. Therefore, while both taxes cause population to centralize, there is more centralization under the gasoline tax, because under the gasoline tax the effect of remaining in the suburbs is more onerous than under the congestion toll. The impact of two policies on the aggregate fuel consumption and CO_2 emissions are similar, and both policies reduce aggregate fuel by 17.1% and 18%, respectively.

In chapter 6, the urban growth boundary (UGB) is examined as an alternative anti-congestion policy. The UGB is designed so that the some of the vacant land in the suburban zones is excluded from development. Although the UGB protects open space, I do not model the importance of open space since it does not enter the consumer's utility, but only watch how people change their location choices and how the fuel consumption and CO_2 emissions are affected. As expected, the UGB causes centralization of both residences and jobs. When such pairs of residence-work locations are moved to the center, many also change their mode from auto to other modes. Thus fuel consumption and CO_2 emissions are also decreased. I compare the results with those of quasi-Pigouvian tolling. Between UGB and quasi-Pigouvian toll, the difference of impact on fuel consumption and CO_2 emission is larger than the difference of impact on jobs and residential location. The contribution of the UGB to reduce fuel consumption and CO_2 emissions is less than the quasi-Pigouvian tolls. For example, when 60% of the initially vacant suburban land is available for development under the UGB, the jobs increase by 19,810 in the city and decrease by 19,515 in the suburbs. Residents increase by 32,665 in the city and decrease by 32,665 in the suburbs. Under the quasi-Pigouvian toll, jobs increase by 17,596 in the city and decrease by 19,721 in the suburbs. Residents increase by 44,228 in the city and decrease by 44,228 in the suburbs. On the other hand, the fuel consumption and CO_2 emissions decrease but by only 0.7% under the same UGB while they decrease by a much larger 17.1% under quasi-Pigouvian toll.

When the toll revenue is distributed, consumers make more non-work trips and the fuel consumption and CO_2 emissions change from a 17.1% reduction to a 14.8% reduction.

Chapter 7 is the concluding chapter. The chapter summarizes the results explained above in more detail and presents tables that show all of the policy results.

Chapter 2. The Structure of the RELU-TRAN2 Model

The purpose of this chapter is to explain the structure of RELU-TRAN [Anas and Liu (2007)] and how RELU-TRAN2 is an extension of RELU-TRAN. As already explained, RELU-TRAN is a spatially disaggregated computable general equilibrium model of a regional economy, its land use and its transportation. The RELU-TRAN model's details were explained in an article by Anas and Liu (2007). The purpose of RELU-TRAN2 is to make two significant extensions to RELU-TRAN, so that the power and accuracy of this model in examining certain policies can be improved.

These extensions are the following: a) To add the choice of automobile gasoline efficiency (i.e. fuel economy) for consumers; b) To add road traffic congestion for trips that occur within geographic zones, not just between two different geographic zones. Extension (a) is important because it allows me to test more realistically and accurately the effects of policies such as the gasoline tax. When such a policy is imposed in RELU-TRAN, consumers cannot react to the policy by adjusting their vehicle types (e.g. switching to a vehicle with a higher fuel economy), but in RELU-TRAN2 they will be able to make such adjustments alongside the other adjustments (i.e. change in travel route, travel mode, or changes in location and in trip frequency that RELU-TRAN already captures). Extension (b) is also important because it allows for an increase in congestion on trips that occur locally (i.e. mostly within one's geographic zone of residence) when congestion is tolled on regional highways. This is more realistic than the assumption in RELU-TRAN that there is no intra-zonal congestion.

I will first address the extension of car-efficiency choice by consumers. This is done in the course of presenting the structure of the RELU-TRAN2 model, pointing out along the way, how car-efficiency has been introduced into the original RELU-TRAN. Since consumer behavior (except for the choice of travel mode and route) is modeled in RELU and RELU2, but mode choice and route choice are modeled in TRAN, the choice of car-efficiency is introduced in RELU. The second extension, that of intra-zonal travel calculations is introduced into the original TRAN sub-model and will be discussed next in similar fashion, namely presenting the new TRAN, explaining along the way how the new calculations modify the model.

2.1 RELU and RELU2

In RELU [Anas and Liu (2007)], the economy consists of $f = 1...F$ types of consumers who differ by skill in the labor market. $r = 1...\Re$ industries that engage in exchanging goods with each other, that is industry 1 uses the output of industry 2 as an input and vise versa. Of these industries, agriculture, manufacturing, and business services are called basic industries that can export their outputs from the region (imports are also allowed), while the fourth industry is retail and sells to the region's consumers. The model treats $k = 1...\aleph_1$ housing types. $\aleph_1 = 2$, representing housing in single-family type and in multiple-family type buildings (e.g. apartments and condos), $k = \aleph_1 + 1...\aleph_2$ represent floor space to be used by the model's industries (see above) that will be located in business buildings (e.g. industrial and commercial buildings) and k represents urban land that is undeveloped and empty but available for development.

There are $\Im' \equiv \wp + \Im$ geographic zones in the metropolitan area (that is the Chicago MSA), where $\Im$ are the zones internal to the model, and $\wp$ are peripheral zones that represent an exurban area surrounding the internal zones (see Figure 2(a)).

The difference between an internal zone and the peripheral zone is that all internal zones are equilibrated in all respects within the model, while the peripheral zones represent "the rest of the world". In these zones, the prices of the goods that are endogenously determined for the internal zones are taken as exogenous. By excluding $\wp$, the model becomes the closed city. In this book I will simulate the closed city model.

Chapter 2   13

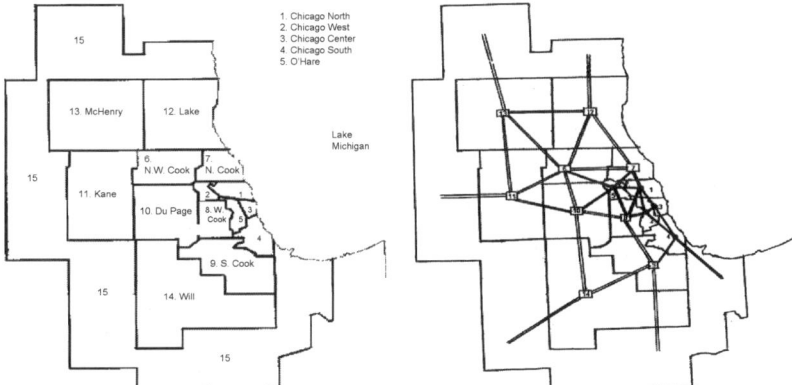

Figure 2 (a) Modeled Chicago as represented in RELU-TRAN and RELU-TRAN2 (Zone 3 is the Central Business District; zones 2-5 are the rest of the City of Chicago; zones 6-10 are the inner ring suburbs; zones 11-14 are the outer suburbs and zone 15 is the peripheral zone).

Figure 2 (b) The road network of the TRAN model.

The peripheral zone used in the current application is just one superzone (zone 15) shown in Figure 2 (a). In 1990 and also in the year 2000 census, this zone contained the residences of about 5% of the population that had jobs in one of the 14 internal model zones. It is assumed that all building types k could be constructed in an internal model zone or may already initially exist in these zones. The same building types are subject to demolitions. How construction and demolition occur will be discussed below. In addition, consumers of all skill-types and all industries can setup production in any internal zone. Consumers can choose the external zone as a place of residence or as a place of work, but not both (since in that case they would not be observed by the model), consumers can also shop from the retail industry in the external zone. As explained above, external zones are not equilibrated within the model. Therefore, rents, wages, retail prices and all other variables relevant to consumers are taken as given for the external zones but are endogenously determined for the internal zones.

In this modeled city, consumers, producers, landlords and developers behave so as to achieve their own economic objectives, namely they maximize their utility or their profit as is appropriate. For example, landlords of each building type rent out the floor space. Depending on how high the rent is, they may choose to keep some floor space vacant, which determines the short run supply of rentable floor space in the relevant real estate market. Developers maximize profit under perfect foresight and construct or demolish floor space in each type of building in each zone. Construction reduces the amount of land that is initially vacant, whereas demolition increases it.

Businesses in each industry have geographic-zone specific constant returns to scale technologies and are price takers (perfectly competitive) in all input and output markets. In this situation, RELU cannot determine the number of firms in an industry, only the aggregate size of each industry in each zone. Any firm is profit maximizing and produces by using exogenous capital, building space and labor of each skill type and by purchasing inputs from all the industries in all the other zones. Thus, implicitly, the outputs of the same industry produced in different zones are imperfect substitutes and the production function of each firm exhibits a Dixit-Stiglitz (1977) (or Ethier (1982)) bias for input-variety, whereby all the geographic variants of the same input are combined in the production process, namely more output can be produced by using all the variants of the same input, no matter what the delivered prices of these variants may be. This assumption, that the same goods produced in different locations are imperfect rather than perfect substitutes, is also known as the Armington (1969) assumption from international trade theory.

RELU consumers make a complex set of utility maximizing choices which will be described in more detail, below. They take as given average transport cost and times across the different travel modes that are available and feasible to use between each zone pair: highway (i.e. trips by car), transit, and a non-motorized mode consisting of walking and bicycling for the most part. Consumers also take as given all wages, rents and retail prices offered in the region's zones. Given this information and also their skill types and their unearned incomes, they decide whether to be workers or non-workers (i.e. whether to be in or out of the labor market), in which zone to work (if in the labor market) and how many hours of labor to supply there, in which zone and what type of residential housing to reside in. These two decisions of job-location and residence-location determine the commuting arrangement of the consumer.

The consumer is indifferent about industry of employment since it is an assumption of the model that all industries being competitive, offer the same wage in the same zone. Wages differ by zone of employment and skill level but not by industry. In addition, the consumer decides how many shopping trips to make from his zone of residence over a unit time period. Consumers are endowed with a Dixit-Stiglitz (1977) utility function in which retail goods at different zones are treated as imperfect substitutes. Hence, each consumer will travel to all zones offering retail goods, although more such trips will occur to nearby zones. As explained earlier, in RELU2, one more decision is added, that of choosing the fuel-efficiency level of one's automobile.

The rest of this section 2.1 describes the technical details of the four types of economic agents included in RELU. In 2.1.1 consumers, in 2.1.2 producers (i.e. businesses or firms), in 2.1.3 landlords and in 2.1.4 developers are described.

2.1.1 Consumers/Potential Workers

There are two serious limitations about how the consumers are treated in the model which should be mentioned at the outset. This was mentioned only briefly in Anas and Liu (2007).

1) Consumers are individuals not households, so that household behavior is not explicitly modeled. It can only be pieced together hypothetically, from the choices of consumers. For example, the housing consumption of a household composed of a worker with skill level 4 and a non-worker with skill level 1, would be the sum of their personal choices of floor space assuming they have chosen to reside in the same zone i and the same housing type, k. Similarly, the fuel economy utilized by a hypothetical household would be the weighted average fuel economy of the individual consumers comprising that household.

2) Consumers are myopic and spend all their income annually. Thus, saving and capital accumulation by consumers is ignored in the model. This assumption avoids a great many complications such as the fact that the savings rate will vary by location and other choices and consequently, wealth levels will be dependent on the location history of a particular consumer.

In the modeled Chicago, there are $N = \sum_f N_f$ consumers/potential workers, where $f = 1...F$ indicates the ability or skill in the labor market. Skill is such that at the model's equilibrium, the higher skilled workers will have higher earned incomes. I refer to consumers as potential workers because they might choose to be non-workers relying exclusively on their unearned income. For simplicity I will hereafter just say "consumers" understanding that work/do-not-work, and where-to-work and how-much labor-to-supply, are standard decisions of such consumers. As mentioned earlier, they consume products retailed in every model zone $\Im$ by traveling to that zone. The quantity purchased implies a certain number of trips at a fixed rate per quantity. The shopping travel incurs both monetary travel cost and a time opportunity cost valued at the wage rate, which are added to the "mill price" of the shopped good to get a "delivered price", according to the residence location of the consumer. Another choice of the consumer is how much housing floor space and in what type of residential building to rent in the zone of residence. And finally, as explained earlier, there is the choice of fuel economy for one's car which is done in the context of the consumer's comprehensive travel pattern. It is assumed that each consumer can rationally consider his utility as being conditional on the combination of possible choices that are discrete in the model: residing in zone $i = 1...I$, working in zone $j = 0, 1...J$, (where $j = 0$ represents choosing not to work and thus having no workplace), having housing type $k = 1...K$ and vehicle type $c = 1...C$. The combination of these discrete choices is (i, j, k, c). It is assumed that each consumer will choose that combination that offers the highest utility, after optimizing each combination for those choice variables that are continuous in the model. These continuous choices are how many shopping trips to make to each zone, how much labor to supply at the zone of employment (for

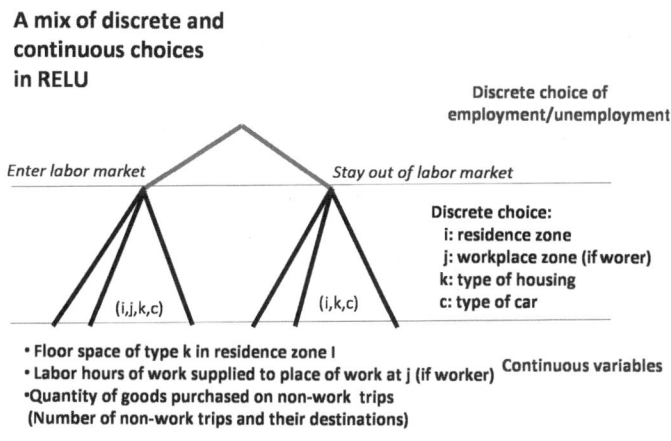

Figure 2.1.1 Consumer's mix of discrete and continuous choices.

consumers choosing to be workers) and how much housing floors pace to rent.

Figure 2.1.1 describes the decision tree of the consumer as a three stage choice process where the stage at the bottom (third stage) is the choice of the continuous variables and the top two stages are the choice of the discrete variables.

Note that the top level choice (stage 1) is whether to work or not. That is, the consumer chooses between the expected utility of $j = 0$ and the expected utility of $j > 0$. In the middle (stage 2) of the tree, the consumer chooses among the combinations $(i, k, c | j = 0)$ if not working and among the combinations $(j, i, k, c | j > 0)$ if working. In the third (bottom) stage, the consumer optimizes the continuous variables for each combination of discrete choices from the top two stages. As shown in Figure 2.1.1, these are the shopping trips originating from a residence in i and the quantities of goods purchased associated with these shopping trips, the floor space quantity to be rented in the chosen housing type k. If the consumer is working, the commuting time and cost is implicitly determined by the choice of work zone j and residence zone i, so that the labor supply is also determined by the total amount spent commuting and shopping being deducted from a fixed amount of time available for work plus all travel. Leisure is not directly modeled, but a kind of leisure effect can be captured by adding the disutility of commuting time as a separate term in the utility function. It is shown below that the model of the consumer also includes idiosyncratic tastes (i.e. constant terms in the utility function for each combination of discrete choices, that are distributed randomly in the population of consumers). These are necessary to include so that consumers with the same non-idiosyncratic utility function will not all choose the same alternative. Such dispersion of choices for seemingly identical consumers is prevalent in the data.

The utility function and its maximization

In the third stage, consumers maximize the following utility function with respect to the continuous variables b (floor space) and Zz (quantity of retail goods purchased from zone z), for each combination of discrete choices (i, j, k, c) which, as explained, are determined in the earlier stages:

(2.1.1)

$$U_{ijkc|f} = \alpha_f \ln \underbrace{\left(\sum_{\forall z} \iota_{z|ijfc} (Z_z)^{\eta_f} \right)^{\frac{1}{\eta_f}}}_{\substack{\text{Dixit–Stiglitz C.E.S.} \\ \log \text{ of Cobb–Douglas}}} + \beta_f \ln b - \gamma_{1f} G^{work}_{ijc|f} + \gamma_{2f} (ineff_c)$$

$$+ E_{ijkc|f} + e_{ijkc|f}.$$

The taste coefficients and other terms appearing in this utility function are as follows:

$\alpha_f, \beta_f, \alpha_f + \beta_f = 1$ are the shares of the consumer's disposable income (to be seen below) for a consumer of skill-level f that are spent on the retailed goods $Z_1, Z_2,..., Z_3$ purchased from all the zones and on housing floor space b rented in type k housing in the zone of residence i, respectively. The imperfectly substitutable retail goods are in the Dixit-Stiglitz (1977) C.E.S. sub-utility function, where $0 < \eta_f < 1$. In this sub-utility function, the elasticity of substitution among the retail varieties is $1/(1-\eta_f)$. This sub-utility structure for retailed goods implies that the consumer views the goods in the various locations as different and imperfectly substitutable as in Anas and Xu

(1999). The consumers travel to every location to enjoy the location specific varieties regardless of the prices of the goods and the travel cost. Of course, pricier locations will be shopped less frequently and It is shown shortly how shopping frequency attenuates with the full price (i.e. delivered opportunity cost or delivered price) of a retail good and how that full price entails travel time and cost. The coefficients $\iota_{z|iij} \geq 0$ are constants that measure the *inherent attractiveness* of the retail location z for consumers conditional on (i, j, k, c). If $\iota_{z|iij} = 0$, the retail location is not attractive for the consumers and excluded from the travel.

The third term, $-\gamma_{1f} G_{ijc|f}^{work}$, where $G_{ijc|f}^{work}$ measures the commuting time for a consumer who has a job at some zone $j > 0$ resides in zone i, and travels via a car that has fuel-economy level c. $\gamma_{1f} > 0$ thus measures the disutility of time spent in commuting separately from any monetary opportunity cost of such commuting (that is, lost wages). Non-workers have no commutes and are treated by the model as if they had a job at the dummy zone $j = 0$. But, by definition, $G_{i0c|f}^{work} = 0$, for all $(i, c|f)$. Hence, this consistently reflects the fact that non-workers would experience no disutility from commuting since they do not commute. As shown later in discussing TRAN, the expected travel times $G_{ijc|f}^{w}$ and costs $g_{ijc|f}^{w}$, conditional on skill type f and vehicle type c, are formed as expected values over travel modes such as car, public transit and a composite of "other modes", and incorporate the efficient (cost minimizing) route choices which are treated in TRAN (to be seen later). The purpose of trips is expressed by the upper script $w = 1 = work$ for commuting and $w = 2 = non$-$work$ for shopping trips. Consumers form those expected travel times and costs by taking into account the congestion over the road network. It is assumed that when consumers make the RELU choices, which include as already described residential location, job location, housing type, vehicle type and choosing to work or not to work, they only know the average travel time and cost by vehicle type for each (i, j, c). This assumption may be interpreted so that consumers mix all of the modes with some probability, rather than being committed to the same mode of travel every day.

The fourth term, $\gamma_{2f}(ineff_c)$ represents the sub-utility with respect to one's car. $ineff_c$ is an index number that increases as the fuel un-economy (gallons of gasoline per mile of travel) of the car increases. Relatively less fuel efficient cars are also larger and safer on average. Hence, by $\gamma_{2f} > 0$ it is assumed that consumers like less efficient cars reflecting the fact what they like about such cars are things like comfort and safety that happen to be correlated with fuel inefficiency. The monetary cost associated with higher inefficiency will appear in the budget of the consumer. As mentioned earlier, this term is not present in RELU (that is RELU may be regarded as having $\gamma_{2f} = 0$), but I have introduced in RELU2 because I want to make the model capable of capturing the effects of policies in which car choice plays an important role directly and indirectly.

The fifth term, $E_{ijkc|f}$, is a constant taste-effect for the combination of the discrete choices (i, j, k, c), for all consumers of skill-level f. Such constant taste effects can be ordered in some way across the different discrete combinations to reflect such systematic effects as the fact that high income (high skill) consumers *ceteris paribus* prefer residing in a suburban zone, in a single family home and owning an SUV (low fuel efficient car) due to things other than those which are captured in the rest of utility function. To put it differently, the terms $E_{ijkc|f}$ can be varied among different skill-types to represent the fact that their tastes are vertically differentiated, due to systematic effects that are unobserved in the rest of the utility function.

The sixth term, $e_{ijkc|f}$, is the idiosyncratic utility constant. Unlike the $E_{ijkc|f}$ which has the same value for all consumers of skill-f, $e_{ijkc|f}$ varies among the consumers of the same f for the combination of discrete choices (i, j, k, c). Thus, $e_{ijkc|f}$ helps capture horizontal taste differences among consumer of the same f-type who face the same choices. Therefore, the variances of these terms will be crucial in achieving a dispersion of choices among consumers of the same f-type.

The labor supply of the employed consumer, $H_{ijc|f}$, is decided from time constraint as $H_{ijc|f} = H - dG^{work}_{ijcf} - \sum_{\forall z} c_{ijf} Z_z G^{non-work}_{izcf}$, once the consumer has solved the continuous problem and has found the $Z \equiv [Z_1...Z_3]$ for each combination of discrete choices (i, j, c). In this labor supply equation, H is the total number of annual hours available for allocation between work and travel. d is the exogenous number of commutes per year and G_{ijcf}^{work}, the round trip travel time during a daily commute. $\sum_{\forall z} c_{ijf} Z_z G_{izcf}^{non-work}$ is the total travel time taken up in shopping trips, where the coefficients $c_{ijf} > 0$ are the number of shopping trips required per unit of quantity of retail output the consumer in the situation (i, j, f) buys. Hence, the remaining time is allocated to work in the job located in zone j.

To summarize, in stage three, the consumers maximize their utility conditional on the discrete choices of work-residence-housing-vehicle (i, j, k, c) with respect to the continuous variables: (i) the floor space of type type-k housing to rent; (ii) the aggregate annual quantity of retail goods to buy at each zone z. When consumers decide the quantity of retail goods to consume, non-work travel time is immediately decided at the same time. Then the time constraint shows the annual labor supply at the chosen workplace at some $j > 0$ where the consumer is employed.

The utility maximization problem is written as,

(2.1.2)
$$MAX_{Z_z, b} \quad U_{ijkc|f} = \alpha_f \ln\left(\sum_{\forall z} \iota_{z|ijfc}(Z_z)^{\eta_f}\right)^{\frac{1}{\eta_f}} + \beta_f \ln b - \gamma_{1f} G_{ijc|f}^{work}$$
$$+ \gamma_{2f}(ineff_c) + E_{ijkc|f} + e_{ijkc|f}$$

subject to: $\sum_{\forall z} \psi_{z|ijcf} Z_z + b R_{ik} = \Psi_{ijcf}$ (income budget)

$$H - dG_{ijc|f}^{work} - \sum_{\forall z} c_{ijf} Z_z G_{ijc|f}^{non-work} \geq 0 \quad (time\ budget).$$

In more detail, the budget constraint of the consumer is:

(2.1.3)
$$\sum_{\forall z}(p_{\Re z}+c_{ijf}g_{izc|f})Z_z+bR_{ik}=$$
$$\Delta_j w_{jf}\left(H-dG^{work}_{ijc|f}-\sum_{\forall z}c_{ijf}Z_z G^{non-work}_{izc|f}\right)-\Delta_j dg^{work}_{ijc|f}+M^e_f-O^e_{cf}.$$

The consumers are price takers. Those prices are, p_{Rz}, the unit price of retail goods sold in zone z, R_{ik}, the rent per unit of type k floor space in zone i, w_{jf}, the hourly wage rate for skill f labor employed in a zone $j > 0$. $\Delta_j = 0$ when $j = 0$ (that is for a non-working consumer) and $\Delta_j = 1$ for all $j > 0$ (that is for a working consumer).

$G^w_{ijc|f}$ and $g^w_{ijc|f}$ are the expected travel time and monetary travel cost, respectively, averaged over all the available travel modes of a round trip from zone i to zone j for a consumer of type f and using vehicle type c. It is assumed that these times and costs remain constant over the day. But as explained later, travel time and monetary cost could be different for trip purposes such as commuting and shopping.

M^e_f is the exogenous non-wage income of the employed and unemployed (upper script) consumer of type f. It might be interpreted as the normal investment return from all of the consumer's assets within or outside the regional economy.

On the left side, $(p_{\Re z}+c_{ijf}g^{non-work}_{iz})$ is the price of the good purchased at retail zone z, plus the monetary cost of travel. The second term is the rent for the floor space. On the right, the first term is the annual income from work, and the second term is the annual monetary cost of commuting, and the third term is income from non-work sources. O^e_{cf} is the personal annual cost of owning a vehicle of inefficiency level c that rises with the level of the car's inefficiency because less fuel efficient cars are also more comfortable and safer on average. In American Automobile Association (2005), it is given by,

(2.1.4)
$$O^e_{cf}=120{,}000\times(0.01421\times ineff_c+0.04386)/n^e_f$$

annual cost of owning a vehicle

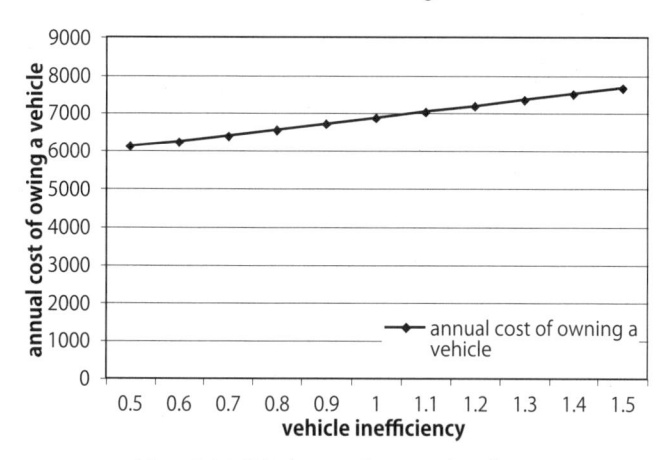

Figure 2.1.2: Vehicle ownership cost when $n_f^e = 1$.

where *ineff$_c$* is vehicle type index number. n_f^e contains two meanings. Those are adults who share a vehicle (on average) in a skill-type f household of employed and unemployed (upper script) and the cost difference of different cars of the same inefficiency. This cost curve (numerator) is illustrated in Figure 2.1.2.

It is possible to rewrite the budget constraint in (1) by rearranging terms so that each retail good quantity bought is multiplied by the full price of the good which includes the value of the travel time. Thus, $\psi_{z|ijfc}$ is the unit full price of the retail goods sold in zone z that for a consumer of type f residing in i and working in j and owning vehicle type c.

(2.1.5)
$$\psi_{z|ijfc} \equiv p_{\Re z} + c_{ijf}\left(g_{izc|f}^{non\text{-}work} + \Delta_j w_{jf} G_{izc|f}^{non\text{-}work} \right).$$

Travel time is valued at the wage rate for the employed consumers and not valuable for the unemployed consumers.

Ψ_{ijcf} is the full economic income of the consumer, net of commuting expenditure inclusive of the value of commuting time and the annualized vehicle cost.

(2.1.6)
$$\Psi_{ijcf} = \Delta_j w_{jf}(H - dG^{work}_{ijc|f}) + M_f - \Delta_j dg^{work}_{ijc|f} - O^e_{cf}.$$

The full income is conditional on the discrete choice (i, j, c), that is the pair of residence and job location and the type of car. This is full economic income because it represents the total income the consumer could get if all his time after commuting could be allocated to earning a wage. But, because the consumer spends some time on non-work travel, the actual income from work is lower than the full income. Note that all variables in (2.1.5) and (2.1.6) are taken as exogenous for the consumer in the consumer's problem, once (i, j, c) have been decided.

In the model, non-wage incomes M^e_f are assumed to be exogenous constants. These non-wage incomes reflect the aggregate discounted annual return from real estate ownership and any other payments from all other sources inside and outside the region, owned by consumers in the region. See Anas and Liu (2007) for a way to make these non-wage incomes partially endogenous. By grouping terms and rearranging, the budget constraint can be written in the form that is familiar and appears in textbooks, where the full price of each good multiplies its quantity, and the full income appears on the right side:

(2.1.7)
$$\sum_{\forall z} \psi_{z|jifc} Z_z + bR_{ik} = \Psi_{ijfc}.$$

The inner stage continuous choice problem

By solving the innermost stage of the problem, the *Marshallian demands* of the consumer for the continuous variables conditional on (i, j, k, c) are derived. These are the demands for the quantity of floor space of housing type k to rent and the annual quantity of goods to shop at retail zone z:

(2.1.8)
$$b_{ijke|f} = \beta_{ijf} \frac{\Psi_{ijef}}{R_{ik}},$$

(2.1.9)
$$Z_{z|ijfc} = \frac{\iota_{z|ijf}^{\frac{1}{1-\eta_f}} \psi_{z|ijfc}^{\frac{1}{\eta_f}-1}}{\sum_{\forall s} \iota_{s|ijf}^{\frac{1}{1-\eta_f}} \psi_{s|ijfc}^{\frac{\eta_f}{\eta_f}-1}} \alpha_f \Psi_{ijfc}.$$

Meanwhile, the labor supply is given by subtracting the total travel time for commuting and retail trips from the annual time endowment:

(2.1.10)
$$H_{ijc|f} = H - dG_{ij|fc}^{work} - \sum_{\forall z} c_{ijf} Z_{z|ijfc} G_{ij|fc}^{non-work}.$$

The indirect utility of this continuous problem of the innermost stage, conditional on the discrete choice set (i, j, k, c) is:

(2.1.11)
$$\overline{V}_{ijkc|f} = \alpha_f \ln\alpha_f + \beta_f \ln\beta_f + \ln\Psi_{ijfc} - \beta_f \ln R_{ik} + \frac{\alpha_f(1-\eta_f)}{\eta_f} \ln\left(\sum_{\forall z} \iota_{z|ijfc}^{\frac{1}{1-\eta_f}} \psi_{z|ijfc}^{\frac{\eta_f}{\eta_f}-1}\right).$$

The second stage discrete choice problem

For the consumer who knows the indirect utility of the inner stage, the second stage discrete choice problem is[2];

---

[2] In recent years, several papers have been published that have discussed vehicle choice. For example, see Golob et al.(1996), Bhat and Sen (2006), Bhat and Guo (2007), Fang(2008), Bhat et al (2009). Within those, Bhat and Guo(2007) studies the impact of the built environment (which includes land-use, urban form and street network attributes), characteristics of household residential choice and auto owner ship decisions. Bhat et al (2009) analyses the impact of demographics, vehicle characteristics and gasoline price in addition to the built environment on household vehicle holdings and use.

(2.1.12)
$$U_{ijkc|f} = Max_{\forall(i,j,k,c)} \left\{ \overline{\overline{V}}_{ijkc|f} - \Delta_j \gamma_{1f} G^{work}_{ij|fc} + \gamma_{2f} ineff_c + E_{ijkc|f} + e_{ijkc|f} \right\}.$$

The utility maximizing population distribution among the discrete choice combinations (*i, j, k, c*) is given by the nested multinomial logit choice probabilities. The upper level (marginal) probabilities of being employed or non-working are:

(2.1.13)
$$Pr^{up}_{e|f} = \frac{\exp((1-\sigma_f)I_{e|f})}{\exp((1-\sigma_f)I_{e|f})+\exp((1-\sigma_f)I_{u|f})}, \quad Pr^{up}_{u|f} = \frac{\exp((1-\sigma_f)I_{u|f})}{\exp((1-\sigma_f)I_{e|f})+\exp((1-\sigma_f)I_{u|f})},$$

where $I_{e|f} = \frac{1}{\lambda^e_f} \ln \sum_{ijkc} \exp(\lambda^e_f \tilde{U}^e_{ijkc|f})$, $I_{u|f} = \frac{1}{\lambda^u_f} \ln \sum_{ikc} \exp(\lambda^u_f \tilde{U}^u_{ikc|f})$ are the expected utilities of the lower level discrete choices. The lower level (conditional) probabilities of choosing (*i, j, k, c*) for the employed and unemployed are,

(2.1.14)
$$Pr^{low|e}_{ijkc|f} = \frac{\exp(\lambda^e_f \tilde{U}^e_{ijkc|f})}{\sum_{ijkc} \exp(\lambda^e_f \tilde{U}^e_{ijkc|f})}, \quad Pr^{low|u}_{ikc|f} = \frac{\exp(\lambda^u_f \tilde{U}^u_{ikc|f})}{\sum_{ikc} \exp(\lambda^u_f \tilde{U}^u_{ikc|f})}.$$

The joint probabilities of employment status and (*i, j, k, c*) choice are then:

(2.1.15)
$$Pr^e_{ijkc|f} = Pr_{ij(>0)kc|f} = Pr^{up}_{e|f} Pr^{low|e}_{ijkc|f}, \quad Pr^u_{ikc|f} = Pr_{i0kc|f} = Pr^{up}_{u|f} Pr^{low|u}_{ikc|f}$$

where $\sum_{\forall(i,j,k,c)} Pr_{ijkc|f} = 1$. The indirect utility is:

(2.1.16)
$$\begin{aligned}\tilde{U}_{ijkc|f} &= \overline{V}_{ijkc|f} - \Delta_j \gamma_{1f} G^{work}_{ij|fc} + \gamma_{2f} ineff_c + E_{ijkc|f} \\ &= \alpha_f \ln \alpha_f + \beta_f \ln \beta_f + \ln \Psi_{ijfc} - \beta_f \ln R_{ik} \\ &+ \frac{\alpha_f(1-\eta_f)}{\eta_f} \ln \left(\sum_{\forall z} \iota_{z|ijfc}^{\frac{1}{1-\eta_f}} \psi_{z|ijfc}^{\frac{\eta_f}{\eta_f - 1}} \right) - \Delta_j \gamma_{1f} G^{work}_{ij|fc} + \gamma_{2f} ineff_c + E_{ijkc|f} .\end{aligned}$$

2.1.2 Producers

I will keep the same treatment of producers as Anas and Liu (2007). Industries can potentially produce in any zone and can import any of their inputs from all other zones. In the economy, there are $r = 1...\Re$ industries. The first $\Re$-1 of these are defined as industries that produce various goods and services, either to sell as intermediate inputs to any other industries producing in the region or to export to the outside world. Agriculture, manufacturing and business services would be highly aggregated examples and they are in fact the ones used by Anas and Liu (2007). The $\Re$ *th* basic industry is retail trade. Retail trade obtains intermediate inputs from the first $\Re$-1 industries but it sells its output only to consumers in the region, or exports part of its output.

In addition to the basic industries, I also define two specialized industries for each building type. Thus there are $2\aleph$ such industries where $\aleph = \aleph_1 + \aleph_2$. One of these provides construction and the other demolition of that type of building. It will be assumed that these industries use the primary inputs of business capital, labor and buildings, as well as the intermediate inputs from potentially all basic industries, while selling their services (construction and demolition) only to building developers. The detail discussion of these construction-demolition industries is in developers section.

The firms of industry r ($r = 1...\Re + 2\aleph$) in zone j produce output X_{rj} by Cobb-Douglas constant returns production functions.

(2.1.17)
$$X_{rj} = A_{rj} K^{v_r} \left(\sum_{f=0}^{F} \kappa_{f|rj} L_f^{\theta_r} \right)^{\frac{\delta_r}{\theta_r}} \left(\sum_{k=0}^{\aleph} \chi_{k|rj} B_k^{\zeta_r} \right)^{\frac{\mu_r}{\zeta_r}} \prod_{s=1}^{\Re} \left(\sum_{n=0}^{\Im'} \upsilon_{sn|rj} Y_{sn}^{\varepsilon_{sr}} \right)^{\frac{\gamma_{sr}}{\varepsilon_{sr}}}.$$

The inputs, K, L_f, B_k, Y_{sn}, are business capital, labor, buildings (floor space) and intermediate inputs from the other industries. $f=0$, $k=0$ and $n=0$ stand for labor hired, buildings rented and intermediate inputs purchased by the firm outside the region that contribute to production in this region. The intermediate inputs Y_{sn} potentially come from all the industries $s=1,...,\Re$ and $n=0,1,...,\Im$ zones, including industry r and zone j itself, because outputs of the same industry s produced in different model zones are treated as imperfectly substitutable intermediate inputs as per the Armington (1969) assumption of trade theory.

The exponents of each term v_r, δ_r, μ_r, $\gamma_{sr} > 0$ are the cost shares of each of the input goods. The constant returns means that $v_r + \delta_r + \mu_r + \sum_{s=1}^{\Re} \gamma_{sr} = 1$. $1/(1-\theta_r)$, $1/(1-\zeta_r)$, $1/(1-\varepsilon_{sr}) > 1$ are elasticity of substitution between the labor skills f, building types k and inputs from industry s, respectively. $\kappa_{f|rj}$, $\chi_{k|rj}$, $\upsilon_{sn|rj} \geq 0$ allow to specify input-specific biases including the ruling out of specific inputs from being used in production. Typically, residential buildings might be excluded as production inputs by setting $\chi_{k|rj} = 0$ with such k that stands for residential building. The leading scale factor A_{rj} is a constant that is calibrated not only by industry but also by location in order to account for place-specific Hicksian-neutral productivity effects.

Each firm solves the cost minimization problem:

(2.1.18)
$$Min_{[L_f],[B_k],[Y_1],...,[Y_\Re]} \quad \rho K + \sum_{f=0}^{F} w_{jf} L_f + \sum_{k=0}^{\aleph} R_{jk} B_k + \sum_{s=1}^{\Re} \sum_{n=0}^{\Im'} \left(p_{sn} + \sigma_s g_{nj} \right) Y_{sn}$$

subject to a target output X_{rj} given by the production function (2.1.17). In the objective function, ρ is the exogenous real interest rate for business capital and, W_{jf} are hourly wage rates per unit of labor, R_{jf} are rents per unit of floor space and P_{sn} are the prices of the output sold at the place of production s. $\hat{p}_{snj} \equiv p_{sn} + \sigma_s g_{nj}$ is the delivered price of the same output purchased by other producers located at some zone j. Recall that g_{nj} are the monetary costs of commuting from n to j for producers and σ_s are the factors that convert this passenger transport cost to the monetary cost of freight transport per unit of industry s output[3]. Firms are competitive in all markets and take all these prices as given.

The inputs choices expressed as the conditional (i.e. cost-minimizing) input demand functions of the industry $r = 1...\Re + 2\aleph$ producing in zone j are as follows:

(2.1.19)
$$L_{f|rj} = \frac{\kappa_{f|rj}^{\frac{1}{1-\vartheta_r}} w_{jf}^{\frac{1}{\vartheta_r - 1}}}{\sum_{z=0}^{F} \kappa_{z|rj}^{\frac{1}{1-\vartheta_r}} w_{jz}^{\frac{\vartheta_r}{\vartheta_r - 1}}} \delta_r p_{rj} X_{rj},$$

(2.1.20)
$$B_{k|rj} = \frac{\chi_{k|rj}^{\frac{1}{1-\varsigma_r}} R_{jk}^{\frac{1}{\varsigma_r - 1}}}{\sum_{z=0}^{\aleph} \chi_{z|rj}^{\frac{1}{1-\varsigma_r}} R_{jz}^{\frac{\varsigma_r}{\varsigma_r - 1}}} \mu_r p_{rj} X_{rj},$$

(2.1.21)
$$Y_{sn|rj} = \frac{\upsilon_{sn|rj}^{\frac{1}{1-\varepsilon_{sr}}} \hat{p}_{snj}^{\frac{1}{\varepsilon_{sr} - 1}}}{\sum_{y=0}^{\Im'} \upsilon_{sy|rj}^{\frac{1}{1-\varepsilon_{sr}}} \hat{p}_{syj}^{\frac{\varepsilon_{sr}}{\varepsilon_{sr} - 1}}} \gamma_{sr} p_{rj} X_{rj}.$$

---

3 Freight cost congestion could also be modeled explicitly as related to the flow of intermediate goods between zones but this is ignored in the present as it is also ignored by Anas and Liu (2007).

The capital input is treated as an exogenous variable[4]. By substituting the conditional demands (2.1.19)-(2.1.21) into the direct cost expression (2.1.18), I find the output level. Because constant returns to scale production is assumed, firms make zero-profit with the output price equaling average (or marginal) cost, independent of the level of output.

(2.1.22)

$$p_{rj} = \frac{\rho^{v_r}}{A_{rj}\delta_r^{\delta_r}\mu_r^{\mu_r}v_r^{v_r}\left(\prod_{s=1}^{\Re}\gamma_r^{\gamma_r}\right)} \left(\sum_{f=0}^{F}\kappa_{f|rj}^{\frac{1}{1-\theta_r}}w_{if}^{\frac{\theta_r}{\theta_r-1}}\right)^{\frac{\delta_r(\theta_r-1)}{\theta_r}} \left(\sum_{k=0}^{\aleph}\chi_{k|rj}^{\frac{1}{1-\varsigma_r}}R_{jk}^{\frac{\varsigma_r}{\varsigma_r-1}}\right)^{\frac{\mu_r(\varsigma_r-1)}{\varsigma_r}}$$

$$\times \prod_{s=1}^{\Re}\left(\sum_{n=0}^{\Im'}v_{sn|rj}^{\frac{1}{1-\varepsilon_{sr}}}\hat{p}_{sn|rj}^{\frac{\varepsilon_{sr}}{\varepsilon_{sr}-1}}\right)^{\frac{\gamma_{sr}(\varepsilon_{sr}-1)}{\varepsilon_{sr}}}.$$

For a discussion on the interpretation of the inter-industry demands from the perspective of input-output analysis, see Anas and Liu (2007).

2.1.3 Landlords

I take the same assumptions about landlord behavior as did Anas and Liu (2007). The landlords own the $k = 1...\aleph$, $\aleph \equiv \aleph_1 + \aleph_2$ types of residential and commercial buildings. The landlords can let in the rental market a unit of floor space of those buildings to be occupied, or they can keep it vacant. The landlords are rent taker and make this decision annually.

Landlord profits per unit floor space are given as the rent revenue minus a maintenance cost, $R_{ik} - D_{iko} + d_{iko}$, if the space is occupied and minus another maintenance cost if the space is kept vacant, $-D_{ikv} + d_{ikv}$. Here D_{iko} and D_{ikv} are the maintenance costs and $(d_{iko}, d_{ikv}) \in (-\infty, +\infty)$ are i.i.d. Gumbel idiosyncratic maintenance costs that vary across these landlords with dispersion parameter ϕ_{ik}. Subscripts shows type k buildings in zone i for occupancy and vacancy.

Then, q_{ik} is the probability that a landlord will let a unit amount of

---

4   In Anas and Liu (2007), the capital input is endogenous variable, $K_{rj} = \left(\frac{1}{\rho}\right)v_r p_{rj} X_{rj}$.

space to be occupied.

(2.1.23)
$$q_{ik}(R_{ik}) = \frac{\exp\left[\phi_{ik}(R_{ik} - D_{iko})\right]}{\exp\left[\phi_{ik}(R_{ik} - D_{iko})\right] + \exp\left[\phi_{ik}(-D_{ikv})\right]}.$$

The probability of unit floor space remaining vacant is then $1-q_{ik}$. ϕ_{ik} are the dispersion parameters.

The landlords' ex-ante expected rental profit from a unit amount of floor space is

(2.1.24)
$$\omega_{ik}(R_{ik}) = \frac{1}{\phi_{ik}}\ln\left(\exp\left[\phi_{ik}(R_{ik} - D_{iko})\right] + \exp\left[\phi_{ik}(-D_{ikv})\right]\right).$$

The rental on vacant land, that is for $k = 0$, is taken as exogenous.

2.1.4 Developers

I keep the same assumptions on developers' behavior as Anas and Liu (2007). Developers are profit maximizing risk neutral firms which have perfect foresight. The market is competitive and developers take building asset prices, unit construction and demolition prices and other costs as given.

At the beginning of the period, developers buy vacant lands and buildings. During the period, those assets are operated in the rental asset market by landlords. In the end of the period, the idiosyncratic uncertainty is realized. Buildings might then be demolished or constructed on vacant land in the most profitable way. Developers buy the services of specialized (non-basic) industries that construct or demolish buildings. Building must be constructed on vacant land. To make a new building on the land where a building of a different type exists, developers need to demolish the existing building, then construct the new building in the next period. At the end of each period all building assets are valued at the market prices produced by the model.

The *stationary state* market prices (per unit of floor space or land) are V_{ik}. Subscript i denotes the zone and $k=0$ denotes vacant land as an asset and $k>0$ stands for floor space in each of the building types in the model. It is assumed that there are $k=1...\aleph$ predetermined building types. The exogenous structural densities (square feet of floor space per acre of lot size) of building type k in zone i are m_{ik}. By constructing a type k building on a square foot of vacant land, m_{ik} square feet of floor space are made available. Conversely, to make a square foot of vacant land, m_{ik} acres floor space of type k building need to be demolished. In other words, to construct a square foot floor space of type k building, $1/m_{ik}$ acres of land are used up and become unavailable in the next market period.

Per unit floor space construction and demolition prices for each industry and zone are given by $p_{\Re+k,i}$ and $p_{\Re+\aleph+k,i}$. In addition to those monetary costs, developers incur non-financial costs of constructing and demolishing type k building, $\mathbb{C}_{i0k}$ and $\mathbb{C}_{ik0}$. Also, ς_{i0k} and ς_{ik0} are uncertain (fluctuating) non-financial idiosyncratic costs.

The developers' profits from possible construction and demolition choices are expressed in the following equations, where the asset purchasing costs are ignored because those are sunk cost for developers operating at this moment. Those profits are discounted with the real interest rate ρ to the beginning of the time period. The profits expressed in (2.1.25a) are from keeping the vacant land undeveloped, in (2.1.25b) are from constructing type k building on vacant land, in (2.1.25c) are from keeping a building unchanged and in (2.1.25d) are from demolishing a type k to make vacant land.

(2.1.25a)
$$\Pi_{i00} = \tilde{\Pi}_{i00} + \varsigma_{i00} = \frac{1}{1+\rho}V_{i0} - \mathbb{C}_{i00} + \varsigma_{i00},$$

(2.1.25b)
$$\Pi_{i0k} = \tilde{\Pi}_{i0k} + \varsigma_{i0k} = \frac{1}{1+\rho}(V_{ik} - p_{\Re+k,i})m_{ik} - \mathbb{C}_{i0k} + \varsigma_{i0k},$$

(2.1.25c)
$$\Pi_{ikk} = \tilde{\Pi}_{ikk} + \varsigma_{ikk} = \frac{1}{1+\rho} V_{ik} - \mathbb{C}_{ikk} + \varsigma_{ikk},$$

(2.1.25d)
$$\Pi_{ik0} = \tilde{\Pi}_{ik0} + \varsigma_{ik0} = \frac{1}{1+\rho}\left(\frac{V_{i0}}{m_{ik}} - p_{\aleph+\aleph+k,i}\right) - \mathbb{C}_{ik0} + \varsigma_{ik0},$$

where $\tilde{\Pi}_{i00}, \tilde{\Pi}_{i0k}, \tilde{\Pi}_{ikk}, \tilde{\Pi}_{ik0}$ are the non-idiosyncratic parts of the developers' profits.

Assume that the non-financial idiosyncratic construction costs for each i, ($\varsigma_{i00}, \varsigma_{i0k}; k=1...K)\in(-\infty, +\infty)$~i.i.d. Gumbel with dispersion coefficient Φ_{i0} and also that for each (i, k), the idiosyncratic demolition costs ($\varsigma_{ikk}, \varsigma_{ik0}; k=1...K)\in(-\infty, +\infty)$~i.i.d. Gumbel with dispersion coefficient Φ_{ik}.

A developer who owns vacant land will build a type-k building on it when $\Pi_{i0k} > \Pi_{i00}$. The probability that this will occur is the ($\aleph+1$) nominal logit (2.1.26a). For any building type ($k>0$):

(2.1.26a)
$$Q_{i0k}(V_{i0}, V_{i1}, ..., V_{i\aleph}) = \frac{\exp\left(\Phi_{i0}\tilde{\Pi}_{i0k}\right)}{\exp\left(\Phi_{i0}\tilde{\Pi}_{i00}\right) + \sum_{s=1...\aleph}\exp\left(\Phi_{i0}\tilde{\Pi}_{i0s}\right)}.$$

A developer who owns a type k building will demolish it if $\Pi_{ik0} > \Pi_{ikk}$. The probability that this will occur is the binomial logit:

(2.1.26b)
$$Q_{ik0}(V_{i0}, V_{ik}) = \frac{\exp\left(\Phi_{ik}\tilde{\Pi}_{ik0}\right)}{\exp\left(\Phi_{ik}\tilde{\Pi}_{ik0}\right) + \exp\left(\Phi_{ik}\tilde{\Pi}_{ikk}\right)}.$$

For investors in land and type k building, the expected economic profit known from the logit calculus is

(2.1.27a)
$$E\left[\max(\Pi_{i00}, \Pi_{i0k}; k=1...\aleph)\right] = \frac{1}{\Phi_{i0}}\ln\left(\exp(\Phi_{i0}\tilde{\Pi}_{i00}) + \sum_{s=1...\aleph}\exp(\Phi_{i0}\tilde{\Pi}_{i0s})\right)$$

for construction, and

(2.1.27b)
$$E\left[\max(\Pi_{kk}, \Pi_{k0})\right] = \frac{1}{\Phi_{ik}}\ln\left(\exp(\Phi_{ik}\tilde{\Pi}_{ik0}) + \exp(\Phi_{ik}\tilde{\Pi}_{ikk})\right),$$

for demolition.

The zero ex-ante expected economic profits discounted to the beginning of the year including the expected rents are then equal to the asset prices:

(2.1.28a)
$$V_{i0} = \frac{1}{\Phi_{i0}}\ln\left(\exp(\Phi_{i0}\tilde{\Pi}_{i00}) + \sum_{s=1...\aleph}\exp(\Phi_{i0}\tilde{\Pi}_{i0s})\right) + R_{i0},$$

(2.1.28b)
$$V_{ik} = \frac{1}{\Phi_{ik}}\ln\left(\exp(\Phi_{ik}\tilde{\Pi}_{ik0}) + \exp(\Phi_{ik}\tilde{\Pi}_{ikk})\right) + \omega(R_{ik}).$$

In RELU2 I have slightly changed the setting of a developer's behavior. Suppose that the developer takes multiple-years to complete demolition and construction. In the simulations to be reported in this book, the length of time for a developer's period is 5 years as opposed to a single year in Anas and Liu (2007). Define the number of years required to complete a project as *year* (*e.g. year* = 5). Then, the profits from construction and demolition are modified as follows.

(2.1.25'a)
$$\Pi_{i00} = \tilde{\Pi}_{i00} + \varsigma_{i00} = \left(\frac{1}{1+\rho}\right)^{year} V_{i0} - \mathbb{C}_{i00} + \varsigma_{i00},$$

(2.1.25'b)
$$\Pi_{i0k} = \tilde{\Pi}_{i0k} + \varsigma_{i0k} = \left(\frac{1}{1+\rho}\right)^{year} (V_{ik} - p_{\Re+k,i})m_{ik} - \mathbb{C}_{i0k} + \varsigma_{i0k},$$

(2.1.25'c)
$$\Pi_{ikk} = \tilde{\Pi}_{ikk} + \varsigma_{ikk} = \left(\frac{1}{1+\rho}\right)^{year} V_{ik} - \mathbb{C}_{ikk} + \varsigma_{ikk},$$

(2.1.25'd)
$$\Pi_{ik0} = \tilde{\Pi}_{ik0} + \varsigma_{ik0} = \left(\frac{1}{1+\rho}\right)^{year} \left(\frac{V_{i0}}{m_{ik}} - p_{\Re+\aleph+k,i}\right) - \mathbb{C}_{ik0} + \varsigma_{ik0},$$

where $\mathbb{C}_{i00}, \mathbb{C}_{i0k}, \mathbb{C}_{ikk}, \mathbb{C}_{ik0}$, and $\varsigma_{i00}, \varsigma_{i0k}, \varsigma_{ikk}, \varsigma_{ik0}$ are discounted.

The zero profit condition is changed accordingly

(2.1.28'a)
$$V_{i0} = \frac{1}{\Phi_{i0}} \ln\left(\exp\left(\Phi_{i0}\tilde{\Pi}_{i00}\right) + \sum_{s=1\ldots\aleph} \exp\left(\Phi_{i0}\tilde{\Pi}_{i0s}\right)\right) + \sum_{y=1}^{year}\left(\left(\frac{1}{1+\rho}\right)^{y-1} R_{i0}\right),$$

(2.1.28'b)
$$V_{ik} = \frac{1}{\Phi_{ik}} \ln\left(\exp\left(\Phi_{ik}\tilde{\Pi}_{ik0}\right) + \exp\left(\Phi_{ik}\tilde{\Pi}_{ikk}\right)\right) + \sum_{y=1}^{year}\left(\left(\frac{1}{1+\rho}\right)^{y-1} \omega(R_{ik})\right).$$

In both cases, if $year = 1$ the equations become the same as (2.1.25a)-(2.1.25d) and (2.1.28a)-(2.1.28b).

2.1.5 General equilibrium of RELU2

There are several modifications from the general equilibrium formulated in Anas and Liu (2007). First, in RELU2 consumers have vehicle type c choice in addition to the other choices treated by Anas and Liu (2007). Second, the travel time and cost is different by consumer type f and vehicle type c, whereas in Anas-Liu travel time and cost are the same for all consumers since, implicitly, consumers own the same vehicle type. Third, non-wage incomes are treated as exogenous constants in RELU2 whereas in Anas-Liu they were endogenous.

The other general equilibrium conditions are the same as Anas and Liu (2007). At the equilibrium (i) labor markets, (ii) product markets, and (iii) floor-space/land markets are cleared in all zones. (i) In the labor market, zero excess demands for all skill types are achieved, (ii) in the product market, the aggregate output produced by each primary industry in each zone covers exports and inter-industry demands for the product, and the retail good's output covers consumer demands and exports. (iii) In the building floor space markets (residential and commercial), zero excess demands for all building types are achieved. In addition, the constructed and demolished floor spaces of each building types are equalized to maintain the stock of each building type at its stationary equilibrium.

The vectors of product prices (**p**), wages (**w**) and rents (**R**), the vector of industry outputs (**X**), the vector of real estate asset prices (**V**), the vector of stationary real estate stocks (**S**) are all solved at the stationary general equilibrium.

(i) Labor Markets

The annual labor demand in hours is equalized to the labor supply in hours for each $f = 1...F$ skill group in each of the $j = 1...\Im$ model zones, by $F\Im$ equations.

(2.1.29a)
$$L_{jf}^{demand} = L_{jf}^{supply},$$

where the aggregate labor demand over industries for each f in zone j is, by using the labor demand functions given by (2.1.19),

(2.1.29b)
$$L_{jf}^{demand} = \sum_{r=1}^{\Re+2\aleph} L_{j|rf}.$$

The aggregate labor supply of type f in zone j is, by using the personal labor supply in (2.1.10) and consumers' choice probability in (2.1.15),

(2.1.29c)
$$L_{jf}^{supply} = \sum_{kic} \left(N_f \Pr^e_{ijkc|f} H_{ijc|f} \right).$$

(ii) Goods Product Markets
Retail Industry:

In the case of the retail industry, some outputs are purchased by consumers who travel shop at that zone. Other parts of outputs are exported. There are $\Im$ such equations, one for each model zone:

(2.1.30a)
$$X_{\Re i} = Z_i^{demand}$$

where the aggregate demand over all consumers and export for the product of industry r made in zone i is, by using the personal demands in (2.1.9) and consumers' choice probability (2.1.15), and the exogenous export demands, $\Xi_{\Re i}$,

(2.1.30b)
$$Z_i^{demand} = \sum_{\forall f} N_f \left(\sum_{\forall(n,s,k,d)} \Pr_{nskd|f} Z_{i|nsfd} \right) + \Xi_{\Re i}.$$

The aggregate supply of the product of the retail industry $\Re$ made in zone i $X_{\Re i}$, is given in (2.1.17).

Basic Industry:

For each basic industry, some of the aggregate output in zone j will be shipped to be used as an intermediate input to any basic industry including the same industry or to any construction/demolition industry in any model zone. The remaining aggregate output is exported to the outside world. Let Ξ_{ri} be the exogenous export demands. The following $\Im(\Re-1)$ equations are cleared for the basic product markets in each zone:

(2.1.31a)
$$X_{ri} = Y_{ri}^{demand}.$$

For the product of type r industry made in zone i, the aggregate intermediate goods demand is the demand for all zone $S=1,...,\Im$ and all industries $n = \Re + 2\aleph$ and for export. By using intermediate goods demand of the firm (2.1.21),

(2.1.31b)
$$Y_{rj}^{demand} = \sum_{s}^{\Im} \sum_{n}^{\Re+2\aleph} Y_{sn|rj} + \Xi_{ri}.$$

The aggregate supply of intermediate good of type r industry made in zone i, X_{ri}, is derived in (2.1.17).

(iii) Real Estate Market
Real Estate Rental Markets:

The floor space demand and supply must be equal for each housing building of type $k=1...\aleph_1$ and commercial building of type $k=1...\aleph_2$ in each zone $\Im$. There are $\Im\aleph_1 + \Im\aleph_2$ such equations:

For the residential floor space,

(2.1.32a)
$$b_{ik}^{demand} = b_{ik}^{supply},$$

where the aggregate demand for residential floor space of building type k in zone i is, by using personal floor space demand (2.1.8) and consumers' choice probability,

(2.1.32b)
$$b_{ik}^{demand} = \sum_{fjc} \left(N_f \Pr_{ijkc|f} \beta_f \frac{\Psi_{ijef}}{R_{ik}} \right).$$

The aggregate expected supply of residential floor space in building type k in zone i is obtained by multiplying the stock with the probability that the landlord will let the space be occupied (2.1.23),

(2.1.32c)
$$b_{ik}^{supply} = S_{ik} q_{ik}.$$

For the buisiness floor spase,

(2.1.33a)
$$B_{k|j}^{demand} = B_{k|j}^{supply}$$

where the aggregate demand for business floor space in buildings of type k in zone j is obtained by using the aggregate floor space demands of firms (2.1.20),

(2.1.33b)
$$B_{k|j}^{demand} = \sum_r B_{k|rj}.$$

The aggregate supply for business floor space in buildings of type k in zone j is obtained by multiplying the stock with the probability that the landlord will let the space in the rental market (2.1.23),

(2.1.33c)
$$B_{k|j}^{supply} = S_{kj} q_{kj}.$$

Normal returns in real estate

All firms in the model make zero economic profit. This also means that investors make a normal return equal to the interest rate ρ by lending financial capital to the firms. There are $\Im(\Re+2\aleph)$ zero profit equations (2.1.22).

In every zone there are there are $\aleph+1$ potential real estate markets, one for each asset, i.e. the $\aleph$ building types and the vacant land. Investors in these assets make zero expected profits. There are $\Im$ such equations (2.1.28a) for the vacant land in each zone and $\Im\aleph$ such equations (2.1.28b) for each building type.

Construction/Demolition and Building Stock Conversions

The newly produced floor space of building type $s = 1,...,\aleph$ by construction on vacant land in zone i is obtained by multiplying the stock of vacant land in zone i with the probability that construction of type s floor space will occur and then multiplying by the structural density of the type s building.

(2.1.34a)
$$X_{\Re+s,i} = m_{is}S_{i0}Q_{i0s}(V_{i0}, V_{i1},...,V_{i\aleph}).$$

The newly produced floor spaces of vacant land from demolishing each building type $s = 1,...,\aleph$ in zone i are obtained by multiplying the stock of floor space with the probability of demolition,

(2.1.34b)
$$X_{\Re+\aleph+s,i} = S_{is}Q_{is0}(V_{is}, V_{i0}).$$

At the stationary equilibrium, the available floor space of each building types in each zone i is stationary. For this to happen, the floor space of demolition and construction of the same building type in all zones in (2.1.34) must be equalized each period. There are $2\Im\aleph$ such equations ($\Im\aleph$ for each construction and demolition). See Anas-Arnott (1997). Recall that subscript $\Re+s$ is for construction of type $s = 1,...,\aleph$ building and $\Re+\aleph+s$

is demolition of type $s = 1,...,\aleph$ building.

(2.1.35a)
$$X_{\Re+s,j} = X_{\Re+\aleph+s,j}.$$

In addition, the total amount of land in each zone $\Im$ that is utilized for each building type and remains vacant must be equalized to the exogenous land space of each zone, J_i.

(2.1.35b)
$$\sum_{k=0,...,\aleph} \frac{1}{m_{ik}} S_{ik} = J_i. \ (m_{i0} \equiv 1).$$

For the relationship between the stationary state and the non-stationary dynamics, see Anas and Arnott (1997).

Summary

The general equilibrium contains $\Im(7\aleph + 2\Re + F + 2)$ unknowns. These unknowns are: **w** ($\Im F$ wages for each skill type of labor in each model zone), **p** ($\Im(\Re + 2\aleph)$ prices of output for the basic and construction/demolition industries in each model zone), **X** ($\Im(\Re + 2\aleph)$ outputs of the basic and construction/demolition industries in each model zone), **R** ($\Im \aleph$ rents for each type of floor space in each model zone), **V** ($\Im(\aleph + 1)$ stationary asset prices of each type of floor space and vacant land in each model zone), **S** ($\Im(\aleph + 1)$ stationary stocks of each type of floor space and vacant land in each model zone).

To find those variables I will solve $\Im(7\aleph + 2\Re + F + 2)$ equations. These equations are: $\Im F$ equations form labor market clearing condition (2.1.29a). $\Im$ equations from retail goods market clearing condition (2.1.30a). $\Im(\Re-1)$ equations form basic industry market clearing condition (2.1.31a). $\Im(\Re + 2\aleph)$ equations from intermediate goods market clearing condition (2.1.31b). $\Re\aleph_1 + \Re\aleph_2$ equations from housing and commercial building market clearing condition (2.1.32a) and (2.1.33a). $\Im$ equations from zero profit condition of investor on vacant land (2.1.28a). $\Im\aleph$ equations from zero profit condition of investor on building (2.1.28b). $2\Im\aleph$ equations from construction and demolition industry market clearing condition (2.1.34a) and (2.1.34b). $\Im\aleph$ equations from construction and demolition consistency condition (2.1.35a). $\Im$ equations from total land market clearing condition (2.1.35b).

2.2 TRAN2

Anas and Liu (2007) described in detail how the RELU model was linked with the TRAN model of mode choice and route choice on the road network. I will here refer to their TRAN model as TRAN1. In what follows, I described how TRAN2, developed in this book, differs from TRAN1. There are four reasons why TRAN1 had to be modified. (i) As described earlier, one modification was necessary because TRAN1 did not model the choice of car fuel economy by consumers, whereas this becomes crucial in evaluating the effects of the fuel tax, congestion tolls and emission control policies which are all studied in this book; (ii) The other modification that was necessary to make is the modeling of congestion not only on the major roads but also on local streets. Any policy of pricing travel on major roads would cause traffic to spill over to local roads and congestion on those local roads to increase. More precisely, the major roads in the TRAN1 network link various zones and are important in accommodating zone-to-zone, that is, inter-zonal traffic. Intra-zonal traffic which is significant is also important, but TRAN1 ignores the congestion that can occur due to travel within zones. In TRAN1, the travel times and travel costs of trips that occur within zones are taken as constants that are exogenous; (iii) Thirdly, the values of time (VOT) in TRAN1 are the same for any consumer type f. But higher f type consumers evaluate time highly as compared to lower f types; (iv) Fourthly, the travel time and monetary cost of the same O-D pair are the same for work and non-work trips in TRAN1. But those could be different for different purpose and this is remedied in TRAN2.

TRAN2 remedies the above shortcomings by doing two things. First, as already shown, car trips from RELU2 come to TRAN2 by car type. For example, some higher income consumers may like the comfort and safety of larger cars that are less fuel efficient, and will experience higher gasoline consumption and higher monetary cost as they travel on the network. More precisely, RELU2 produces a zone-to-zone trip matrix for each income group f of consumers and each car type, c. Consumers of different (f, c), choosing the same routes of travel on the network, will not experience the same monetary costs due to the fact that they are using vehicles differing in fuel economy and will not experience the same time cost due to the fact that they have different values of time (VOT) by f. This differs from TRAN1 of Anas-Liu (2007) where it was assumed that all cars are implicitly of the same fuel economy and VOT are the same for any f. Hence, consumers experienced the same monetary costs on the road network, if they chose the same route. TRAN2 retains the assumption of TRAN1 that all trips traveling on the same network link take the same amount of time, hence also all trips traveling on the same route also take the same amount of time (the time on a route is the sum of the times on the link and intra-zone roads that form that route for the same purpose). But TRAN2 departs from TRAN1 in that the time cost and monetary costs of travel on the same link will differ according to the consumer type and the car-type of the consumer doing the travel. Hence, consumers on the same link and route will experience different monetary costs and because of these differences, the choice of the optimal route will depend on consumer type and car type, since consumers choose their optimal routes by minimizing generalized cost, a weighted average of monetary cost and travel time.

The purpose of TRAN is to find the expected travel time and expected travel monetary cost for each consumer and car type combination. TRAN2 to RELU2 are connected by passing the relevant variables between the two models. I begin with RELUTRIPS, the matrix of trips that connects RELU2 to TRAN2. RELUTRIPS stands for the conventional origin to destination trip matrix of travel forecasting. Taking RELUTRIPS from RELU2, TRAN2 executes several steps to find the expected travel time and monetary travel cost by car and consumer type (f, c).

The *first* procedure is to classify the trips into auto, transit and other modes, that is to perform the mode-choice step of the travel forecasting.

Second, the trips by the auto mode traveling from zone i to zone j are split among the routes connecting i and j, by a stochastic user equilibrium and the numbers of auto trips on the local roads and the major highway links are determined. Travel on local roads and major highway links are both subject to congestion, so in the course of doing the stochastic user equilibrium assignment, congestion and the congested equilibrium travel time on each local road or major highway link is also determined. I do not model the congestion in the non-auto modes, nor do I model the intraday variation in road congestion.

Third, in TRAN2, three variables are traced from the link and route level up to the level of modal choice and then back to RELU2. The three variables are time, monetary cost and generalized cost which is a linear combination of time and monetary cost. Generalized cost is used by each consumer to decide the route choice as well as the choice of travel mode.

2.2.1 Mode Choice

TRAN2 receives the following daily trip matrices from RELU2. These are: 1) a matrix of the daily commutes from residence zone i to job zone j for all consumers of type f who work, by each car type c ; 2) a matrix of daily non-work trips (shopping trips), by both employed and non-working consumers, that originate at residence zone i and terminate at shopping zone j by type of consumer f and car type c.

(2.2.1)
$$TRIPS^w_{ijfc} = \begin{cases} N_f \sum_{k=1}^{\aleph_1} \Pr_{izjkc|f} & \text{if } w=1 (\text{work trip}) \text{ for } j>0 \\ \left(\frac{1}{d}\right)\left(N_f \sum_{s=0}^{\aleph'} \sum_{k=1}^{\aleph_1} \Pr_{iskc|f} C_{isf} Z_{zj|isfc}\right) & \text{if } w=2(\text{non-work trip}) \text{ for } j>0, s \geq 0. \end{cases}$$

The number of trips for work and non-work are categorized for each vehicle type c and traveler type f in addition to zone origin-destination pairs, i and j. This is because the different vehicle types have the different travel monetary cost as already explained, and the different types of travelers have different values of time (VOT) for travel, according to their consumer type.

TRAN2 calculates the probabilities of mode choice, $\pi^w_{mij|fc}$. $\pi^w_{mij|fc}$ is the probability that a trip by a type f consumer with work or non-work trips w having car c, originating in zone i and terminating in zone j will choose mode m. There are three possible modes. $m = 1$ is the auto mode, $m = 2$ is the transit mode (including bus and/or rail) and $m = 3$ is all other modes primarily walking and bicycling. The mode choice probabilities are used to calculate $MODETRIPS^w_{mijfc}$ which are the trips by mode of travel originating at zone $i = 1...\Im$, terminating at zone $j > 0$, by traveler type f, and vehicle type c. Note that $MODETRIPS^w_{mijfc}$ consist of trips that are outbound and inbound from the residence location. It is assumed, however, that on the same round trip the outbound and inbound trips always use the same mode:

(2.2.2)
$$MODETRIPS^w_{mijfc} = \{(TRIPS^w_{ijfc}) + (TRIPS^w_{jifc})\} \times \pi^w_{mij|fc}.$$

The mode choice probabilities will be discussed later.

2.2.2 Traffic Flow

$IFLOW_i$, $i = 1...I$, and $FLOW_l$, $l = 1...L$, are the *vehicle* traffic-flows (that is, aggregate traffic) on local roads in zone i and on a highway link (representing major roads) l respectively. These flows are determined in the highway network equilibrium endogenously. In TRAN2, the congested equilibrium network flows and travel times on each local road and highway link are calculated by using the Anas-Kim (1990) stochastic user equilibrium formulation and their algorithm.

In order to understand how the congested equilibrium flows are calculated it is first important to understand how the model treats intra-zonal versus inter-zonal trips. If a trip originates and terminates in the same zone (e.g. consumers commute from a residence in zone i to a job in zone i or from a residence in zone i to a shopping destination in zone i), the trip is an intra-zonal trip. In the model, it is assumed that all intra-zonal trips use local roads only. But for inter-zonal trips, it is assumed that a trip uses local roads in the zone of origin and the zone of destination but also at least one link on the major road network. One may think of this type of trip-making in several different ways. For example, a trip going from one zone to another has to make use of local roads to get on the nearest highway, then travel on that highway, exiting the highway network at the destination zone and then, finally, traveling on the local roads of the destination zone to reach a specific destination there. The part of such a trip that uses the major road contributes to the traffic flow on all the network links that the trip uses.

The aggregated flow on a particular link of the major road network is then calculated as follows by making use of the route choice probabilities, *RPROB*:

(2.2.3a)
$$FLOW_\ell = \frac{1}{\tilde{\eta}} \sum_{w=1,2} \sum_{\forall f, \forall c} \sum_{\forall (i,j)} \sum_{r \in ROUTES_{ij}} \left(MODETRIPS^w_{1ij|fc} \times RPROB^w_{r \in ROUTES_{ij}|fc} \times a_{\ell \in r \in ROUTES_{ij}} \right).$$

$\tilde{\eta}$ is a constant car occupancy rate in persons (adults) per vehicle. The equation sums the trips utilizing all the routes that share the same link. More precisely, $a_{\ell \in r \in ROUTES_{ij}} = 1$ if the link ℓ belongs to $route_{r \in ROUTES_{ij}}$, $a_{\ell \in r \in ROUTES_{ij}} = 0$ otherwise. The set of routes, $ROUTES_{ij}$, which comes from the route choice model, contains all feasible sequences of links connecting the origin zone i and the destination zone j.

The aggregated flow of all trips using the local roads in zone i is calculated as follows:

(2.2.3b)
$$IFLOW_i = \frac{1}{\tilde{\eta}} \sum_{w=1,2} \sum_{\forall f, \forall c} NWR_i^w \times \left[MODETRIPS_{1ii|fc}^w + \sum_{\forall j \neq i} GWR_{ij} \left(MODETRIPS_{1ij|fc}^w + MODETRIPS_{1ji|fc}^w \right) \right],$$

where $GWR_{ij} = 1$ *if* $i = j$ and $GWR_{ij} > 0$ *if* $i \neq j$ are the ratio of average travel distance over the local roads for the inter-zonal traveler ($i \neq j$) relative to the intra-zonal traveler ($i = j$). $NWR_i^w = 1$ *if* $w = 1$ (*work trip*) and $NWR_i^w > 0$ *if* $w \neq 1$ (*non–work tip*) are the ratio of average travel distance over the local roads for non-work trips relative to work trips. The adjustments reflected in the values of GWR_{ij} are meant to capture that most inter-zonal travelers use the local roads just to reach the major roads, while those who travel intra-zonally may travel longer (or shorter, since GWR can be less than 1.) distances over the local roads. The adjustments in NWR_i^w reflect the fact that non-work trips take longer (or shorter) distances over the local road network. For example I might interpret this as people do trip-chaining, comparison shopping and searching. In reality, travelers have more than one purpose for each trip. Travelers often stop by several locations in one trip. For a theory of trip-chaining, see Anas (2007). But in the RELU-TRAN model, there is one purpose for each trip. To compensate for the gap created by ignoring trip-chaining which happens mostly intra-zonally, I put higher weights on zone trips, by using the coefficients NWR_i^w.

2.2.3 Time, Monetary Cost and Generalized Cost
Zone and Link Level

I now describe how the model calculates the travelers' required travel time, monetary cost and generalized cost at the zone and link level. $ITIME_\ell$ and $TIME_\ell$ are the congested one-way travel times (in minutes) on local roads i and major road link l, respectively. They are calculated from the following congestion functions:

(2.2.4a)
$$TIME_\ell = ALPHA_\ell \times LENGTH_\ell \left(1 + BETA_\ell \left[\frac{FLOW_\ell}{CAP_l}\right]^{CEXP}\right),$$

(2.2.4.b)
$$ITIME_i = IALPHA_i \times ILENGTH_i \left(1 + IBETA_i \left[\frac{IFLOW_i}{ICAP_i}\right]^{ICEXP}\right),$$

where $ILENGTH_i$ and $LENGTH_l$ are the "lengths" of the local road and highway link in miles, $IALPHA_i$ and $ALPHA_l$ are the inverse vehicle free-flow (uncongested) speeds (i.e., minutes per mile) on local roads i and on highway links l. $IBETA_i$, $BETA_l$, $ICEXP$ and $CEXP$ are coefficients. $ICAP_i$ and CAP_l are the capacity of local road i and highway link l.

To derive the monetary cost, I need some more information. The travel speed on major road links and local roads is immediately found from $ITIME_i$ and $TIME_l$.

(2.2.5a,b)
$$Ispeed_i = \frac{ILENGTH_i}{ITIME_i / 60} \quad \text{and} \quad speed_\ell = \frac{LENGTH_\ell}{TIME_\ell / 60}.$$

Fuel consumption in gallons per mile for a vehicle with fuel inefficiency factor $e_c = 1$ is a function of the vehicle's speed as follows:

(2.2.6a)
$$Ifuel_i = \begin{pmatrix} 0.122619 - 0.0117211 \times Ispeed_i + 0.0006413 \times Ispeed_i^2 \\ -0.000018732 \times Ispeed_i^3 + 0.0000003 \times Ispeed_i^4 \\ -0.0000000024718 \times Ispeed_i^5 \\ +0.000000000008233 \times Ispeed_i^6 \end{pmatrix},$$

(2.2.6b)
$$fuel_\ell = \begin{pmatrix} 0.122619 - 0.0117211 \times speed_\ell + 0.0006413 \times speed_\ell^2 \\ -0.000018732 \times speed_\ell^3 + 0.0000003 \times speed_\ell^4 \\ -0.0000000024718 \times speed_\ell^5 \\ +0.000000000008233 \times speed_\ell^6 \end{pmatrix}.$$

Figures 2.2.1 and 2.2.2 are relevant illustrations. The first figure reproduced from Davis and Diegel (2004) shows the variation in the basic shape of the above polynomial for nine different vehicle types, while the next figure shows the above polynomial equation which has been fitted to the Geo Prizm by Hyok-Joo Rhee. In RELU-TRAN2, the Geo Prizm corresponds to a vehicle type with a unit inefficiency factor.

To get the gasoline consumption per mile for a car of any inefficiency factor, I just multiply by that inefficiency factor,

(2.2.7a,b)
$Ifuel_i \times ineff_c$ and $fuel_l \times ineff_c$.

The monetary cost in dollars per vehicle mile by vehicle type for travel on local roads and major roads are,

(2.2.8a)
$IUCOST_{i|c} = p_{FUEL} \times Ifuel_i \times ineff_c + Io_i \times ineff_c$,

(2.2.8b)
$UCOST_{\ell|c} = p_{FUEL} \times fuel_\ell \times ineff_c + o_\ell \times ineff_c$,

where, p_{FUEL} is the price of fuel in $/gallon and $o_\ell \times ineff_c$ is other than fuel costs per mile for each vehicle type. $IMCOST_{i|c}$ and $MCOST_{i|c}$ are the one-way *per traveler* monetary cost on local and major road links by vehicle type.

(2.2.9a)
$$IMCOST_{i|c} = IUCOST_{i|c} \times ILENGTH_i \times \frac{1}{\tilde{\eta}},$$

(2.2.9b)
$$MCOST_{\ell|c} = UCOST_{\ell|c} \times LENGTH_\ell \times \frac{1}{\tilde{\eta}}.$$

$IGCOST_{i|fc}$ and $GCOST_{l|fc}$ are the zone and link generalized cost of the travel by auto per person. Generalized costs are the total cost of traveler's time value and monetary cost on local roads and major road links by traveler and vehicle type.

(2.2.10a)
$$IGCOST_{i|fc} = IMCOST_{i|c} + VOT_f \times ITIME_i,$$

(2.2.10b)
$$GCOST_{l|fc} = MCOST_{\ell|c} + VOT_f \times TIME_\ell.$$

VOT_f is *the value of travel time* for each traveler type f.

Route Level

By adding across all the intra-zonal roads and highway links (major roads) on the route, I can find the route level time, costs and generalized cost. The route travel time is calculated as follows by adding up the travel times on the links making up the route and the intra-zonal travel times on the local roads:

(2.2.11)
$$Rt^w_{1ij|fc} = \left\{ \left(\sum_{\forall \ell} a_{\ell \in r \in ROUTES_{ij}} TIME_\ell \right) + GWR_{ij} \times NWR^w_i \times ITIME_i + GWR_{ji} \right.$$
$$\times NWR^w_j \times ITIME_j \text{ if } i \neq j$$
$$\left. NWR^w_i \times ITIME_i \text{ if } i = j. \right.$$

Similarly, for monetary costs and generalized costs, I have:

(2.2.12)
$$Rv^w_{1ij|fc} = \left\{ \left(\sum_{\forall \ell} a_{\ell \in r \in ROUTES_{ij}} MCOST_{\ell|c} \right) + GWR_{ij} \times NWR^w_i \times IMCOST_{i|c} \right. \\ + GWR_{ji} \times NWR^w_j \times IMCOST_{j|c} \text{ if } i \neq j \\ \left. NWR^w_i \times IMCOST_{i|c} \text{ if } i = j. \right.$$

(2.2.13)
$$RGCOST^w_{r \in ROUTES_{ij}|fc} = \left\{ \left(\sum_{\forall \ell} a_{\ell \in r \in ROUTES_{ij}} GCOST_{r \in ROUTES_{ij}|fc} \right) + GWR_{ij} \right. \\ \times NWR^w_i \times IGCOST_{i|fc} + GWR_{ji} \times NWR^w_j \\ \times IGCOST_{j|fc} \text{ if } j \neq i \\ \left. NWR^w_i \times IGCOST_{i|fc} \text{ if } j = i. \right.$$

2.2.4 Route Choice Probability

The route choice probability is developed based on the stochastic route choice model of Anas and Kim (1990). I start the route choice model with defining the notations. $i = 1 \ldots \Im$ are possible travel origin zones and $j = 1 \ldots \Im$ are possible travel destination zones. $\ell = 1 \ldots L$ are the links on the aggregated network of major roads. Let $ROUTES_{ij}$ be the *set* of permissible highway routes connecting from i to j. $r \in ROUTES_{ij}$ is such a route that belongs to the above set. $a_{\ell \in r \in ROUTES_{ij}} = 1$ if link l belongs to route $r \in ROUTES_{ij}$ or $a_{\ell \in r \in ROUTES_{ij}} = 0$ otherwise. It is assumed that the travelers choose the route to minimize the generalized cost of a one way trip. Let $RPROB^w_{r \in ROUTES_{ij}|fc}$ be the route choice probability given by the multinomial logit that an *auto vehicle trip* from zone i to j will choose route $r \in ROUTES_{ij}$.[5]

The route choice probability by traveler and vehicle type is:

---

5 See, for example, Daganzo and Sheffi (1977) for an early use of such a model. Zhu et al. (2007) propose an agent-based route choice model that tracks the decision maker's choices on the road network. The model is applied on the Sioux Falls network and the Chicago sketch network. Bar-Gera (2006) presents the condition of consistency for sets of minimum-cost routes and shows how it helps to choose similar routes as user-equilibrium routes.

(2.2.14)
$$RPROB^w_{r \in ROUTES_{ij}|fc} = \frac{\exp\left(-LAMDA_f \times RGCOST^w_{r \in ROUTES_{ij}|fc}\right)}{\sum_{s \in ROUTES_{ij}} \exp\left(-LAMDA_f \times RGCOST^w_{s \in ROUTES_{ij}|fc}\right)}.$$

$LAMDA_f > 0$ is the cost-dispersion coefficient in the route choice model. Notice that $RPROB^w_{r \in ROUTES_{ij}|fc}$ need not to be the same to go and to return. There is no route choice in the model's intra-zonal travel, since the model does not distinguish among routes within a zone.

2.2.5 One-Way Trip

Note that for the non-auto modes, $m = 2,3$, regardless of any differences in the travelers' f and c, the travel time, monetary cost and generalized cost are the same for the same m, i, j.

$t^w_{mij|fc}$ is the expected one-way travel time by auto, calculated from the congested major road link and local road equilibrium.

(2.2.15)
$$t^w_{1ij|fc} = \sum_{r \in ROUTES_{ij}} PROB^w_{r \in ROUTES_{ij}|fc} \times Rt^w_{1ij|fc}.$$

$t^w_{mij|fc}$ for $m = 2,3$ are the zone-to-zone times for the non-auto modes. Those are constants since congestion in non-auto modes is not modeled.

Similarly the expected one-way travel, monetary cost is given by:

(2.2.16)
$$v^w_{1ij|fc} = \sum_{r \in ROUTES_{ij}} PROB^w_{r \in ROUTES_{ij}|fc} \times Rv^w_{1ij|fc}.$$

$v^w_{mij|fc}$ for $m = 2,3$ are the zone-to-zone monetary cost for the non-auto mode. Those are constants since congestion in non-auto modes is not modeled. It is assumed that those who travel by $m = 2,3$ will incur the same time and cost for non-work and work travel.

$\tilde{c}^w_{1ij|fc}$ is the one-way expected minimized generalized cost to travel from i to j over all the routes in the set of routes, $ROUTES_{ij}$, by traveler and vehicle types.

(2.2.17a)
$$\tilde{c}^w_{1ij|fc} = -\frac{1}{LAMDA_f} \ln \sum_{s \in ROUTES_{ij}} \exp\left(-LAMDA_f \times RGCOST^w_{s \in ROUTES_{ij}|fc}\right).$$

$\tilde{c}^w_{mij|fc}$ for m = 2,3 are the one-way generalized costs for the non-auto modes:

(2.2.17b)
$$\tilde{c}^w_{mij|fc} = VOT_f \times t^w_{mij|fc} + v^w_{mij|fc} \; ; m = 2,3.$$

2.2.6 Mode Choice Probabilities

The expected *round trip generalized costs of travel* per person by mode m from zone i to zone j *for each f and c* is,

(2.2.18)
$$C^w_{mij|fc} = \tilde{c}^w_{mij|fc} + \tilde{c}^w_{mji|fc}.$$

The mode choice probability, $\pi^w_{mij|fc}$, is derived by minimizing the expected round trip generalized cost in the mode choice model. Recall that $\pi_{mij|fc}$ are the probabilities that a trip from i to j will choose mode m for traveler type f and vehicle type c.[6]

(2.2.19)
$$\pi^w_{mij|fc} = \frac{\delta_{m|ij} \exp \hat{\lambda}_f \left(C^w_{mij|fc} + \hbar^w_{mij|c}\right)}{\sum_{n=1}^{3} \delta_{n|in} \exp \hat{\lambda}_f \left(C^w_{nij|fc} + \hbar^w_{nij|c}\right)}.$$

$\hat{\lambda}_f < 0$ is the mode choice cost dispersion coefficient and $\hbar_{mij|c}$ are the mode-

---

[6] De Salvo and Huq (1996) study the commuters' mode choice, where the mode is defined in terms of continuous speed and travel time.

specific constants. Travelers choose only one mode for a round trip, which is different from route choice where they can choose different inbound and outbound routes.

2.2.7 Composite Trip Travel Times and Costs

The expected travel time over all modes, for round trip travel from i to z and back for consumer of type f and vehicle type c are:

(2.2.20)

$$G^w_{ij|fc} = \sum_{m=1,2,3} \pi^w_{mij|fc} \left(t^w_{mij|fc} + t^w_{mji|fc} \right),$$

(2.2.21)

$$g^w_{ij|fc} = \sum_{m=1,2,3} \pi^w_{mij|fc} \left(v^w_{mij|fc} + v^w_{mji|fc} \right).$$

These expected times and costs, as shown before, are passed to the consumer's indirect utility function in RELU2 and thus make the connections between TRAN2 and RELU2.

2.3 Post-equilibrium calculations

In this section I describe the calculations that are done after the RELU-TRAN2 model converges to an equilibrium.

2.3.1 Basic calculations

Since the aggregate demand and supply are equalized at the equilibrium, equilibrium quantities can be calculated from either supply or demand. For example, the aggregate labor supply is,

(2.3.1a)
$$L^{supply} = \sum_{if} L_{if}^{supply} = \sum_{if} L_{if}^{demand}.$$

The same variable can also be calculated for various geographic areas or market segments, such as the aggregate labor supply of type f consumers and the aggregate labor supply in each zone j.

(2.3.1b)
$$L_f^{supply} = \sum_f L_{if}^{supply} = \sum_f L_{if}^{demand},$$

(2.3.1c)
$$L_j^{supply} = \sum_j L_{if}^{supply} = \sum_j L_{if}^{demand}.$$

It is usuful to discript average or per capita values. Thus, continuing with the labor example, the region-wide per capita labor supply would be,

(2.3.1d)
$$^{ave}L^{supply} = \frac{\sum_{ijkcf} \Pr^e_{ijkc|f} N_f L_{if}^{supply}}{\sum_{ijkcf} \Pr^e_{ijkc|f} N_f}.$$

For some purposes it is interesting to categorize some values by city and suburbs. In such a case, define which zone i belongs to city and which to suburb. In this case zones 1-5 comprise the City of Chicago and zones 6-14 are the suburban areas.

(2.3.1e,f)
$$L_{city,f}^{supply} = \sum_{j \in city} L_{if}^{supply} = \sum_{j=1}^{5} L_{if}^{supply} \text{ and } L_{suburb,f}^{supply} = \sum_{j \in suburb} L_{if}^{supply} = \sum_{j=6}^{14} L_{if}^{supply}.$$

In a similar way, it is also possible to categorize the city in different parts, such as the Central Business District (CBD, or zone 3), the Rest of the City (zones 1,2,4,5), the Suburbs (zones 6-14), and the Exurban Area peripheral (zone 15).

Another type of calculation involves interactive output, such as, for example, the average travel time between and within the city and suburb. For example, I will calculate travel times for work and non-work trips by auto.

(2.3.2a)
$$ave\,t^{w}_{1,city,city|fc} = \frac{\sum_{i \in city}\sum_{j \in city}\sum_{fc} MODETRIPS^{w}_{1ijfc} \times t^{w}_{1ij|fc}}{\sum_{i \in city}\sum_{j \in city}\sum_{fc} MODETRIPS^{w}_{1ijfc}},$$

(2.3.2b)
$$ave\,t^{w}_{1,city,suburb|fc} = \frac{\sum_{i \in city}\sum_{j \in suburb}\sum_{fc} MODETRIPS^{w}_{1ijfc} \times t^{w}_{1ij|fc}}{\sum_{i \in city}\sum_{j \in suburb}\sum_{fc} MODETRIPS^{w}_{1ijfc}},$$

(2.3.2c)
$$ave\,t^{w}_{1,suburb,city|fc} = \frac{\sum_{i \in suburb}\sum_{j \in city}\sum_{fc} MODETRIPS^{w}_{1ijfc} \times t^{w}_{1ij|fc}}{\sum_{i \in suburb}\sum_{j \in city}\sum_{fc} MODETRIPS^{w}_{1ijfc}},$$

(2.3.2d)
$$ave\,t^{w}_{1,suburb,suburb|fc} = \frac{\sum_{i \in suburb}\sum_{j \in suburb}\sum_{fc} MODETRIPS^{w}_{1ijfc} \times t^{w}_{1ij|fc}}{\sum_{i \in suburb}\sum_{j \in suburb}\sum_{fc} MODETRIPS^{w}_{1ijfc}}.$$

2.3.2 The calculations related to gasoline consumption

Important measures of transportation performance form the basis of policy thinking. Therefore, from the model's equilibrium, the traffic flows are used to calculate various measures all related to the use of automobiles. These are:

1. Vehicle Miles Traveled (VMT):

$$VMT = \sum_{l} FLOW_l \times Length_l + \sum_{i} IFLOW_i \times ILength_i .$$

2. Gasoline consumption:

$$Gallons = \sum_{c} \left(\begin{array}{l} \sum_{l} fuel(speed_l) \times ineff_c \times FLOW_{cl} \times Length_l \\ + \sum_{i} fuel(Ispeed_i) \times ineff_c \times IFLOW_{ci} \times ILength_i \end{array} \right) .$$

3. Average Car Fuel Economy (miles per gallon, or MPG):

$$AveMPG = \frac{VMT}{Gallons} .$$

The Average Vehicle Inefficiency can also be calculated, and conveys information that is closely related to *AveMPG*:

$$AveIneff = \frac{\sum_{fikjc} Ineff_c \times P_{ijkc|f} \times N_f}{\sum_{f} N_f} .$$

4. Gasoline Tax Revenue (*GTR*):

$$GTR = t_{fuel} \times p_{fuel} \times gallons .$$

5. Average Car Speed (miles per hour, or *mph*):

$$AveSpeed = \frac{\sum_{l} Speed_l \times FLOW_l \times Length_l + \sum_{i} ISpeed_i \times IFLOW_i \times ILength_i}{\sum_{l} FLOW_l \times Length_l + \sum_{i} IFLOW_i \times ILength_i} .$$

6. Aggregate emissions of CO_2

To estimate the aggregate carbon dioxide emissions from car trips, there was initially a dilemma that was resolved. Chemists knowledgeable about the internal combustion engine inform that the CO_2 content of fuel is a constant that does not vary with driving conditions, but should be strictly proportional to gasoline consumption which as seen does depend on driving conditions such as speed and car type. Therefore aggregate CO_2 is found by making a proportional adjustment to the polynomial equation giving fuel consumption as a function of speed. That is, equation (2.3.3) is multiplied by a leading constant to convert gasoline per mile to CO_2 per mile.

(2.3.3)
$$CO_2\ emmision = EGR \times fuel.$$

EGR is emission gasoline ratio. It is reported that $EGR = 8788$ (grams/gallon)[7].

Barth and Boriboonsomsin (2007), report direct measurements of CO_2 emissions under Southern California cruising driving conditions at each speed, as well as under actual urban driving conditions. Figure 2.3.3 plots their CO_2 curve against the fuel consumption polynomial fitted to Davis and Diegel's 2004 data (which was discussed earlier). The difference in the curvature of the two polynomials reflects possible experimental differences which come from the vehicle type (recall that the polynomial fitted to the data of Davis and Diegel is for the Geo Prizm as well as the fact that Davis and Diegel's data reflects actual urban driving not cruising speeds.

---

[7] U.S. Enviromental Protection Agency, http://www.epa.gov/oms/climate/420f05001.htm#calculating

Chapter 2 59

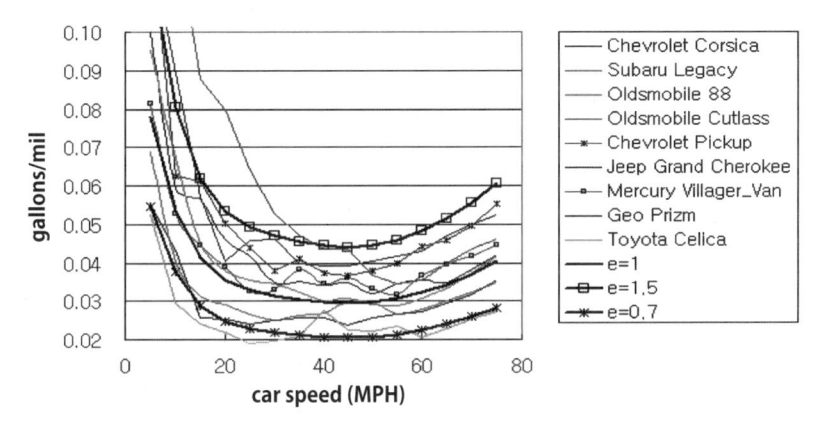

Figure 2.3.1: Car speed versus fuel consumption per mile by car model type (actual driving conditions). Source: Davis and Diegel (2004)

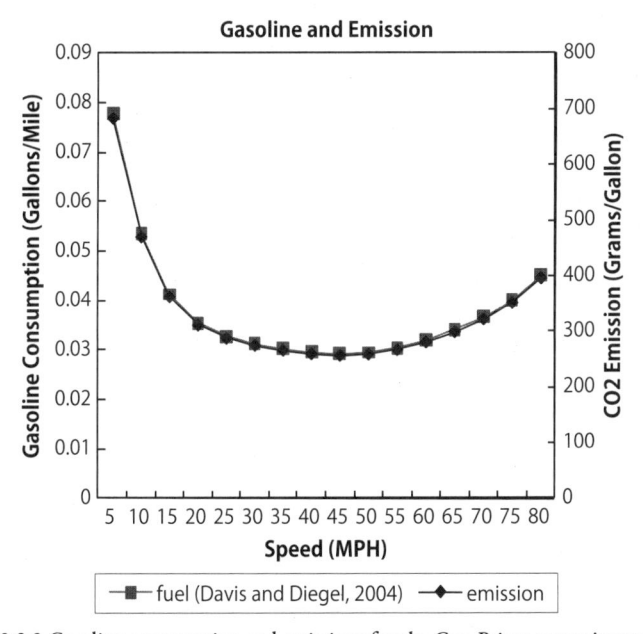

Figure 2.3.2 Gasoline consumption and emissions for the Geo-Prizm approximated by the fitted polynomial.

Gasoline and Emission

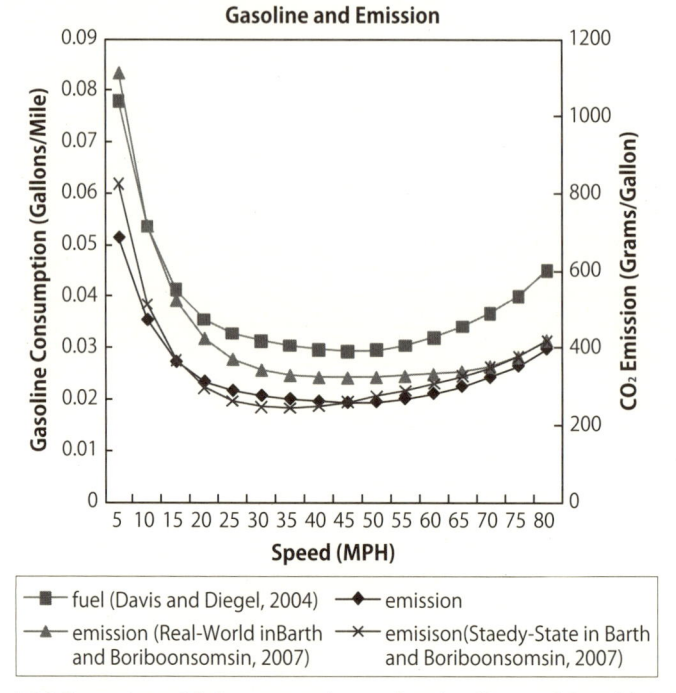

Figure 2.3.3 Comparison of fuel versus speed curves based on Davis and Diegel (2004) and Barth and Boriboonsomsin (2007).

Appendix 2. Measurement of Welfare

There is difficulty on measurement of welfare. In the model, there are three variables accounted in the social welfare; consumer's utility, government revenue from policies and the discounted changing of total value of stocks. To measure the social welfare, there are two main discussions. (i) How to measure the social welfare and (ii) how government utilizes revenue from policies. In the text, consumer's utility function is not measured by money. Thus I examined the consumer utility, government revenue and changing of value differently. There are a few other suggested measurements.

A2.1 Measurement of Social Welfare
Welfare Measurement by consumer's utility (CU)

Consumer utility of type f employed and unemployed consumer are

$$CU_f^e = \left(\frac{1}{\lambda_f^e}\right) \times \log\left[\sum_{ijk} \exp(\lambda_f^e \tilde{U}_{ijkc|f}^e)\right],$$

$$CU_f^u = \left(\frac{1}{\lambda_f^u}\right) \times \log\left[\sum_{ik} \exp(\lambda_f^u \tilde{U}_{ikc|f}^u)\right].$$

This is accurate measure and it is possible to compare the changing of utility within each f types of employed and unemployed. But this utility function cannot be aggregated to measure the social welfare. In addition, since this is unit is not money, it is not possible to compare with revenue or value of stock. Hence I examine consumer utility, government revenue and discounted total stock value separately. In addition, CO_2 emission could be evaluated in money. Glaeser and Kahn (2008) use a social cost figure of 43 dollars per ton of carbon dioxide[8].

A2.2 Alternative Measurement of Welfare

Anas and Rhee (2006) uses consumer surplus (CS), the equivalent variation (EV), and compensative variation (CV), for welfare analysis. The idea of EV is to money should be subsidized (or taxed) to the base welfare before the policy to achieve the welfare after the policy. CV is how much money must be subsidized (or taxed) to the welfare after policy to recover the welfare before policy. I will see the CS and CV here.

---

8   CO_2 emission per day is 58.4 thousand ton in the base (and 54.8 thousand ton in my target data). If social cost of a ton of CO_2 emission is $43 as Glaeser and Kahn (2008), whole CO_2 emission is evaluated as those are evaluated as $2,511 thousand (and $2,356 thousand). The number of consumer, that in the model includes possible labor participants per day, is 4,690,847. Thus the per capita social cost of CO_2 emission per day is $0.535 and per year is $195.31 (and $183.35). If policy could save 1% of emission, it increases additional $1.95 (and $1.83) of social welfare per capita.

A2.2.1 Welfare Measurement by Consumer's Surplus (CS)

One of the alternative methods is to convert consumer utility to consumer surplus by measuring money unit. Consumer surplus for employed, unemployed for each f are:

$$CS_f^e = \frac{CU_f^e}{AMUI_f^e} \text{ and } CS_f^u = \frac{CU_f^u}{AMUI_f^u},$$

where $AMUI_f^u$ and $AMUI_f^e$ are average marginal utility of income for employed and unemployed of each f. Thus consumer surplus is not exact measure and approximation. Average marginal utility of income are defined as,

$$AMUI_f^e = \sum_{ikjc} \frac{\Pr_{fikjc}^e}{\Psi_{fikjc}^e} \text{ and } AMUI_f^u = \sum_{ikc} \frac{\Pr_{fikc}^u}{\Psi_{fic}^u}.$$

Since consumer surplus is measured by money unit, this could be added to other variables that is measured by money unit. Thus the social welfare is the sum of total consumer surplus, the annual gain from real estate market, and government revenue.

$$SW = TCS + \frac{\rho}{1+\rho} \sum_{ik} \left(Stock_{ik} \times Value_{ik} \right) + Revenue.$$

A2.2.2 Measurement by Compensative Variation (CV)

The idea of CV is how much compensation is needed for consumers after policy execution to recover the same welfare before policy execution. For the clear notation, I denote consumer's utility in base case as,

$$CU_f^{e|BASE} = \left(\frac{1}{\lambda_f^e}\right) \times \log\left[\sum_{ijk} \exp(\lambda_f^e \tilde{U}_{ijkc|f}^{e|BASE})\right],$$

$$CU_f^{u|BASE} = \left(\frac{1}{\lambda_f^u}\right) \times \log\left[\sum_{ik} \exp(\lambda_f^u \tilde{U}_{ikc|f}^{u|BASE})\right].$$

And the utility of employed is

$$\tilde{U}_{jkc|f} = \alpha_f \ln\alpha_f + \beta_f \ln\beta_f + \ln\Psi_{ijfc} - \beta_f \ln R_{ik} + \frac{\alpha_f(1-\eta_f)}{\eta_f} \ln\left(\sum_{\forall z} \iota_{z|ijfc}^{\frac{1}{1-\eta_f}} \psi_{z|ijfc}^{\frac{\eta_f}{\eta_f - 1}}\right)$$

$$- \Delta_j b2_f G_{ij|fc}^{work} + \gamma_f \text{ineff}_c + E_{ijkc|f}.$$

Now I define the full income under any policy Ψ_{ijfc}^{POLICY} and Ψ_{ifc}^{POLICY} for employed and unemployed. Then I define the full income under any policy with CV_f^e and CV_f^u as,

$$\Psi_{ijfc}^{CV} = \Psi_{ijfc}^{POLICY} - CV_f^e,$$

$$\Psi_{ifc}^{CV} = \Psi_{ifc}^{POLICY} - CV_f^u.$$

The surplus under policy with compensative valuation are rewritten as

$$\tilde{U}_{jkc|f}^{CVcu} = \alpha_f \ln\alpha_f + \beta_f \ln\beta_f + \ln\Psi_{ijfc}^{CVcu} - \beta_f \ln R_{ik}$$
$$+ \frac{\alpha_f(1-\eta_f)}{\eta_f} \ln\left(\sum_{\forall z} \iota_{z|ijfc}^{\frac{1}{1-\eta_f}} \psi_{z|ijfc}^{\frac{\eta_f}{\eta_f - 1}}\right) - \Delta_j b2_f G_{ij|fc}^{work}$$
$$+ \gamma_f \text{ineff}_c + E_{ijkc|f}.$$

and similar for surplus of unemployed. Using this, the employed and unemployed consumer's utility for each type f are

$$CU_f^{e|CV} = \left(\frac{1}{\lambda_f^e}\right) \times \log\left[\sum_{ijk} \exp(\lambda_f^e \tilde{U}_{ijkc|f}^{e|CV})\right],$$

$$CU_f^{u|CV} = \left(\frac{1}{\lambda_f^u}\right) \times \log\left[\sum_{ik} \exp(\lambda_f^u \tilde{U}_{ikc|f}^{u|CV})\right].$$

The CV as a welfare measurement is such CV that equalize the consumer's utility under policy compensated by CV to base consumer's utility

$$CU_f^{e|BASE} = CU_f^{e|cv} \text{ and } CU_f^{u|BASE} = CU_f^{u|CV}.$$

The total CV is then:

$$TCV = \sum_f (U\text{Prob}_f^e \ N_f \times CV_f^e) + \sum_f (U\text{Prob}_f^{x\,x} \ N_f \times CV_f^u).$$

The CV per capita is:

$$CV^{pc} = \frac{TCV}{\sum_f N_f}.$$

The total social welfare is the sum of CV and the difference of annual gain of total stock value from the base and government revenue:

$$SW^{CV} = TCV + \left(\sum_i \sum_{k=0,1,2,3,4} \frac{\rho}{1+\rho}\left(S_{ik}V_{ik} - S_{ik}^{BASE}V_{ik}^{BASE}\right)\right) + \text{Revenue}.$$

A2.3 Revenue Utilization

In the simulation, government keeps the revenue from policies. By using the revenue in better way, the welfare would increases. Since the quasi-Pigouvian toll is designed to remove the negative externality of congestion, I expect it is possible to improve the social welfare from base case by using revenue in a proper way. In this Appendix, I discuss about the revenue distribution and the investment in public goods. For more discussion, for example, see Bento et al.(2006), Eliasson and Mattsson (2006), Parry and Bento (2001) and Santos and Rojey (2004).

A2.3.1 Revenue Distribution

To distribute the revenue to consumers equally is the most intuitive way. The better way of distribution, however, would be such that the social welfare maximizing distribution. Assuming concave consumer surplus, this will require the marginal consumer surplus of income would be the same for all types of consumers, if the revenue were enough. If revenue is not enough, who has the higher marginal surplus of income would get and who would have the lower marginal surplus income would not get the distribution. Who get the revenue have the same marginal surplus of income. Although there is equality problem, to distribute in a way that marginal utility of income are equalized will increase consumer utility the most. In this case, who pay more would be higher income group who travel more and who gain more would be lower income group whose marginal utility of income is higher. The other way of distribution is to the traveler by public transportation to reduce the travel cost each time.

A2.3.2 Invest in Public Good

The revenue can be the financial resource for government to execute any other policy. This could be more beneficial for consumer. For example, government could invest in public transport to reduce money cost of public transport or to increase speed of public transportation. Differently from redistribution to the travelers, the marginal cost of traveler is zero in public transport in the model. Other kind of public goods could be examined. In such case I would add public goods term in utility function or welfare function.

// Chapter 3. The Short- and Long-Run Price Elasticity and Fuel Economy Elasticity of Gasoline Consumption and CO_2 Emission: Calibration and Application of the RELU-TRAN2 Model

3.1 Introduction

Imposition of a gasoline tax and the technological advances in vehicle fuel economy are two scenarios that have the promise of significantly reducing gasoline consumption in urban travel. These policies would naturally target the reduction of CO_2 emissions as well, since CO_2 emissions are strictly proportional to gasoline consumption. Unlike congestion tolls and other taxes that are politically difficult to implement, a tax on gasoline is relatively much more feasible and has been implemented at high levels in Europe. It would reduce not only fuel consumption and thus directly carbon emissions but also, it would indirectly reduce the externalities of time delay and excess fuel consumption involved in driving by acting as a second-best to Pigouvian congestion tolling. Technological advances in vehicle fuel economy are expected to improve emissions and reduce the magnitude of the excess fuel consumption externality associated with driving.

The price elasticity and the fuel economy elasticity of fuel consumption play an important role in determining the potential success of these policies. For example, if the price elasticity of fuel consumption is low, the gasoline tax that would have to be levied would be high, since a low gasoline tax would not significantly alter driving behavior or the number of car-trips.

The optimal gasoline tax to improve welfare in Britain and the United States is examined by Parry and Small (2005). Their optimal tax is composed of several components: (i) a toll for the congestion externality; (ii) a part to internalize the accidents externality; (iii) a part to internalize the air pollution externality; (iv) a Ramsey component that accounts for excise and labor taxes. They found that although the optimal gasoline tax in Britain is higher than in the United States, the observed tax is too high in Britain and too low in the United States.

Hughes et al. (2006) observe that the short-run elasticity is caused by driver's responses. Those responses are reducing vehicle miles traveled (VMT), adjusting vehicle maintenance, speed adjustment and slower acceleration, and household vehicle stock utilization. They find that the price elasticity of gasoline is getting smaller, ranging from -0.21 to -0.34 in the period 1975 to 1980, and from -0.034 to -0.077 during 2001 to 2006. The income elasticity of gasoline ranges from 0.21 to 0.75 but does not show a significant change between the two periods.

Espey (1998), Graham and Glaister (2002) and Goodwin et al. (2004) reviewed the international research and summarized the short- and long-run fuel price elasticity and income elasticity of gasoline consumption. Goodwin et al. (2004) reviews the definitions. Short term is 1 period of data, within 1 year in most cases. Long term refers to a time horizon long enough that all economic responses to the higher gas price are completed and is 5-10 years.

The above authors give a good summary of price effects and income effects of a rise in the price of gasoline. The price effects are: (a) falling volume of traffic, (b) falling of volume of fuel consumption, (c) rising of the efficiency of fuel use (that is rising fuel economy), and (d) a decrease in the total number of vehicles owned. (c) and (d) are the results of technical improvements to vehicles, more fuel-conserving driving styles and driving in easier traffic conditions, and the differential effect between high- and low-consumption vehicles. The income effects are: (a) the rise in the number of vehicles and the total amount of fuel consumed, and (b) an increased volume of traffic.

Puller and Greening (1999) report an interesting consumer response to gasoline price change. They report that their consumers show an initially larger response than that implied by the total elasticity. For example, households adjust vehicle miles traveled (VMT) more than they adjust fuel economy (miles per gallon, MPG) in the first year after the price change.

The gasoline income and price elasticity as an application of nonparametric regression models are estimated in Hausman and Newey

(1995). They also estimate the consumer surplus and the deadweight loss. There are several studies on demographic differences in the price and income elasticity of gasoline demand. Schmalensee and Stoker (1999)[9], using United States data, studied the variation of the income elasticity across different income groups, the number of licensed drivers and age effects. They showed that there is no evidence that higher income groups have a lower income elasticity of demand for gasoline. Yatchew and No (2001), using Canadian data, and support to these findings. They report that the price elasticity is about -0.9 and the income elasticity is about 0.29. Nicol (2003), using United States and Canadian data, concluded that family size and housing tenure status have a bigger effect on elasticity, than regional differences.

Kayser (2000) estimates household gasoline demand and the price and income elasticities. The author attempts to include car stock in the estimation since car efficiency and gasoline demand have a close relation. The results show that the short-run price elasticity is -0.23, and the income elasticity is 0.49. The higher income households can afford to have newer cars and are, therefore, more fuel efficient. Differences in gasoline demand across the population are shown. For example, rural location, and having no access to public transportation are affected more by the gasoline price.

As Berkhout et al. (2000) point out, for energy saving, the technology is the most important factor. By the technological improvement of the energy efficiency, if the economic activity does not change, the energy consumption must decrease. For example, if the energy consumption per unit of any economic activity becomes 10% less than before, and this does not change any other economic activity, the energy consumption should decrease by 10%. But actually, economic activity would increase and change along many margins in an economy that is becoming more energy efficient. This increment of economic activity along many margins is called the rebound effect. The rebound effect may be defined as *the increase in energy use because of improved technology and more efficient energy consumption, ceteris paribus.*

---

9 Although they also estimate the price elasticity, it is figured out in their paper that their data is not suitable to use to estimate the price elasticity.

Berkhout et al. (2000) defined three kinds of rebound effects: (i) the own price effect (also called the substitution effect, the first-order effect, or the direct effect); (ii) the income effect (also called the second-order effect, or the indirect effect), and (iii) the macro effect (also called the structural effect, the economy-wide effect, or the general equilibrium effect)[10]. In the model, RELU-TRAN2, the price effect corresponds to the effect of the cheaper gasoline price or the fuel economy on traveling a mile, the income effect corresponds to the incremental increase in travel by using the saved cost of the gasoline or any savings from the fuel economy improvement, and the macro effect corresponds to the changing of the vehicle types used, or to changes in residence-work locations and any other adjustment in prices, rents or wages that occur in the economy through the general equilibrium adjustments that would follow a fuel economy improvement. In the general discussion, but not only in the transportation sector, if the rebound effect is very large (more than 100%), the economy consumes more energy than it did before the technological progress. This phenomenon is called Jevons' paradox[11].

The gasoline consumption is mainly composed of MPG (miles per gallon), in the intensive margin, and VMT (vehicle miles travel), in the extensive margin. The incremental increase in VMT, when vehicle gasoline efficiency is improved, is called the rebound effect. Thus, the increment of VMT when the vehicle gasoline consumption is improved creates the rebound effect. If the rebound effect is very large, the gasoline consumption could increase to more than what it was before the improvement of vehicle efficiency. But in the literature on vehicle gasoline consumption efficiency, I could not find anything that observes the presence of such a strong rebound effect that it could support to Jevons' paradox. Rather, there is some evidence that the rebound effect is actually getting smaller over time.

Small and Van Dender (2007a,b) estimate the short- and long- run

---

10 See the survey of Greening et al. (2000) for the discussion of each kind of rebound effect. Madlener and Alcott (2007) also provide a discussion on the rebound effect.
11 The survey of Alcott (2005) says that the empirically measured rebounds range from less than 1% to several hundred percent. Brookes (1990) insists that technological improvements will increase the use of energy, but not decrease it, because of the huge rebound effects that are built into economic behavior.

rebound effect. They find that the rebound effect is getting smaller in both the short- and long-run. This is occurring as real income increases and fuel price falls. See the Appendix to this Chapter for a more detailed exposition of the results of Small and Van Dender (2007a,b). The rebound effect for household vehicle travel is also estimated in Greene et al. (1999). They showed that a long-run "take-back" caused by the rebound, amounts to about 20% of potential energy savings.

As explained in Chapter 2, RELU-TRAN2 is a general equilibrium model that takes into account land use and transportation adjustments along a variety of margins and markets. Comparative statics results with the model show the combined response after every variable has adjusted to the higher fuel price or to the improved fuel economy. Thus, the response predicted by RELU-TRAN2 would be a long run response. However, it is possible to run only some parts of the model keeping constant variables determined by other parts. I could then study the shorter-run responses by running to equilibrium only those processes in the model that would adjust relatively quickly in the real world. For example, when the gasoline price rises, RELU-TRAN2 shows that relatively long-run responses including how consumers change their residence-work place pairs and how developers change the construction pattern, and then how the price-wage-rent structure changes, after these variables have fully affected each other through the general equilibrium adjustments. But in the short-run, the economy could not change so drastically. Consumers could change their commute routes to save gasoline or they could change their travel modes from auto to the public transport or other for the same purpose. It would take a longer time for consumer-workers to change their residence or work locations.

The purpose of this chapter is to calibrate those parts of RELU-TRAN2 that deal with travel that were explained in Chapter 2 (and which did not exist in RELU-TRAN1 and therefore were not calibrated), and thus properly include the sensitivity to gasoline prices and to fuel efficiency. In Chapter 2, I saw how RELU-TRAN1 was extended to include these aspects. In the next section the year 2000 travel data for the Chicago MSA is used to update the calibration of RELU-TRAN1. Following that I use other data sources to calibrate RELU-TRAN2's predictions of fuel consumption, vehicle miles traveled and CO_2 emitted by cars. With this recalibrated and updated model, I am ready to examine, in the remaining parts of this chapter, the short-run and long-run responses to an increase in the price of gasoline and to improvements in fuel economy.

3.2 Data

RELU-TRAN1 was calibrated to Chicago by Alex Anas and Yu Liu. Because RELU-TRAN2 includes several changes to RELU-TRAN1, as discussed in Chapter 2, it was necessary to recalibrate all of the model's most important relationships including the new ones. For this purpose, several data sources were utilized, that were not previously used in the calibration of RELU-TRAN1. These data sources were especially important in calibrating the RELU-TRAN2 relationships dealing with commuting in the year 2000, fuel consumption and Greenhouse Gas emissions. The data sets are the following:

1) The Regional Transportation Assets Management System (RTAMS) websites[12] from which the category "Demographics and Travel Patterns" provides data on the distribution of daily commute trips by mode among the different areas of the Chicago, MSA.

2) The Illinois Travel Statistics, Illinois Department of Transportation, Office of Planning and Programming, 2000.

3) World Resources Institute, 2007, Addendum 1 to the Illinois Greenhouse Gas Emissions Inventory and Projections, Overview Report: Detailed Greenhouse Gas Emissions, Illinois Sectors, Prepared for the Illinois Climate Change Advisory Group.

Key data from the above sources are used as "targets" to be matched by the calibration. In the model's calibration, the targeted data is matched either exactly or approximately. Below, the specific data tabulations that serve as

---

12 The Regional Transportation Assets Management System (RTAMS) websites; http://www.rtams.org/ui/homepage.asp

targets are described for each data set.

3.2.1 Target data from RTAMS

The RTAMS data are used to target the number of jobs in the city of Chicago and in the suburbs as evidence by the commute destinations of the number of workers traveling to work in those places; the number of residents in the city and in the suburbs as evidence by the commute origins traveling to work from those places; the number of commuters between and within city and suburb by their mode of travel (car, public transit, other) and the average travel time for each mode of travel and by origin and destination place (that is city to city, city to suburb, suburb to city and suburb to suburb). The RTAMS provide data for each zone that corresponds to a RELU zone. I use their zone data for population and for employed workers, but I use this data aggregated to the city and suburb level as for the purposes of mode choice.

Table 3.2.1 shows the data taken from RTAMS. The number of jobs is the population that works in the corresponding zone and it includes those who commute from the "outside zone" which represents the exurban area. The number of employed residents is the population of workers who reside in the corresponding zone and it does not include those who work in the "outside zone" which represents the exurban area. The total number of workers and employed residents are 3,548,387 and 3,738,292. In the model, it is needed to have a balance of employed residents and jobs. To do so, I redistribute the difference between the total employed-residents and total jobs to residences in each zone, in proportion to the residential population of that zone. The total redistributed in this way is 189,905 employed residents, or 5.1% of the total number of employed residents. Thus, this is the percentage of those employed residents who occupy housing within the RTAMS and the RELU-TRAN2 areas but who work outside the 14-zone area (that is outside the City and its suburbs), in the peripheral RELU zone 15 which represents the exurban area.

Table 3.2.2 is the target data of residence-to-work commuters between the city (zone 1-5) and the suburbs (zone 6-14) matrix. Table 3.2.3 are the target data for the mode choices expressed as the percent of workers

74 Simulation Analysis of Urban Economy

Table 3.2.1. Population distribution by RELU zone in the Chicago,
MSA (2000) Source: RTAMS demographic and travel statistics.

RELU-zone		Jobs	Employed residents
1	City of Chicago	313,009	541,464
2		84,976	51,120
3	(CBD)	543,154	31,088
4		246,763	400,193
5		120,460	124,576
6	Suburbs	413,241	368,121
7		208,760	139,195
8		270,646	268,862
9		292,286	350,706
10		517,944	445,756
11		168,811	179,856
12		312,856	297,245
13		91,587	124,990
14		153,802	225,215
Total	City of Chicago	1,308,362	1,148,441
	Suburbs	2,429,933	2,399,946
Total	City and Suburbs	3,738,295	3,548,387

Table 3.2.2. The number of commuters by residence-job pair.

Aggregated Commuting Matrix		Jobs	
		City	Suburbs
Employed Residents	City	814,268	334,173
	Suburbs	494,094	2,095,760

commuting between the city and the suburbs. From the table 3.2.3, within the commuters who reside in the city and work in the city, 57.4% of workers commuted by auto, 32.9% of workers commuted by public transit and 9.7% commuted by the non-motorized ("other") mode from city to city, for example. Table 3.2.4 are the target data of average travel times in hours of commuting per trip in the commuting matrix.

Table 3.2.3. The mode choice relative frequencies for commuting between city and suburb.

Aggregated Mode Choice Matrix		Mode		
		Auto	Public Transport	Other
Reside-Job pair	City-City	0.574	0.329	0.097
	City-Suburbs	0.871	0.098	0.032
	Suburbs-City	0.686	0.29	0.025
	Suburbs-Suburbs	0.952	0.013	0.036

Table 3.2.4. The round trip commuting time (hour) between city and suburb by each mode.

		Mode		
		Auto	Public Transport	Other
Reside-Job pair	City-City	0.967	1.433	0.267
	City-Suburb	1.367	1.9	0.433
	Suburb-City	1.467	2	1.2
	Suburb-suburb	0.933	1.5	0.283

3.2.2 Target data from the Illinois Travel Statistics.

(i)*Vehicle Miles Traveled*: The target data of Vehicle Miles Traveled (VMT), Fuel Consumption and Miles per Gallon (MPG) are taken from the Illinois Travel Statistics. These are annual totals for the year 2000. I categorize VMT data as "Regionwide Total VMT" (RVMT), "Total Link VMT" (LVMT) and "Total Zone VMT" (ZVMT). From the obtained Chicago data for the year 2000, these totals are roughly as follows: RVMT is 55,923 million miles/year; LVMT is 15,820 million miles/year; and ZVMT is 40,103 million miles/year, with RVMT = LVMT + ZVMT. The LVMT originates from traffic that occurs on major roads and expressways and the ZVMT originates from traffic that occurs on local roads. The data is categorized for interstate highways, other principal arterials, minor arterials, collectors and local roads & streets. I categorize interstate highways as LVMT and others as ZVMT.

For RELU-TRAN2 I need data on VMT per day by passenger vehicles.

To get a reasonable estimate of this I first multiply the above numbers by 90%. Doing so, I believe, excludes those miles of travel generated by trucks. To convert the annual VMT numbers to daily I divide by 365 days. The target values of the total, major road and intra-zonal VMT per day, after the above adjustments, are: RVMT = 137.9, LVMT = 39.0, and ZVMT = 98.9 million miles, respectively.

(ii) *Fuel consumption*: From the Illinois Statistics, aggregate fuel consumption for the State of Illinois in the year 2000 was 4,329 million gallons. Chicago's consumption of fuel by cars is 54.9% (= 61% x 0.9) of that of the State of Illinois[13]. The 2000 number was then multiplied by this percentage to get the adjusted annual year 2000 consumption of motor fuel by passenger vehicles. After dividing the adjusted annual with 365 days, the fuel consumption per day is 6,511 thousand gallons.

(iii) The Illinois Statistics also give the average miles per gallon, that is the fuel economy that applies to cars in the region. That is 21.2 miles per gallon.

(iv) *CO_2 Emissions*: The Illinois statistics include an annual estimate of CO_2 emissions for on-highway and off-highway travel for the State, of 60.189 million tons in the year 2005. From this I arrive at the target number for the year 2000, by taking 35.4% of it. CO_2 emissions are 58,374 tons per day. The calculations follow the same adjustments that were made in the case of VMT. In that case, the year 2005 number was multiplied by 0.94 to get an estimate of the year 2000 level, then by 0.686 to get the level applicable to passenger vehicles and then by 0.549 to get Chicago's portion[14].

How does the number 58,374 tons per day derived from the data agree with the output from RELU-TRAN for the calibrated base in the year 2000? The gasoline consumed by cars predicted by the model is 6.235 million gallons of gasoline per day. According to the USEPA one gallon of gasoline

---

13   I estimate those by using the year 2000 motor fuel consumption from the Illinois Travel Statistics. I assume that 10% of VMT is made by trucks in Chicago.
14   On- and off- highway CO_2 emissions and the adjustment from Illinois year 2005 to Chicago year 2000 is made by using 2000 motor fuel from Illinois Travel Statistics and the 2005 motor fuel from Addendum 1 to the "Illinois Greenhouse Gas Emissions Inventory and Projections Overview Report: Detailed Greenhouse Gas Emissions Illinois Sectors."

contains 8,788 grams of carbon dioxide. Hence, multiplying, I get 54,792 million grams of CO_2 which is 54,792 tons per day. Note that this number is close but lower than the 58,374 tons per day implied by the data as discussed above. Part of the difference is that the data number reflects the fact that some of the fuel is diesel, but I assumed only gasoline. Diesel has a higher CO_2 content. Another possibility is that the adjustment for trucks could be off a bit.

3.3 Calibration

The model's calibration is based on the principle that the key elasticities of the CGE model obtain reasonable values, supported by estimates from the relevant literature and that alternative specific constants of the multinomial logit model are adjusted so that the predicted demands fit the observed demands. Following this principle, some of the coefficients of the utility function or the developer's profit function etc are adjusted to get the desired elasticities using the observed values of the relative choice frequencies. This section explains how this is done. Then, the alternative-specific constants or dummy variables of the multinomial logit probability functions are adjusted so that the probabilities predicted by the model match exactly the relative choice frequencies that were observed in the data. The data observations, therefore, are assumed to be observations of an equilibrium state.

Meanwhile, the model's predictions of travel times, vehicle miles traveled, fuel consumption and CO_2 emissions must match what was observed or inferred from the data. To achieve these, the coefficients of the road traffic congestion function and other parameters and coefficients used in TRAN are adjusted by a trial and error process until a reasonable matching is observed.

3.3.1 Key Elasticities of the Mode
a) The consumer

In this subsection I discuss the key elasticities and other measures on the consumer side of the model that were paid close attention to in the calibration. These are: (i) the value of commuting time (that is, the MRS between commuting time and disposable income); (ii) the elasticity of location demand with respect to commuting time; (iii) the elasticity of housing demand with respect to rent; and (iv) the elasticity of labor supply with respect to wage. The elasticitis of consumers' behavior could be adjusted by the dispersion coefficient of consumer's location choice probability, (that is λ_f^e or λ_f^u). Since the number of elasticities is more than the number of λ_f^e and λ_f^u, the freedom of adjusting the elasticity is not enough. λ_f^e and λ_f^u are adjusted by seeing the balance of those elasticities.

(i) The MRS (marginal rate of substitution) between commute time and disposable income

The MUI (marginal utility of income) from the indirect utility function and the MUT (marginal utility of the expected commuting travel time used in RELU) are,

$$MUI_{ijkc|f} = \frac{d\widetilde{U}_{ijkc|f}}{d\Psi_{ijfc}} = \frac{1}{\Psi_{ijfc}},$$

$$MUT_{ijkc|f} = \frac{d\widetilde{U}_{ijkc|f}}{dG^{work}_{ij|fc}} = \Delta_j \left(-\gamma_{1f} + \frac{-w_{jf}(1-\vartheta_f)d}{\Psi_{ijfc}} \right).$$

Then, the MRS (the marginal rate of substitution between commuting time and disposable income) is the ratio of MUT and MUI. This MRS then measures, how many dollars of annual disposable income increase an employed commuter in group f would demand as compensation for each hour of commuting time increase per day. Since this MRS will vary for each location/car situation (i, j, k, c) I take its probability-weighted average and call it $AveMRS$:

$$MRS^{\Psi_{ijfc}, G^{work}_{ij|fc}}_{ijkc|f} = -\frac{MUT_{ijkc|f}}{MUI_{ijkc|f}} / day,$$

$$AveMRS_f^{\Psi_{ijfc},G^{work}_{ij|fc}|emp} = \sum_{ijkc} \Pr^{low|emp}_{ijkc|f} MRS_{ijkc|f}.$$

(ii) The elasticity of location demand with respect to commute time

The location demand of an employed consumer of type f who resides in zone i, works in zone j and owns car type c is,

$$D^{location|emp}_{ijc|f} = N_f \Pr^{upper|emp}_f \sum_k \Pr^{low|emp}_{ijkc|f}.$$

By assuming that the upper probability is constant, the elasticity of location demand with respect to the commuting time of the (i, j, f, c) combination is,

$$\eta^{D^{location|emp}_{ijkc|f}, G^{work}_{ij|fc}}_{ijfc} = \frac{dD^{location|emp}_{ijkc|f}}{dG^{work}_{ij|fc}} \frac{G^{work}_{ij|fc}}{D^{location|emp}_{ijkc|f}}$$

$$= \lambda^e_f \left(-\frac{w_{ij}d}{\Psi_{ijfc}} - b2_f \right) \left(1 - \sum_k \Pr^{low|e}_{ijkc|f} \right) G^{work}_{ij|fc}.$$

If the commuting time of a specific residence-work location pair increases, keeping the non-work travel time the same, and the commuting times of all other pairs constant, then the demand for the corresponding location decreases. An unemployed does not react to changes in commuting time. The average elasticity of a type f consumer is,

$$\eta^{D^{location|emp}_{ijkc|f}, G^{work}_{ij|fc}}_f = \sum_{ijkc} \Pr_{ijkc|f} \eta^{D^{location|emp}_{ijkc|f}, G^{work}_{ij|fc}}_{ijfc}.$$

(iii) Elasticity of the consumer's housing demand with respect to rent

The housing demand for type k building in zone i by a consumer of type f is,

$$D_{ik|f}^{HD} = N_f \sum_{\forall c, j > 0} \Pr_{e|f}^{up} \Pr_{ijkc|f}^{low|e} \frac{\beta_f \Psi_{ijfc}}{R_{ik}} + N_f \sum_{\forall c, j = 0} \Pr_{u|f}^{up} \Pr_{ikc|f}^{low|u} \frac{\beta_f \Psi_{ijfc}}{R_{ik}}.$$

By assuming that the outer probability is constant, the elasticity is calculated to get:

$$\eta_{ik|f}^{HD|emp} = \frac{dD_{ik|f}^{HD}}{dR_{ik}} \frac{R_{ik}}{D_{ik|f}^{HD}} = -1 - \lambda_f^e \left(1 - \sum_{jc} \Pr_{ijkc|f}^{low|e}\right) \beta_f < -1,$$

$$\eta_{ik|f}^{HD|unemp} = \frac{dD_{ik|f}^{HD}}{dR_{ik}} \frac{R_{ik}}{D_{ik|f}^{HD}} = -1 - \lambda_f^e \left(1 - \sum_c \Pr_{ikc|f}^{low|unemp}\right) \beta_f < -1.$$

When the rent of a particular housing type in a zone increases, keeping the rents in all other housing alternatives constant, the housing demand decreases. The second term represent resident moves out from this type of building or this region. The probability-weighted average elasticities are

$$\eta_f^{HD|emp} = \sum_{ik} \left(\sum_{jc} \Pr_{ijkc|f}^{low|emp}\right) \eta_{ik|f}^{HD|emp},$$

$$\eta_f^{HD|unemp} = \sum_{ik} \left(\sum_c \Pr_{ikc|f}^{low|unemp}\right) \eta_{ik|f}^{HD|unemp},$$

$$\eta_f^{HD} = \Pr_f^{upper|emp} \eta_f^{HD|emp} + \Pr_f^{upper|unemp} \eta_f^{HD|unemp}.$$

(iv) Elasticity of the consumer's labor supply with respect to wage

The labor supplied to employers in zone j by consumers of type f who reside in zone i and use car type c is

$$H_{ijc|f} = H - dG_{ij|fc}^{work} - \sum_{\forall z} c_{ijf} Z_{z|ijfc} G_{iz|fc}^{non-work}.$$

The total labor supply from all residence zones and using all car types is

$$L_{jf}^{supply} = \sum_{kic}\left(N_f \Pr_{e|f}^{up} \Pr_{ijkc|f}^{low|e} H_{ijc|f}\right).$$

By assuming that the upper probability is constant, the elasticity of labor supply with respect to wage is,

$$\frac{dL_{jf}^{supply}}{dw_{jf}} = \sum_{kic}\left(N_f \Pr_f^{up|emp} \frac{d\Pr_{ijkc|f}^{low|emp}}{dw_{jf}} H_{ijc|f}\right) + \sum_{kic}\left(N_f \Pr_{ijkc|f} \frac{dH_{ijc|f}}{dw_{jf}}\right),$$

where, in the first term,

$$\frac{d\Pr_{ijkc|f}^{low|e}}{dw_{jf}} = \lambda_f^e \Pr_{ijkc|f}^{low|e}\left(\frac{H_{ijf}}{\Psi_{ijfc}} - \sum_{ikc}\left(\Pr_{ijkc|f}^{low|e}\frac{H_{ijf}}{\Psi_{ijfc}}\right)\right)$$

and in the second term,

$$\frac{dH_{ijc|f}}{dw_{jf}}\bigg|_{ijcf} = -\sum_{\forall z}c_{ijf}\left(\left(\frac{1}{\eta_f - 1}\frac{c_{ijf}G_{izc|f}^{non-work}}{\Psi_{z|ijcf}} - \frac{\eta_f}{\eta_f - 1}\frac{\left[\sum_{\forall s}c_{ijf}G_{izc|f}^{non-work}Z_{z|ijf}\right]}{\alpha_f \Psi_{ijcf}} + \frac{(H - dG_{ijc|f}^{work})}{\Psi_{ijcf}}\right)Z_{z|ijcf}\right)G_{iz|fc}^{non-work}.$$

In the bracket of the first term, the derivative of the lower level probability is the increment of probability that the labor chooses a job in zone j. H is the labor endowment per person and the other part is the number of employed laborers. Thus the first term is the amount of labor supply in hours that changes to jobs located in zone j from other zones, when the wage increases in zone j. In the second term, the derivative of H is the change of the labor supply per employed laborer when the wage increases. This is negative in this definition because when income increases, consumers spend more time on non-work trips. The other part in the second term is the number of employed laborers in zone j before the wage increases. Thus the second term is the changing of the supply of the laborers who originally worked in zone j.

b) Producers

I now turn to the elasticities of the firms. I evaluate the elasticity of the demand for labor with respect to wage.

(i) Average elasticity of total labor demand with respect to wage

The demand for type f labor in industry r and zone j is

$$L_{f|rj} = \frac{\kappa_{f|rj}^{\frac{1}{1-\vartheta_r}} w_{jf}^{\frac{1}{\vartheta_r-1}}}{\sum_{z=0}^{F} \kappa_{z|rj}^{\frac{1}{1-\vartheta_r}} w_{jz}^{\frac{\vartheta_r}{\vartheta_r-1}}} \delta_r p_{rj} X_{rj}.$$

The elasticity of labor demand with respect to wage, assuming that wage increased in only one employment location staying constant in the others, is

$$\eta_{f|rj}^{L_{f|rj}, w_{jf}} = \frac{1}{\vartheta_r - 1}\left(1 - \vartheta_r \frac{w_{jf} L_{f|rj}}{\delta_r p_{rj} X_{rj}}\right) = \frac{1}{\vartheta_r - 1}\left(1 - \vartheta_r \underbrace{\frac{\kappa_{f|rj}^{\frac{1}{1-\vartheta_r}} w_{jf}^{\frac{\vartheta_r}{\vartheta_r-1}}}{\sum_{z=0}^{F} \kappa_{z|rj}^{\frac{1}{1-\vartheta_r}} w_{jz}^{\frac{\vartheta_r}{\vartheta_r-1}}}}_{\text{LOGIT FORM =cost share } f}\right).$$

The labor-demand-weighted average elasticities are,

$$\eta_f^{L_{f|rj}, w_{jf}} = \frac{\sum_{rj} L_{f|rj} \eta_{f|rj}^{L_{f|rj}, w_{jf}}}{\sum_{rj} L_{f|rj}},$$

$$\eta_r^{L_{f|rj}, w_{jf}} = \frac{\sum_{fj} L_{f|rj} \eta_{f|rj}^{L_{f|rj}, w_{jf}}}{\sum_{fj} L_{f|rj}}.$$

c) Real estate

Next I have the elasticities in the real estate side of the model. These are:

(i) the elasticity of floor space supply with respect to rent in the short-run; (ii) the elasticity of construction with respect to the asset value of floor space; (iii) the elasticity of demolition with respect to the asset value of floor space; (iv) the elasticity of building stock with respect to the asset value of floor space. The elasticity of floor space supply is adjusted by changing ϕ_{ik}. The average elasticity of construction is adjusted by changing Φ_{i0}, but since the number of Φ_{i0} is less than the number of elasticity of construction, the elasticity of construction for each building type are not separately adjustable and the adjustment must be done across building types in each zone. The elasticity of demolition is adjusted by Φ_{ik}.

(i) **Floor space supply elasticity with respect to rent.**

The floor supply of type k building in zone i is $S_{ik}q_{ik}$ where q_{ik} is the probability that the unit amount of floor space will be put on the market for rent during a period. Then, the elasticity and the supply-weighted average elasticity of floor supply with respect to rent are

$$\eta_{ik}^q = \phi_{ik}(1-q_{ik})R_{ik},$$

$$\overline{\eta_{ik}^q} = \frac{\sum_{\forall i} S_{ik} q_{ik} \eta_{ik}^q}{\sum_{\forall i} S_{ik} q_{ik}}.$$

(ii) **The elasticity of construction with respect to asset value**

The flow of new construction of type k building is $S_{i0}Q_{i0k}$ where S_{i0} is the stock of developable land in zone i, and Q_{i0k} is the probability that a type k building will be constructed in zone i. The elasticity is

$$\eta_{i0k}^{S_{i0}Q_{i0k},V_{ik}} = \Phi_{i0} \frac{m_{ik}}{1+\rho_{long}}(1-Q_{i0k})V_{ik} > 0.$$

The average elasticity is

$$\eta_{0k}^{S_{i0}Q_{i0k},V_{ik}} = \frac{\sum_{\forall i} S_{i0}Q_{i0k}\eta_{i0k}^{S_{i0}Q_{i0k},V_{ik}}}{\sum_{\forall i} S_{i0}Q_{i0k}}.$$

(iii) Elasticity of demolition with respect to value

The flow of demolition of type k building is $S_{i0}Q_{i0k}$. The elasticity and the stock-weighted average elasticity are:

$$\eta_{ik0}^{S_{ik}Q_{ik0},V_{ik}} = -\frac{\Phi_{ik}}{1+\rho_{long}}Q_{ikk}V_{ik} < 0,$$

$$\eta_{k0}^{S_{ik}Q_{ik0},V_{ik}} = \frac{\sum_{\forall i} S_{ik}Q_{ik0}\eta_{ik0}^{S_{ik}Q_{ik0},V_{ik}}}{\sum_{\forall i} S_{ik}Q_{ik0}}.$$

(iv) Elasticity of stock with respect to value

I examine the elasticity of the stocks when the value of the corresponding building increases but the other types of buildings' values do not change. If the values of all building types in a zone increased simultaneously then the elasticity would be smaller. Recall that at equilibrium,

$$S_{ik} = \underbrace{S_{ik}Q_{ikk}}_{\substack{\text{existing stock}\\\text{that did not change}}} + \underbrace{m_{ik}S_{i0}Q_{i0k}}_{\text{new construction}}.$$

The elasticity of the stock with respect to value is,

$$\begin{aligned}\eta_{ik}^{S_{ik},V_{ik}} &= \frac{dS_{ik}/dV_{ik}}{S_{ik}/V_{ik}}\\ &= \frac{S_{ik}(dQ_{ikk}/dV_{ik}) + m_{ik}S_{i0}(dQ_{i0k}/dV_{ik})}{S_{ik}/V_{ik}}\\ &= -(1-Q_{ikk})\eta_{ik0}^{S_{ik}Q_{ik0},V_{ik}\,(\text{demolition})} + Q_{ik0}\eta_{i0k}^{S_{i0}Q_{i0k},V_{ik}\,(\text{construction})} > 0.\end{aligned}$$

When the asset price increases, the stock increases. The stock-weighted average elasticity is

$$\eta_k^{S_{ik},V_{ik}} = \frac{\sum_{\forall i} S_{ik}\eta_{ik}^{S_{ik},V_{ik}}}{\sum_{\forall i} S_{ik}}.$$

3.3.2 Comparison with the literature

In this section, some of the elasticities are compared with corresponding estimates that are available in the literatures. Table 3.3.1 shows the calibrated elasticities in RELU-TRAN2.

Anas and Chu (1984), reported estimates based on data from the Chicago SMSA's 1970 US census data. Their travel time elasticity of location demand ranges from -1.462 to -2.190. They also reviewed the result from prior literatures[15] and reported that:

> " The in-vehicle time elasticity ranges from -0.36 to -1.40 for transit and from -0.55 to -1.77 for the drive-alone mode. Out-of-vehicle time elasticities range from -0.23 to -2.7 for transit and are -0.42 in the CSI model. Train and CRA do not report out-of-vehicle time elasticities for the auto mode."

My workers' travel time elasticity of location demand in RELU-TRAN2 ranges from -0.544 to -0.619.

It is reported in Anas and Arnott (1993) that the average price elasticity of housing demand, the price elasticity of white household and the price elasticity of non-white household in the Chicago MSA for 1970 to 1980, are -0.544, -0.516 and -0.683, respectively. In the model, the rent elasticity of housing demand cannot be larger than -1, because of the functional form of the utility function, and ranges from -1.38 to -1.95. Thus my elasticity is

---

15 Lerman(1977), Charles River Association (CRA)(1972), Atherton et al. (1975) and Train (1976).

86 Simulation Analysis of Urban Economy

Table 3.3.1 The calibrated elasticities in RELU-TRAN2

Consumer (f types) f	1	2	3	4
Worker's MRS(Disposable income,Time) by income quartile ($/hour/day)	12.295	21.056	36.204	93.215
Elasticities of worker's location demand with respect to commuting travel time by income quartile	-0.619	-0.602	-0.607	-0.544
Elasticities of housing demand with respect to rent by income quartile	-1.95	-1.76	-1.57	-1.38
Elasticities of labor supply with respect to wage by income quartile	3.83	2.93	2.1	1.32
The first term	4.00	3.10	2.28	1.50
The second term	-0.16	-0.17	-0.18	-0.19
Producer (r types)				
Elasticities of industy's labor demand with respect to wage:	-3.81			
Real Estate (k types)				
k	1 (single family housing)	2 (multi family housing)	3 (industry)	4 (commercial)
Elasticities of short-run supply with respect to rent by building type	0.0991	0.23	0.268	0.138
Elasticities of construction with respect to asset value by building type	0.0521	0.421	0.420	0.0744
City(1-5)	0.0335	0.0564	0.261	0.0396
Suburbs (6-14)	0.0526	0.681	0.452	0.0785
Elasticities of demolition with respect to asset value by building type	-1.612	-0.982	-0.176	-0.523
City(1-5)	-0.0550	-0.528	-0.346	-0.667
Suburbs (6-14)	-1.719	-1.375	-0.0729	-0.465
Elasticities of stock with respect to asset value by building type	0.0535	0.0147	0.00542	0.00872
City (1-5)	0.00102	0.00678	0.00643	0.00786
Suburbs (6-14)	0.0672	0.0218	0.00480	0.00922

more elastic than that in Anas and Arnott (1993).

In Anas and Arnott (1993), the rent elasticity of occupancy is 0.1016 and 0.1136 for the single-family and multiple–family. In my model those are 0.0991 and 0.23. Thus the single-family housing is similarly elastic to theirs, but the multiple-family housing supply is more elastic than theirs.

Kimmel and Kniesner (1998) studied the US households data for the period 1983 to 1986. Their wage elasticity of labor supply in hours worked is 0.51. In the context of my model, their wage elasticity of labor supply would be compared with the second term in the equation of the wage elasticity of labor supply, and those are negative, ranging from -0.16 to -0.19. In my model, the consumer would make more non-work trips when the wage increases (because of the income effect), and this reduces the labor supply.

That the long run price elasticity of the stock is in the 1.2 to 1.4 range and that the construction elasticity is ranging from 1.0 to 1.2 are reported by DiPasquale and Wheaton (1994). Blackley (1999) reports that the long-run price elasticity of new housing supply (supply measured in value terms) in United States for 1950 to 1994 ranges from 1.6 to 3.7. Green et al. (2005) report that the price elasticity of housing supply in the Chicago MSA, for the period 1979 to 1996 is 2.48, although it is not significantly different from zero. Their housing supply is defined as the number of housing units for which building permits were issued, multiplied by 2.5 (average household size), divided by population. My elasticity of housing construction measures what percent of the land available for construction will be developed into type k building (housing) if the asset price of type k building rises by 1%. This elasticity ranges from 0.03 (for single-family housing in city) to 0.68 (for multiple-family housing in the suburbs). One of the reasons why my elasticity of construction is so small is that many of modeled zones are urbanized and there is not much land left to be developed. The area covered by the Chicago MSA in Green et al. (2005) is broader than modeled zone. It is likely that in year 2000 in the model, modeled zone are more developed than their period, and the available land would have decreased significantly. Also, the definition of my elasticity of construction is different than theirs, because they measure the percentage by which a 1% increase in asset price would increase building permits multiplied by the population that would use the newly constructed housing, whereas my elasticity measures the percent by which the available land would decrease.

In addition, there are two assumptions that could be affecting my low elasticity in real estate variables. The first assumption is that the building structural density in space, m_{ik}, is constant. Average structural density in a zone is not constant and can change over time, for example, by demolishing low structural density buildings and constructing higher structural density buildings. But, if the building's floor space amount could be directly chosen by the developer, the stock could be more elastic when the building value increases. This would be especially true in the zones where the vacant land is scarce. Smith (1976) reports that the price elasticity of density is 5.27, where their density is the number of dwelling units built in that land area, by testing the Chicago metropolitan area cross-section data between 1971 and 1972. The second assumption, that could be affecting my low elasticity of stock, is the equilibrium condition that the construction amount and the demolition amount of each in each stock in each zone are equalized by the real estate market being in stationary equilibrium. In reality, the construction would be larger than demolition and stock could therefore increase faster. In any case, the methodology used in the literature to estimate the supply elasticity of housing is not robust. There are important data-driven or definitional differences between any two studies. This suggests that it might be better to evaluate the reasonableness of the housing supply elasticity by actually simulating the model in a comparative static exercise, and observing how the housing stock responds.

In the comparative statics exercise, I simulated a simple urban growth scenario, in which I increased the total population and the net exports by 10%. Table 3.3.2 shows the results in percent change of building stocks, rents and values for the city and the suburb. The vacant land stock ($k=0$) decreases in both the city and the suburbs. The single family housing stock ($k=1$) decreases in the city and increases in the suburbs. The multiple family housing stock ($k=2$) increases in both the city and the suburbs, and increases more in the suburbs than in the city. Both single and multiple family housing

Table 3.3.2 Percent change of building stocks, rent and value from base after population and net exports increase 10%.

		k = 0	k = 1	k = 2	k = 3	k = 4
Building stocks	City	-4.172	-2.434	6.662	4.309	4.028
	Suburbs	-3.904	6.627	8.904	2.789	2.583
Rent	City		12.751	6.725	7.258	7.227
	Suburbs		6.315	4.44	8.429	8.876
Value	City	18.41	28.79	22.85	14.339	16.047
	Suburb	1.195	19.024	12.584	28.11	23.117

stock increases less than the 10% population growth and the average floor space per person decreases. The industrial and commercial buildings ($k = 3$ and 4) also increase in the city and in the suburbs. The rate of increase is more in the city than in the suburbs, but not as much as the rate of increase of the housing stock. In the city, where the available land is limited, some single family housing is demolished and multi family housing, industrial and commercial building are constructed. In suburbs where there is plenty of land, both single and multiple family housing is constructed. Industrial and commercial buildings are also constructed in the suburbs. Thus the building stocks responds reasonably with respect to the increase of the population and net exports. Accordingly, the rents and values of each building type change in a normal way. In the city the rent of single family housing increases by more than 10%, because the supply decreases. The other building rents also increase since demand increases by more than supply. Both rent and value increase more for those building types and locations where the demand increases more and the supply increases less. Thus I evaluate that the building markets, including stocks, rents and values, respond reasonably under the calibrated elasticities of the model.

3.4 The price elasticity of gasoline consumption

In this section I will evaluate the numerically found fuel price elasticity of gasoline consumption, as the time horizon passes from the short-run to the long-run in well-defined steps. The two main factors that contribute to the elasticity of gasoline consumption with respect to the gasoline price, are the elasticity of the average MPG (Miles Per Gallon), with respect to the gas price; and the elasticity of travel, that is the total VMT (Vehicle Miles Traveled), with respect to the gas price.

In the elasticity of MPG, changes that are induced in travel speed and in vehicle inefficiency are the important elements. It should be noted that an average MPG level can be calculated as MPG = VMT/GC, where GC is gasoline consumption. Hence, even if VMT and GC behave as expected, this does not mean that MPG will also behave well. If VMT decreases more on roads where the traffic flow is more gasoline efficient, than on roads where the flow is less efficient, then the average MPG could be disimproved even though the price of gasoline has risen.

In the elasticity of VMT, how the number and the length of trips change are the important elements. Those are strongly affected by the proximities of residence and work locations, on the one hand, and the residences and the retail locations, on the other hand.

In addition, there is a well-known rebound effect which is defined as the increasing of VMT as MPG improves either because driving conditions become more fuel efficient or because cars become more fuel efficient[16]. This is called a rebound effect because if people drive more efficiently, then they can travel more. For example, as the fuel efficiency of driving improves, a trip of the same length as before becomes cheaper in fuel. On the one hand, per-mile less fuel is consumed (the intensive margin), but on the other hand,

---

[16] There are several definitions of the rebound effect. For example, Small and Van Dender (2007) use the elasticity of VMT with respect to fuel cost per mile to identify the rebound effect. Green et al.(1999) say it is the "take back" of potential energy savings from fuel economy improvements as travel increases. For more general discussion, see Berkhout et al.(2000) and Alcott (2005), for example.

the driver may travel longer (more miles) since each mile of driving got cheaper. If driving is done to get to normal goods, then both the income and substitution effects favor more travel occurring. If this effect is large, then more efficient travel could cause more VMT and more fuel consumption. In such a case, the technological improvement from making more efficient cars could have undesirable effects on the environment, by stimulating more not less travel demand and fuel use. As an example carbon dioxide emissions that affect global warming can increase as vehicle fuel economy improves.

In this section, I report the results of several carefully structured simulations in order to evaluate the responsiveness of the calibrated RELU-TRAN2 model to changes in the price of gasoline. These structured simulations are based on the concept that some processes change quickly and would occur soon after the gas price change. For example, it may be expected that trip-making consumers adjust their routes and modes relatively quickly within a matter of days or weeks. But in the longer run, they could also make other adjustments such as buying more fuel efficient vehicles to replace the less efficient vehicles they currently use, or changing their work and or residence or shopping locations to reduce their trip-lengths. Since RELU-TRAN2 includes all of these processes, simulating the entire model and reaching a new equilibrium combines the effects that happen in the short run with those that happen in the longer run. To understand what the effects are over different time horizons, I ought to run only part of the equilibration processes of the model, keeping the others constant. In this way I would move from the very short run to the long run in steps observing how much the response changes at each step. Because demand curves are shifting and not fixed it would be more appropriate to say that I am doing a comparative static simulation using only part of the model, than measuring a true elasticity. In subsequent steps, I will examine complete re-equilibration, meaningful for very long run analysis. In such a way, I will see the model's responsiveness to the price of gasoline per gallon, step by step as the time horizon lengthens.

To be more precise, I make the definitions of short and long run as follows, in the context of the model. In the short run it is assumed that consumer-workers can change their routes of travel on the road network, can change modes by switching from auto to transit or to the non-motorized modes, and can change their non-work trip pattern (e.g. by traveling less or to closer-by places) but not the locations of their commuting arrangements. Such short run adjustments may take anywhere from a few days to a few months to make. In the long run, consumer-workers could change their car-type, housing type, residence location and work location. Such adjustments may take anywhere from one year to many years to make. Even in the long run, I keep constant prices, rents and wages since changes in these variables make it very hard to see how the consumer-worker is responding by adjusting his choices in the face of the gasoline price increase. The effects of rent and wage changes would then be seen in a full comparative static simulation of the entire model.

In addition, it is needed to consider the effect of exogenous technological change on vehicle efficiency. As seen in Chapter 2, the model is formulated in such a way that each consumer-worker type can choose one of several vehicle types which differ in cost and in fuel economy. The fuel economy levels of these car-types are exogenously fixed in the model. While the consumer can change car-type within the model, over the long run, the path of technological improvements would require that I improve vehicle fuel economy for each of the car-types. If the period of interest is more than few years, it would be realistic to count the improvement of such vehicle fuel economy technology. Suppose that everything is fixed and that the fuel price increases by 10%. If technology improvements cause a 2% lower per-mile gasoline consumption for any kind of car, then gasoline consumption will decrease by 2% even without any behavioral reaction to the price change. To someone who did not take into account the technological improvement, it would look as if the price elasticity of gasoline is 0.2.

3.4.1 Impact of fuel price increase

In this section, I measured by structured simulations, the short-run and long-run fuel price elasticity, by re-equilibrating the variables of all shorter-run steps than the current step, keeping the variables of longer-run steps than current step the same. More clearly speaking step by step, in the first stage the traveler's route choice is adjusted. In the second stage, both route choice and mode choice are adjusted, and so on. Figure 3.4.1 (a) and table 3.4.1 (a) show those elasticities.

Price Elasticity of Gasoline

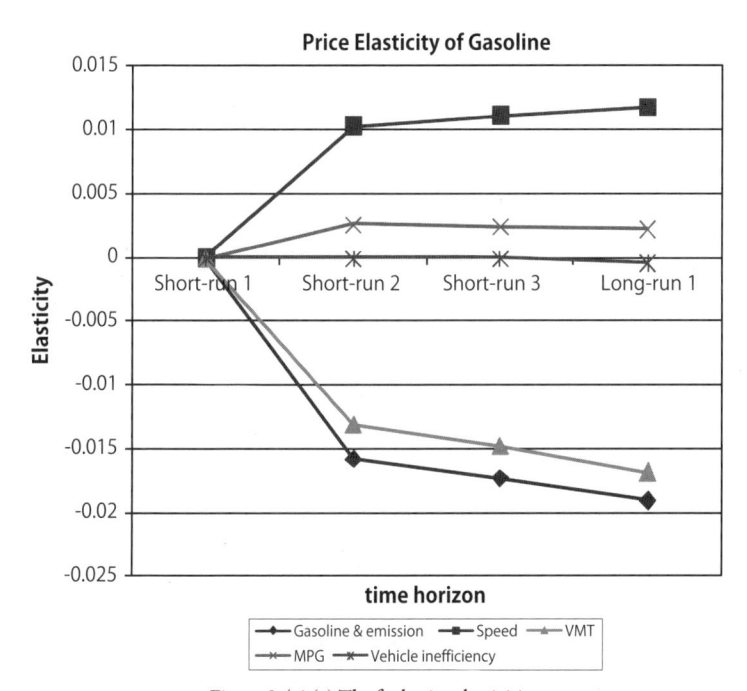

Figure 3.4.1 (a) The fuel price elasticities.

Table 3.4.1 (a) The fuel price elasticities.

	Short run 1 (Route)	Short run 2 (Mode)	Short run 3 (non-work travel)	Long run 1 (RELU Pr)
Gasoline & emission	-0.000066	-0.015783	-0.017281	-0.019052
Speed	0.000014	0.010266	0.011077	0.011763
VMT	-0.000111	-0.013161	-0.01485	-0.016823
MPG	-0.000045	0.002626	0.002435	0.002233
Vehicle inefficiency	0	0	0	-0.000381

Short run 1: Route choice.

By the route choice adjustment, the elasticity of fuel and CO_2 emission, the elasticity of VMT, the elasticity of average MPG, the elasticity of average speed, the elasticity of average vehicle inefficiency are, -0.000066, -0.000111, -0.000045, 0.000014 and 0.

Since only route choices can be changed in this step, some routes of highway trips are switched to other highway routes on TRAN's network. But choices of local roads will not change because whichever route a traveler chooses, the local road trips are not changed in the model, as long as the traveler's origin-to-destination zone pair (O-D pair) and mode of travel is the same. When the price of gasoline increases, the importance of travel monetary cost would increase relative to travel time. Drivers would change route so that their fuel consumption does not increase a lot. Thus, in changing routes they would give more weight to the monetary cost of travel than they did before the gasoline price increased. The monetary cost of a route depends on MPG on the one hand and on the route's length on the other.

On what kind of route would drivers be relatively more tempted to change their driving routes? Suppose that there are four types of routes: (i) fuel saving and time saving; (ii) fuel consuming but time saving, (iii) fuel saving and time consuming, and (iv) fuel consuming and time consuming. The drivers on type (i) and (iii) routes would not be likely change route, since travel cost becomes more important than travel time. The drivers on type (ii) and type (iv) routes would change their routes. Among drivers, those with higher vehicle inefficiency and lower VOT would change routes relatively more than others, if other parameters are the same. For simplicity, I assume that there are only type (ii) and (iii) routes. The type (ii) route is assumed to be the longer distance but shorter travel time because this route is less congested. Suppose that driving speed is fast and MPG is high on route (ii). Thus for the drivers, route (ii) could be the typical detour route. Type (iii) route would be shorter distance but longer travel time because the route is more congested. Driving speed is slow and MPG is low on route (iii). When the fuel price increases and the travel cost becomes relatively more important than travel time, the drivers on route (ii) would change to route (iii). On route (iii) the congestion is increased and speed is decreased. MPG would be decreased. The weight of route (iii) increases. On route (ii), the congestion is mitigated and the speed would increase. MPG increases if the speed is not faster than the fuel efficient speed. Thus average speed and average MPG could be increased or decreased. Some of the drivers on route (iii) would change route to (ii) by reacting to this, and the impact would become moderated. In the result, the average speed increases and average MPG decreases, when the price of gasoline increases. VMT, fuel consumption and CO_2 emissions decrease. Because of the speed adjustment, on the route where the congestion is increased, the speed decreases, travel time increases and MPG decrease. On the other hand, on the route where the congestion is reduced, the speed increases, travel time decreases and MPG increases (if speed is not too fast).

Short run 2: Mode choice.

By the mode choice adjustment, the elasticity of fuel and CO_2 emission, the elasticity of VMT, the elasticity of average MPG, the elasticity of average speed, and the elasticity of average vehicle inefficiency are, -0.0158, -0.0132, 0.00263, 0.0103 and 0.

Since the mode and the routes can both be changed under this structured simulation, people react to the higher gas price by switching from auto trips to transit (and the non-motorized mode). This will in turn cause changes of travel time and cost on both the major road network and the local roads. Note that the number of trips and the origin-destination pairs are not changed in this simulation.

Since some travelers switch their travel mode to transit or other mode, the number of auto trips decrease and congestion is mitigated. VMT, gasoline consumption and CO_2 emissions decrease. Speed improves and MPG improves.

Although the impact of reduced traffic volume is large enough to explain the result, there are other minor effects. As in the route choice case, the drivers in the high fuel consuming route would be more likely to change modes than the drivers in the low fuel consuming routes. In addition, within the drivers on the same route, the drivers whose vehicle is inefficient would change the route more than the drivers whose vehicle is efficient, assuming other factors, such as the value of time, VOT, stayed the same.

Short run 3: Non-work trips

By the non-work travel adjustment, the elasticity of fuel and CO_2 emission, the elasticity of VMT, the elasticity of MPG, the elasticity of speed, and the elasticity of inefficiency are, -0.0173, -0.0149, 0.00244, 0.0111 and 0.

In addition to the route choice and mode choice, now the demand for retail goods and the non-work trips will be adjusted. Since gasoline price is increased, travel cost per-mile is increased. In this structured simulation, work trips remain fixed, but the consumer-worker can adjust to the higher gas price by changing his non-work trip pattern.

Non-work trips can be changed. Some of the long distance trips are decreased, by quitting travel or substituting shorter distance travels. Short distance trips might be increased or decreased, because original short distance trips should be decreased but some of the long distance trips are changed to short distance trips. VMT, gasoline consumption and CO_2 emissions decrease.

Speed increases but MPG decreases from previous stage. I could observe this kind of change when the travels decrease on the very high speed road. MPG increases only slightly as the speed increases from the most efficient speed, but it would decrease more when the speed decreased from a slower speed. In such a case the weight on high speed and high MPG would increase and the weight on slow speed and low MPG would increase. As a result of these changes, it would be observed that the speed increases and the MPG decreases at the same time.

Long run 1: Location, housing and vehicle choices

By the location, housing and vehicle choices adjustment, the elasticity of fuel and CO_2 emission, the elasticity of VMT, the elasticity of average MPG, the elasticity of average speed, and the elasticity of average vehicle inefficiency are, -0.0191, -0.0168, 0.00223, 0.0118 and -0.00381.

In the long run, a year to a few years, some people can change their location patterns as represented by the RELU choice probabilities. These include work location, residence location, housing type and vehicle type choices. In this simulation, other RELU variables, such as wage, rent, price and so on, are not changed. If the fuel price increases, people prefer to live and work in close proximity, since commuting cost is higher due to the gasoline price increase. They prefer to live in places with better access to shops also, so as to reduce the gasoline consumption. This would cause the centralization and the commuting travel distance to be shorter. It is not unlikely that some jobs would move to the suburb where it is easy to access labor and where congestion is lower. The more likely cases are that residences are chosen to be closer to the downtown and to other job centers, and that jobs move closer to labor's residence locations. There is tendency that more people who work in the suburbs work in the same zone where they reside.

VMT, gasoline consumption and CO_2 emissions decrease. Speed increases, average vehicle inefficiency improves and MPG decreases. Average vehicle inefficiency is improved because more efficient cars become more valuable when gasoline is more expensive. Since people travel closer to the downtown, the average speed in the city area is decreased and increased in the suburbs which become less congested. Those who travel near the downtown suffer more congestion. They travel with less efficient speeds and incur more gasoline consumption. Thus similarly to speed, the MPG decreases on city roads. On the suburban roads, the MPG would increase because the congestion is mitigated. But on some of the high speed roads in the suburbs, MPG could decrease because of a speed that is too high. The average speed and average MPG are affected by those changing roads. At the same time, lower aggregate VMT makes vehicle inefficiency less important. Because of this, the overall incentive for getting a more efficient car is ambiguous, but in this case average vehicle efficiency improves.

Long run 2: General equilibrium without technological improvement

Figure 3.4.1 (b) and Table 3.4.1 (b), show that the fuel price elasticities include the longer run in which everything changes. This is the comparative statics analysis of the fuel price change. By the adjustment of all the variables, the elasticity of fuel and CO_2 emission, the elasticity of VMT, the elasticity of average MPG, the elasticity of average speed, and the elasticity of average vehicle inefficiency are, -0.0899, -0.0721, 0.0180, 0.0452 and -0.000016.

98 Simulation Analysis of Urban Economy

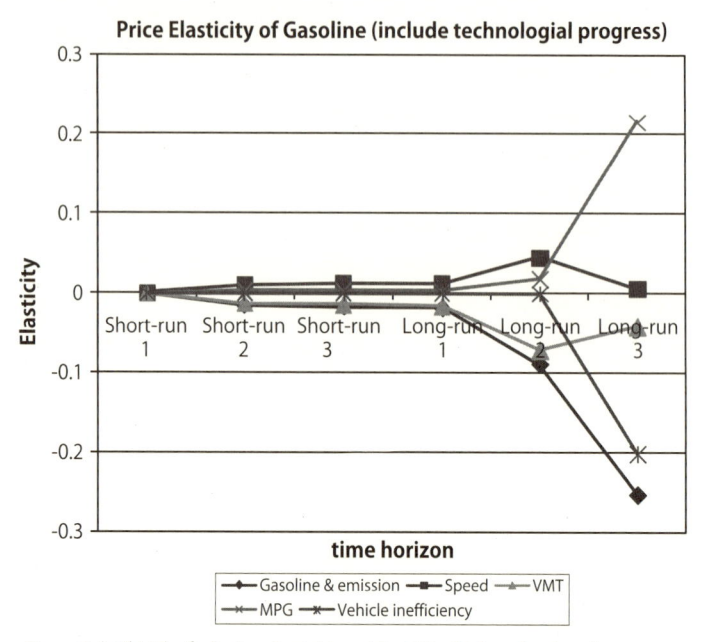

Price Elasticity of Gasoline (include technologial progress)

[Chart: Elasticity vs time horizon (Short-run 1, Short-run 2, Short-run 3, Long-run 1, Long-run 2, Long-run 3) with series: Gasoline & emission, Speed, VMT, MPG, Vehicle inefficiency]

Figure 3.4.1(b) The fuel price elasticities with a 2% vehicle technology improvement.

Table 3.4.1 (b) The fuel price elasticities with a 2% vehicle technology improvement.

	Short run 1 (Route)	Short run 2 (Mode)	Short run 3 (non-work travel)	Long run 1 (RELU Pr)	Long run 2 (all variables)	Long run 3 (Technology)
Gasoline & emission	-0.000066	-0.015783	-0.017281	-0.019052	-0.089877	-0.252927
Speed	0.000014	0.010266	0.011077	0.011763	0.045152	0.005811
VMT	-0.000111	-0.013161	-0.01485	-0.016823	-0.072067	-0.042455
MPG	-0.000045	0.002626	0.002435	0.002233	0.017971	0.215934
Vehicle inefficiency	0	0	0	-0.000381	-0.000016	-0.201483

I let all the variables including prices, wages, rents, values and outputs adjust to their general equilibrium values, The whole economy reacts to the gasoline price change and all markets clear. The increase of the fuel price, reduces congestion on average and makes the city more centralized. Hence travel time is reduced, labor supply increases, and wages decrease.

The increment to travel cost and the wage decrease causes a reduction of disposable income in the simulation. Thus non-work travel decreases. VMT, gasoline consumption and CO_2 emissions decrease, speed up and MPG improves. Vehicle inefficiency is increased.

Long run 3: General equilibrium with a 2% vehicle technology improvement

Under a 2% technological progress, the elasticity of fuel and CO_2 emission, the elasticity of VMT, the elasticity of average MPG, the elasticity of average speed, the elasticity of average vehicle inefficiency are, -0.253, -0.0425, 0.216, 0.00581 and -0.201. In the very long run, more than few years, technological progress improves the fuel economy of cars. I did not consider such an effect in the previous structured simulations. I exogenously decrease vehicle inefficiency by 2%, in addition to the 10% increase of the fuel price, and re-equilibrate. Keeping other things constant, the response of gasoline consumption to the fuel price would be -2%. However, since vehicle efficiency is improved, the rebound effect is observed and VMT increases. The roads are congested and speed decreases. Gasoline consumption and CO_2 emissions decrease because of the technological improvement. The reduction of energy consumption is mostly caused by the technological improvement.

Summary

When fuel price increase, consumers adjust their behavior, but in the short-run consumers do not have many options to change. They would change travel route, travel modes or non-work trips. In the long-run consumer have more option that would be changed. They would change vehicle to be more efficient, reside-work location pair to be closer or even choose to be unemployed. Thus as time horizon becomes longer, consumer could reduce fuel consumption. Lastly, I improve vehicle inefficiency exogenously. The technological progress explains the important part of price elasticity of fuel in the long-run. It is observed when vehicles become efficient, that the increment of VMT from previous step and this is the rebound effect.

3.4.2 Review of Small and Van Dender (2007a, b)

I review the results obtained in the studies of Small and Van Dender (2007a) and Small and Van Dender (2007b) in order to compare with my results. They report that the rebound effect has been getting smaller over time. This tendency is also true for their price elasticity of gasoline. Table 3.4.2 (a) shows their price elasticities of gasoline. Their short-run and long-run price elasticities of gasoline are, -0.0892 and 0.4268 from 1966 to 2001, -0.074 and -0.0363 from 1966 to 2004, -0.0667 and -0.334 from 1997 to 2001 and -0.041 and -0.237 from 2000 to 2004. The second row of the table 3.4.2 (d) shows the fuel price elasticity of gasoline in my simulation when the speed is adjusted. My price elasticity of gasoline in the short-run 3 (route choice, mode choice and non-work trips are adjusted) and Long-run 2 (general equilibrium) and Long-run 3 (the technological progress is introduced) when the time is adjusted are, -0.0173, -0.0899 and -0.253. My short-run 3 and long-run 2 elasticities are still smaller than the elasticities in Small and Van Daner (2007a, 2007b). Thus without the technological progress I would underestimate the fuel price elasticity. In the long-run 3, the 2% improvement of vehicle inefficiency is introduced and the markets are re-equilibriated. This shows that most of the price elasticity of gasoline is explained by the technological progress and the result then becomes similar as Small and Van Dender (2007a ,b).

The VMT effect is the fuel cost per mile elasticity of VMT. Table 3.4.2 (b) shows the VMT effects. Their short-run and long-run VMT effects are, -0.0452 and -0.2221 from 1966 to 2001, -0.041 and -0.21 from 1966 to 2004, -0.0216 and -0.1066 from 1997 to 2001 and -0.011 and -0.057 from 2000 to 2004. The fuel cost per mile is defined as gasoline price by gasoline per mile; thus gasoline price over miles per gallon. Thus I could interpreted that when keeping one of those variables constant, that the elasticity is similar in meaning to the price elasticity of VMT or the vehicle inefficiency elasticity of VMT. They found that their estimates of the rebound effects are smaller than what others found[17]. Short-run and long-run rebound effect are, for

---

17 Small and Van Dender (2007a) insist that the smaller rebound effect might be caused by the endogeneity bias that is ignored in the econometric estimates. Small and Van Dender (2007a,b) ↗

Table 3.4.2 (a). Price elasticities of gasoline in Small and Van Dender (2007a, b).

	Short Run	Long Run
Price Elasticities of Gasoline (1966-2001)	-0.0892	-0.4268
Price Elasticities of Gasoline (1966-2004)	-0.074	-0.363
Price Elasticities of Gasoline (1997-2001)	-0.0667	-0.334
Price Elasticities of Gasoline (2000-2004)	-0.041	-0.237

Table 3.4.2 (b). VMT effect in Small and Van Dender (2007a, b).

	Short Run	Long Run
VMT Effect (1966-2001)	-0.0452	-0.2221
VMT Effect (1966-2004)	-0.041	-0.21
VMT Effect (1997-2001)	-0.0216	-0.1066
VMT Effect (2000-2004)	-0.011	-0.057

Table 3.4.2 (c) Fuel efficiency effect in Small and Van Dender (2007a, b).

	Short Run	Long Run
Fuel Efficiency Effect (1966-2001)	-0.044	-0.2047
Fuel Efficiency Effect (1966-2004)	-0.035	-0.193
Fuel Efficiency Effect (1997-2001)	n.a.	n.a.
Fuel Efficiency Effect (2000-2004)	-0.031	-0.191

Table 3.4.2 (d) The fuel price elasticities of gasoline, VMT and MPG from the RELU-TRAN2 simulations.

	Short run 1 (Route)	Short run 2 (Mode)	Short run 3 (non-work travel)	Long run 1 (RELU Pr)	Long run 2 (all variables)	Long run 3 (Technology)
Gasoline & emission	-0.000066	-0.015783	-0.017281	-0.019052	-0.089477	-0.252927
VMT	-0.000111	-0.013161	-0.01485	-0.016823	-0.072067	-0.042455
MPG	-0.000045	0.002626	0.002435	0.002233	0.017971	0.215934

example, 5% and 15% in Green (1992), 11% and 31% in Jones (1993) and 16% and 22% in Haughton and Sarkar (1996). The third row of the table 3.4.2 (d) shows the fuel price elasticity of VMT in my simulation when the speed is adjusted. My price elasticity of VMT in the short-run 3, the long-run 2, and

---

that their OLS results are similar with the literature and their 3SLS is robust but OLS is sensitive with respect to changes in specification. They also confirm that higher income and urbanization might cause the reduction of the elasticities over time.

the long-run 3 when the time is adjusted are, -0.0149, -0.0721 and -0.0425. Thus when technology progresses, VMT increases. Thus the reduction of gasoline consumption is less than what would be expected on account of the technological progress alone. Thus this increase of VMT is a rebound effect predicted by the model.

The fuel efficiency effect is the elasticity of GPM (= 1/MPG). Table 3.4.2 (c) shows Small and Van Dender's fuel efficiency effects. Their short-run and long-run fuel efficiency effects are, -0.044 and -0.2047 from 1966 to 2001, -0.035 and -0.193 from 1966 to 2004, and -0.031 and -0.191 from 2000 to 2004. The fourth row of the table 3.4.2 (d) shows the fuel price elasticity of MPG in my simulation when the speed is adjusted. My fuel price elasticity of MPG in the short run 3, and the long-run 2 (general equilibrium), and 3 (no technological progress) when the time is adjusted are, -0.00244, -0.018 and -0.216. The reaction of MPG is mostly explained by the technological progress.

Thus, before the technological progress, most of the fuel price elasticities of gasoline is explained by the fuel price elasticity of VMT, and after the technological progress most of the fuel price elasticity in the long-run 3 is explained by the technological progress. The elasticity of VMT decreases because of technological progress (rebound effect). In Small and Van Dender (2007a, b), VMT explains the elasticity of gasoline less than it does in my short-run 3 and my long-run 2. In their result for 2000-2004, MPG explains the price elasticity of gasoline more than for other periods, and this result is similar to mine for long-run 3. In the short-run, my price elasticity of gasoline is mostly explained by VMT and it is smaller than theirs, if I introduce small technological progress that is reasonable to the short-run time period, the result would be similar to theirs.

Hughes et al. (2006) report a result similar to that of Small and Van Dender (2007a,b) for the short-run price elasticity of gasoline demand. They find that from 1975 to 1980, the short-run price elasticity was in the range -0.21 to -0.34 and from 2001-2006 it was in the range from -0.034 to -0.077.

3.5 Fuel economy elasticity of gasoline consumption

In this section, I examine by doing structured simulations, the short- and long-run vehicle efficiency or fuel economy elasticity of gasoline consumption, and related variables, when the inefficiency is improved by technological progress. As explained in Chapter 2, an inefficiency improvement in RELU-TRAN2 is expressed by a smaller vehicle inefficiency level *ineff$_c$*. Thus, to input an exogenous improvement in fuel economy in the simulations, I would reduce the vehicle inefficiency level, *ineff$_c$*, by say 10%. Thus I need to be careful to interpret the result. If the numerically calculated elasticity of a targeted variable is positive, it means that the value of that variable is decreased by the 10% lower inefficiency (that is by the about 10% higher fuel economy). For example, suppose that, keeping other variables constant, fuel consumption decreases by 10% when the vehicle inefficiency decreases by 10%. Thus the reported elasticity of fuel consumption with respect to the vehicle's fuel inefficiency is 1, but not -1. The information should be read as "a 10% reduction in inefficiency resulted in a 10% reduction in fuel consumption."

In this section, the increase in the vehicle miles traveled (VMT) caused by the vehicle inefficiency improvement (technological progress) is called "the rebound effect." The "vehicle inefficiency improvement" means that all the consumer change their vehicles to a more efficient vehicle. In other words, it is assumed that all the vehicles that are available in the market have become less inefficient by 10%. From Chapter 2, the reader will recall that there were 5 vehicle types, $c = 1,...,5$, ranked from the most efficient to the least efficient. So if a consumer-worker chose vehicle type 3 before the improvement and he continues to choose type 3 after the improvement, that consumer-worker will experience a 10% improvement in inefficiency. If a consumer-worker chose 3 before the improvement but chose vehicle type 4 after the improvement, then that consumer-worker will experience an improvement that is less than 10% (or disimprovement), and a consumer-worker who switches from type 3 before the improvement to type 2 after, will experience a more than 10%

Inefficiency Elasticity of Gasoline

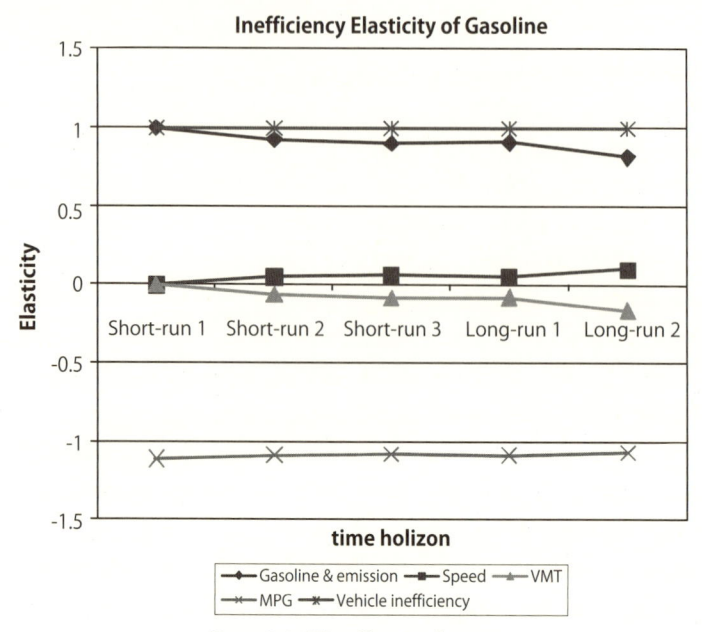

Figure 3.5.1 The efficiency elasticities.

Table 3.5.1 The efficiency elasticities.

	Short-run 1	Short-run 2	Short-run 3	Long-run 1	Long-run 2
Fuel & emission	0.999872	0.924933	0.899626	0.908649	0.819888
Speed	0.000089	0.047917	0.060817	0.053009	0.099756
VMT	-0.000263	-0.064327	-0.087016	-0.083012	-0.163235
MPG	-1.111245	-1.090085	-1.084177	-1.090774	-1.070928
Vehicle Inefficiency	1	1	1	1.001016	1.000392

improvement in fuel inefficiency. However, I may define a short-run scenario in which I do not change the choices of vehicle types but change their inefficiency levels, and I can run such a scenario by means of an appropriate structured simulation. In order to do this, I would keep the trips distribution by vehicle type at the same equilibrium level that occurred prior to the inefficiency improvement.

When the vehicle inefficiency is decreased by 10% and before the travelers can react in any way whatsoever, the elasticity of fuel and CO_2 emissions is 1, but not -1. Because although the fuel and CO_2 emission decrease, inefficiency also decrease $\dfrac{dGalloon}{Galloon} \Big/ \dfrac{dineff}{ineff} = -0.1/(-0.1) = 1$. I need to be careful on sign. The elasticity of vehicle miles traveled (VMT) is 0, the elasticity of miles per gallon (MPG) is -1.111. This is because,

$$MPG_{\ell c} = \dfrac{1}{GPM_{\ell c}} = \dfrac{1}{fuel_\ell(speed_\ell) \times ineff_c}.$$

That is, VMT (= 1 mile in this equation) does not change but fuel consumption decreases by 10%, the elasticity of speed is 0, and the elasticity of inefficiency is 1.

Figure 3.5.1 and Table 3.5.1 show the numerically calculated efficiency elasticities from these structured simulation experiments.

Short-run 1: Route choice.

When trips can choose only their route of travel, while the speed on each road is not changing, then the elasticity of aggregate fuel and CO_2 emissions, the elasticity of aggregate VMT, the elasticity of average MPG, the elasticity of average speed, and the elasticity of average inefficiency are, 0.9999, -0.000263, -1.11, 0.000089 and 1. The aggregate fuel and CO_2 emissions increase, aggregate VMT increases, average MPG increases, average speed decreases and average inefficiency is the same by route choice.

The fuel consumption increases because travelers care less about the fuel consumption after their vehicle's inefficiency is improved. Since the vehicle is now more efficient, travel per mile becomes cheaper because less fuel is required to travel one mile. Because of this, the trips become less sensitive to cost and more sensitive to travel time, since in TRAN a generalized cost combining monetary and time cost of travel is used to choose among routes. When the monetary cost part decreases due to less gasoline being required per mile, the time-cost part becomes more important. In other words, when people decide the route, they pay more attention to the travel time but less attention to the money cost including the fuel consumption. Thus travelers would prefer the route of time saving even if the route is longer. VMT, fuel consumption and CO_2 emission increase. The changing of average speed consists of the changing of speed on each link and the changing of weight of each road. I observe the reduced speed and increased MPG. Those two effects could come up at the same time when the travels on the road of faster speed than the fuel efficient speed increases. The road becomes more congested and the speed decreases towards the more fuel efficient speed. MPG increases. On the other low speed roads, congestion becomes less and speed becomes higher. If travelers increase in high speed roads, keeping speed constant, the weight of high speed roads increases. The average speed goes up. The average MPT would decrease. The results are mixed of those effects and the average speed decreases and the average MPG increases.

Short-run 2: Mode choice.

When trips are allowed to change their modes as well as their routes, then the elasticity of fuel and CO_2 emission, the elasticity of aggregate VMT, the elasticity of average MPG, the elasticity of average speed, and the elasticity of inefficiency are, 0.925, -0.0643, -1.09, 0.0479 and 1. Thus, fuel consumption and CO_2 emissions increase, VMT increases, average MPG decreases, average speed decreases and average inefficiency is the same.

Since all auto trips have improved fuel consumption, more travelers choose auto trips. VMT, fuel consumption and CO_2 emissions increase. The roads are more congested. Relatively more auto would occur by mode choice on time saving roads, probably with high speed. Thus the speed on each road could be decreased by congestion, but the weight on the high speed road increases. As the result the average speed is reduced. Average MPG is also reduced. On most roads MPG is reduced by congestion but MPG is increased by congestion on some high speed road. But such roads are MPG inefficient. It is ambiguous but the weight of high MPG roads would decrease. As a result, average MPG decreases.

Short-run 3: Non-work Trips.

By the non-work travel adjustment, the elasticity of fuel and CO_2 emissions, the elasticity of VMT, the elasticity of average MPG, the elasticity of average speed, and the elasticity of average vehicle inefficiency are, 0.9, -0.087, -1.08, 0.0608 and 1. Thus the fuel consumption and CO_2 emissions increase, VMT increases, average MPG decreases, average speed decreases and average inefficiency is the same.

In the model, the vehicle inefficiency improvement will cause a higher disposable income, because it is assumed that more efficient car is smaller and maintenance cost is cheaper. Thus the consumers use part of this additional income for purchasing more goods and make more non-work travels. The reduction of travel monetary cost by vehicle inefficiency improvement makes full price of goods cheaper. This full price reduction is relatively larger for the goods produced in zones of more distance from the residential zone. Both increased income and decreased full price work to increase non-work trips. Thus non-work travel increases and distance would become longer. VMT, fuel consumption and CO_2 emissions increase. A more congested road will lead to speed and MPG decreasing (except for the MPG on a very high speed road). The reduction of travel cost and increment of travel time would be relatively larger in the longer trips than the shorter trips. It also has an effect on speed and MPG that the non-work auto travels takes more driving distances on zone roads. Thus how the weight of traffic in fast roads or high MPG roads is ambiguous. In this case, the speed and MPG both decrease.

Long-run 1: Location, housing and vehicle choice.

By the adjustment of residence and job location, housing type and vehicle type in RELU, while keeping all prices constant, the elasticity of fuel and CO_2 emission, the elasticity of VMT, the elasticity of average MPG, the elasticity of average speed, the elasticity of average vehicle inefficiency are, 0.909, -0.083, -1.09, 0.053 and 1.001. Thus fuel consumption and CO_2 emission decrease, VMT decreases, average MPG increases, average speed increases and average vehicle inefficiency decreases.

Because the vehicle becomes more fuel efficient, it is expected that the commuting distance becomes longer and more suburbanized. Thus VMT increases. But what is observed is the opposite and the VMT decreases. Although the speed is increased from previous stage, it is slower than base because of congestion. This implies that commuting travel time by auto increases, although commuting travel monetary cost by auto would be decreased from base. Some commuters by auto would feel inconvenience for this speed delay and would change to other modes. As the timing to change the mode, when they change RELU probability is better than other timings, because commuters can choose the location near CBD where it is easy to access other zones by public transport and the other modes. The VMT, fuel consumption and CO_2 emissions decrease. The congestion decreases from the previous stage, but is still higher than the base. The auto commuters would be suburbanized. Increased of speed and MPG from previous stage is the result of the changing of each roads and the weight of the roads.

Long-run 2: General equilibrium.

Here I report the results from re-equilibrating all the markets when vehicle inefficiency is reduced by 10%. This differs from long-run 1 in that all prices, wages and rents are now adjusted to clear the markets.

By allowing all variables to adjust, the elasticity of fuel and CO_2 emission, the elasticity of VMT, the elasticity of average MPG, the elasticity of average speed, the elasticity of average vehicle inefficiency are, 0.82, -0.163, -1.07, 0.0998 and 1.0004. Thus the fuel consumption increases, VMT increases, average MPG decreases, average speed decreases and average vehicle inefficiency increases.

Summary

The first feature of the technological improvement is that keeping other variables constant, the fuel consumption and CO_2 emission decrease by same percentage as technology improves. The second feature is that as the time horizon becomes longer, VMT increases, although the amount of fuel consumption would not exceed the base case since the rebound effect is not that strong. The exception is when the RELU location choice probabilities are endogenously adjusted in the long-run 1. In this case, VMT is more than in the base, but less than the previous step in which the RELU location choice probabilities were fixed. Apparently, compared to the previous step, the consumers prefer to reside near the center and change modes, against what is expected from the lower travel monetary cost by auto. But since auto travel becomes convenient, roads are more congested. Now the auto travel time increases. Thus consumers would choose closer location to center and other modes. In the long-run 2, when all the variables are adjusted, the rebound effect again becomes larger.

Chapter 4. Comparative Statics

To understand how the calibrated general equilibrium model works and if it is reasonable, it is helpful to do some comparative static analysis before it is applied to policy testing. The procedure is to select an exogenous variable (which is a scalar or a vector) and change it by some percentage up or down from its calibrated base value. Then, by comparing the equilibrium with the calibrated base values of the variable, and the equilibrium with the changed value of the variable, it will be possible to see how the parameter change affects the model's predictions.

In this chapter, I will do comparative statics by changing the following exogenous variables: a) The efficiency levels of available automobiles, $ineff_c$; b) the price of fuel, p_{FUEL}; c) The level of monetary travel cost for public transportation, $v^w_{2ij|fc}$ (MCPT); d) The road capacities of the road network's major links and the intra-zonal road capacities representing local roads, CAP_l and $ICAP_j$; e) the dispersion coefficient of the construction probability, Φ_{i0} (phiconv). In each of these cases two runs are made. In one the calibrated values are increased by 10% and the resulting equilibrium is compared to the calibrated base equilibrium. Then, the calibrated value is decreased by 10% and again the results are compared with the base case.

In comparing the results to the calibrated base, I focused on the following groups of variables produced by the model.

(*i*) *Variables related to transportation*: the average level of automobile efficiency, the average speed of car travel, aggregate fuel consumption, aggregate carbon dioxide emissions, average miles per gallon in car travel, and aggregate vehicle miles traveled.

(*ii*) *Variables related to urban sprawl and job dispersion*: the amount of undeveloped land, the number of employed workers in a zone, the workers employed in the CBD, the rest of the central city and in the suburbs, the number of workers that reside in the CBD, in the central city, in the suburbs, and vacant land in the CBD, the central city and in the suburbs.

4.1 Impact on variables related to transportation

The results are shown in Table 4.1 (a). Each row shows the exogenous variables that are changed by 10% (up and down), and each column shows how the transportation related variables are impacted.

Table 4.1 (a). The impact on fuel consumption related variables.

			Fuel (gallon)	CO_2 Emission (ton)	VMT (miles)	MPG (mile)	Speed (mile/hour)
	Base	Value	6,234,858	54,792	132,155,891	21.196	21.773
$ineff_c$ (Vehicle inefficiency)	10%	change	489,224	4,299	-2,132,180	-1.859	0.216
		% change	7.847	7.847	-1.613	-8.772	0.995
	-10%	change	-511,189	-4,492	2,157,247	2.270	-0.217
		% change	-8.199	-8.199	1.632	10.709	-0.998
p_{FUEL} (Fuel price)	10%	change	-56,037	-492.451	-952,403	0.038	0.098
		% change	-0.899	-0.899	-0.721	0.180	0.452
	-10%	change	57,239	503,014	966,489	-0.039	-0.100
		% change	0.918	0.918	0.731	-0.185	-0.458
$v_{2ij|fc}^w$ (MCPT)	10%	change	22,528	197,975	337,789	-0.022	-0.046
		% change	0.361	0.361	0.256	-0.105	-0.209
	-10%	change	-22,659	-199.126	-339,578	0.023	0.046
		% change	-0.363	-0.363	-0.257	0.107	0.212
CAP_l and $ICAP_i$ (Capacity)	10%	change	3,693	32.456	2,361,515	0.366	1.065
		% change	0.059	0.059	1.787	1.727	4.892
	-10%	change	-1,701	-14.946	-2,917,411	-0.462	-1.171
		% change	-0.027	-0.027	-2.208	-2.181	-5.376
Φ_{i0} (phiconv of con)	10%	change	4,578	40,236	125,909	0.005	-0.005
		% change	0.073	0.073	0.095	0.022	-0.022
	-10%	change	-5,020	-44.121	-142,653	-0.006	0.005
		% change	-0.081	-0.081	-0.108	-0.027	0.021

4.1.1 Impact of fuel economy

As vehicle inefficiency, $ineff_c$, increases for all car types, cars consumes more fuel on roads of the same condition. When inefficiency increases by 10%, VMT decreases by 1.6%, but fuel consumption and CO_2 emissions increase by 7.8%. The change in vehicle inefficiency has two effects on VMT in the model. The first effect is the direct effect that occurs because travel cost by auto becomes higher. The second effect occurs because the maintenance cost of cars is a function of the car's fuel efficiency. According to equation (2.1.4) and Figure 2.1.2 in Chapter 2, more inefficient cars cost more to maintain. Hence, if all cars were to become less efficient, consumer workers would have lower disposable income. Keeping other variables constant, when their dsiposable income decreases, consumers reduce their non-work trips. Both effects work in the same direction to reduce aggregate VMT. Fuel consumption and CO_2 emissions would increase by 10% if the traveling behavior did not change. But actually traveling behavior changes and fuel consumption and CO_2 emission still increase, but less than 10%. Keeping other variables the same, the reduction of VMT implies that congestion would become lower and that MPG would increase, especially on roads where the driving speed is slow. In fact, MPG decreases by 8.8% because vehicles have become inefficient, although roads are less congested. Speed increases by 1.0% because congestion decreases. On most roads, the mitigation of congestion improves speed and MPG. But on some roads in the suburbs where the driving speed is too fast, the even higher increasing of speed causes more fuel consumption per mile and lower MPG. This is because of the shape of Figure 2.3.2 of Chapter 2. Fuel consumed per mile of driving decreases rapidly with speed at very low speeds, makes a relatively flat bottom and rises with speed at very high speeds.

When car inefficiency decreases by 10%, VMT by auto increases by about 1.6%. Hence I observe a rebound effect[18]. Fuel consumption and CO_2 emissions decrease by 8.2% and speed decreases by 1.0%. The MPG increases

---
[18] There are several definitions of the rebound effect. For example, Small and Van Dender (2007) use the elasticity of VMT with respect to fuel cost per mile as their rebound effect. Green et al.(1999) define it as the potential energy savings from fuel economy improvements, that are taken back as travel increases. For more general discussions, see Berkhout et al.(2000) and Alcott (2005).

more than the percentage decrease in the inefficiency, that is by 10.7%. It is expected that the roads are more congested because VMT increases. The cheaper travel by auto makes the city more suburbanized. Thus, auto travel in the suburbs increases.

4.1.2 Impact of the Monetary Cost of Public Transportation (MCPT)

When the monetary cost of public transportation (MCPT), $v_{2ij|fc}^{w}$, increases by 10%, VMT increases by 0.3%, and fuel consumption and CO_2 emissions increase by 0.4%. Trips by public transportation respond for in two ways. The first is by reducing their total trips by public transportation, and this has no impact on VMT by auto. The second is by switching travel modes from public transportation to auto or other, because the travel by public transportation has become relatively more expensive. This increases VMT by auto. In addition, the higher cost of trips by public transportation leads to more suburbanization, because the advantage of locations near the center with good access to public transportation is reduced. The suburbanization causes higher VMT, more fuel consumption and CO_2 emissions. MPG decreases by 0.1% and speed decreases by 0.2% because of the higher congestion. The suburbanization can have a positive effect on MPG and speed in general, although the effect from congestion is stronger in this case.

When MCPT decreases by 10%, the results are almost opposite. VMT decreases by 0.3%, fuel consumption and CO_2 emissions decrease by 0.4%, and MPG increases by 0.1% while speed increases by 0.2%.

4.1.3 Impact of road capacity

When the road capacity, CAP_l and $ICAP_j$, are increased by 10%, VMT increases by 1.8%, and fuel consumption and CO_2 emissions increase by 0.1%. VMT increases because the road capacity increases, congestion is mitigated and auto trips become more attractive. Even so fuel consumption increases moderately. The components of fuel consumption are VMT and MPG. Since MPG increases by 1.7% when road capacity increases, fuel consumption is suppressed. Speed increases by 4.9%. The higher MPG and speed are the direct effects of the higher road capacity.

When the road capacity decreases by 10%, the results are almost opposite. VMT decreases by 2.2%, fuel consumption and CO_2 emissions decrease by 0.03%, MPG decreases by 2.2% and speed decreases by 5.4%.

4.1.4 Impact of the fuel price

When the fuel price, p_{FUEL}, increases by 10%, the travel cost by auto increases. VMT decreases by 0.7%. When fuel cost increases, the auto travelers can adjust across many margins: (i) by changing route, (ii) by switching mode, (iii) by changing zones where they shop, (iv) by changing the number of non-work trips, (v) by changing their vehicle inefficiency, (vi) by changing residential location, (vii) by changing employed-unemployed status[19], (viii) by supplying less or more labor hours to the labor market. Since VMT decreases, the congestion would be mitigated. Fuel consumption and CO_2 emission decrease by 0.9%. Small and Van Dender (2007) report that the price elasticity of fuel consumption of in the United States (1997-2001) for the short run and long run are -0.1 and -0.3, respectively. My comparative statics is such a long run that all of the building construction response is completed. MPG increases by 0.2% and speed increases by 0.5%.

When the fuel price decreases by 10%, the results are almost opposite. VMT increases by 0.7%, fuel consumption and CO_2 emissions increase by 0.9%, MPG decreases by 0.2% and speed decreases by 0.5%.

4.1.5 Impact of the construction elasticity

Here, I change the dispersion coefficient of the construction probability, Φ_{i0}. When Φ_{i0} of construction increases by 10%, the construction of buildings with a high value per acre increases, if the other variables (such as construction cost) stay constant. The total amount of construction would become more, especially in the zones with more vacant land. Since the vacant land is plenty in the suburbs (zones 6-14) and limited in the city (zones 1-5), the whole city (zones 1-14) becomes suburbanized. VMT increases by 0.1%, fuel consumption and CO_2 emissions increase by 0.1%, MPG increases by

---

[19] Parry and Bento (2001) mention that the high commuting cost discourages workers from joining the labor market.

0.02% but speed decreases by 0.02%.

When the Φ_{i0} of construction decreases the result is approximately opposite. VMT decreases by 0.1%, fuel consumption and CO_2 emissions decrease by 0.1%, MPG decreases by 0.03% and speed increases by 0.02%.

4.2 Impact on urban sprawl (jobs and residential population distribution, and vacant land)

I now look at jobs, the residential population and the vacant land in the CBD, in the central city and in the suburbs, respectively, in order to observe the impact of the exogenous variables on urban sprawl and decentralization. In the comparative statics of the variables related with the transportation sector, I pay attention to: (i) congestion as a centrifugal force, and (ii) public transportation as a centripetal force.

(i) Congestion is a centrifugal force. If the roads are congested, commuting by auto, for example, takes more travel time and monetary cost. Thus the congestion might cause jobs to move to the suburbs where it is easy to access labor, or the residents to move to the city if by doing so they can be closer to jobs. Anas and Kim (1996) find that there are more job centers in the congested city and jobs are more uniformly dispersed the higher is the congestion.

(ii) Public transportation is a centralization force. Since it is convenient to travel by public transportation between the CBD and any other locations, the locations near the center become popular if the attraction of public transportation increases.

In addition to the two effects of congestion and public transportation, there are other effects on job location, residential location and vacant land. Those effects come through the general equilibrium process and it is not easy to explain them in a simple way.

Other important points would be the gap between jobs and residential population in the CBD and in the city. The residential population in the CBD is smaller than the jobs in the CBD. When the gap of jobs and residential population decreases in a zone, it typically means that more reside and work in that zone and that, therefore, the average distance between jobs and residences is smaller. Tables 4.2 (a) and (b) show the impact on jobs, residential population and vacant land, as the variables related to urban sprawl. In addition, the impact on total stocks, average rents and average values is placed in the Appendix.

Table 4.2 (a) Impact on urban sprawl related variables (Jobs and residential populaiton).

			Jobs			Reside pop		
			CBD	City ex-CBD	Suburb	CBD	City ex-CBD	Suburb
	base		537,861	793,798	2,413,622	39,688	1,413,312	3,237,847
$ineff_c$ (inefficiency)	10%	change	3,290	2,979	-6,546	364	7,967	-8,331
		% change	0.612	0.375	-0.271	0.918	0.564	-0.257
	-10%	change	-3,386	-3,097	6,776	-358	-8,101	8,458
		% change	-0.63	-0.39	0.281	-0.901	-0.573	0.261
p_{FUEL} (Fuel price)	10%	change	1,441	1,285	-2,811	174	3,137	-3,310
		% change	0.268	0.162	-0.116	0.438	0.222	-0.102
	-10%	change	-1,450	-1,326	2,872	-178	-3,331	3,509
		% change	-0.27	-0.167	0.119	-0.448	-0.236	0.108
$v^w_{2ij|fc}$ (MCPT)	10%	change	-900	-316	1,200	-126	-1,143	1,269
		% change	-0.167	-0.04	0.05	-0.316	-0.081	0.039
	-10%	change	900	321	-1,199	132	1,052	-1,184
		% change	0.167	0.04	-0.05	0.332	0.074	-0.037
CAP_l and $ICAP_i$ (Capacity)	10%	change	366	416	-897	-665	948	-283
		% change	0.068	0.052	-0.037	-1.677	0.067	-0.009
	-10%	change	-84	-133	370	854	58	-912
		% change	-0.016	-0.017	0.015	2.151	0.004	-0.028
Φ_{i0} (phiconv of con)	10%	change	-194	-1,052	1,240	-197	-3,552	3,749
		% change	-0.036	-0.133	0.051	-0.497	-0.251	0.116
	-10%	change	231	1,298	-1,519	208	4,123	-4,331
		% change	0.043	0.164	-0.063	0.524	0.292	-0.134

Table 4.2 (b) Impact on urban sprawl related variables (vacant land).

			Vacant Land (acer)		
			CBD	City ex-CBD	Suburb
	base		1,822	15,260	1,178,888
$\mathit{ineff_c}$ (inefficiency)	10%	change	9.771	75.616	8,939
		% change	0.536	0.496	0.758
	-10%	change	-11.455	-87.413	-9,840
		% change	-0.629	-0.573	-0.835
p_{FUEL} (Fuel price)	10%	change	1.519	16.547	2,707
		% change	0.083	0.108	0.23
	-10%	change	-2.764	-24.957	-3,259
		% change	-0.152	-0.164	-0.276
v_{2ijjfc}^{w} (MCPT)	10%	change	0.427	2.163	170.437
		% change	0.023	0.014	0.014
	-10%	change	-1.327	-8.509	-486.702
		% change	-0.073	-0.056	-0.041
CAP_I and $ICAP_i$ (Capacity)	10%	change	14.535	63.23	5,253
		% change	0.798	0.414	0.446
	-10%	change	-20.248	-92.482	-6,860
		% change	-1.111	-0.606	-0.582
Φ_{j0} (phiconv of con)	10%	change	47.964	54.578	-13,336
		% change	2.633	0.358	-1.131
	-10%	change	-60.366	-67.073	14,697
		% change	-3.314	-0.44	1.247

4.2.1 Impact of Fuel Economy

Increasing vehicle inefficiency, *ineff$_c$*, has two main effects. As I already saw earlier those two effects is that there is a higher per mile travel cost by car, and that there is less disposable income because more inefficient cars have higher cost of maintenance. As I saw, both effects reduce VMT which implies that congestion is reduced. As pointed out, the reduction of congestion is a centripetal force. Since auto travel becomes costly, the importance of public transportation increases. To travel by public transport, locations near the center are the most convenient. Thus this is a centripetal force. Hence, both effects act centripetally. Jobs and residential population increase by 3,290 and by 364 in the CBD, and increase by 2,979 and by 7,967 in the city and decrease by 6,546 and by 8,331 in the suburbs, respectively. The vacant land increases by 0.5% in the CBD, by 0.5% in the city and by 0.8% in the suburbs. Since the amount of vacant land in the CBD and in the city is limited, the amount that changes is small. The most important direct reason why the vacant land increases when cars become less efficient is that the disposable income decreases as vehicle maintenance cost increases. If income decreases then housing demand also decreases. In addition, there are indirect effects through other variables in the general equilibrium process. I observe that total travel time decreases, that the labor supply increases and that wage decreases. The travel cost increases, and full income decreases. All building stocks decrease in the city and the suburbs except for the single family residential buildings ($k = 1$) in the city.

When inefficiency decreases by 10%, the results are similar to the exact opposite. Jobs and residential population decrease by 3,386 and 358 in CBD, decrease by 3,097 and 8,101 in the city, and increase by 6,776 and 8,458 in the suburbs, respectively. The vacant land decreases by 0.6% in the CBD, decreases by 0.6% in the city and decreases by 0.8% in the suburbs. I do not go into the details of the general equilibrium process, although the impact is not always just the approximate opposite.

4.2.2 Impact of the Monetary Cost of Public Transportation (MCPT) Change

When the monetary cost of public transportation (MCPT), $v^{w}_{2ij|fc}$, increases, some of the travelers by public transportation change their modes to auto or other. Thus auto trips increase and VMT also increases. This makes the roads more congested and this strengthens the centrifugal force. MCPT also works through other channels influencing the consumers' location choices. For the travelers by public transportation, the location near the center is convenient since there is easy access to (and from) other locations by public transportation in the zones near the center. Since MCPT increases, the importance of public transportation decreases and the advantage of locating near the center decreases. This is a centrifugal effect. Hence both impacts work as centrifugal forces. As a result, both jobs and residential population decrease by 900 and 126 in the CBD and by 316 and 1,143 in the city, and increase by 1,200 and 1,269 in the suburbs, respectively. Vacant land increases moderately, by 0.02% in the CBD, by 0.01% in the city and by 0.01% in the suburbs. In addition, there are indirect effects through other variables in the general equilibrium process. It is observeD that total travel time decreases and labor supply increases. Wage decreases. The travel cost increases. The full income decreases. Producers would substitute land for labor, and rent decreases. Single family housing stock increases in the city, and industrial and commercial building ($k = 3,4$) stocks increase in the suburbs.

When MCPT decreases by 10%, the result is approximately the opposite. Jobs and residential population increase by 900 and 132 in the CBD, by 321 and 1,052 in the city, and decrease by 1,199 and 1,184 in the suburbs, respectively. The total vacant land decreases by 0.1% in the CBD, by 0.1% in the city and by 0.04% in the suburbs.

4.2.3 Impact of Road Capacity

When the road capacity, CAP_i and $ICAP_i$, increases, travel cost by auto becomes cheaper. Although VMT increases, it is expected that the congestion decreases, since the road capacity increases. This is the centripetal force. The travel by auto becomes more convenient and the importance of public transportation decreases. The advantage of locating near public transportation (near the CBD) decreases. This is the centrifugal force. Hence, the effects of the higher road capacity has both centripetal and centrifugal effects. Jobs increase by 366 in the CBD and increase by 416 in the city, but they decrease by 897 in the suburbs. Thus jobs become more centralized. Residential population decreases by 665 in the CBD, increase by 948 in the city and decreases by 283 in the suburbs. The residential population shows a more irregular response. If I look at the CBD and the rest of the central city together, the residential population is becomes more centralized in the city as a whole. But if I separately look at the CBD and other zones in the city, the residential population is decentralizing away from the CBD. Behind this irregular reaction of the residential population, the employed consumers are centralized and unemployed consumers are suburbanized. Vacant land increases by 0.8% in the CBD, by 0.4% in the city and by 0.4% in the suburbs. As a possible reason for the increase in vacant land, there is the increase in the aggregate cost of travel by auto. The aggregate monetary cost of travel by auto in the economy increases, although the aggregate monetary cost of travel by public transportation in the economy decreases. The aggregate travel monetary cost increases, and the average full income of employed consumers decreases. The land demand decreases. In addition, there are indirect effects through other variables in the general equilibrium process. The total travel time decreases and that the labor supply increases. Wage decreases. The travel cost increases, and full income decreases. Producers substitute land to labor, and rent decreases. Single family housing increases in the city, and industrial ($k = 3$) building stock increases in suburb.

The suburbanization accompanied by the decreasing disposable income, thus has two effects. Some of the population in the city moves to the suburbs but housing per person decreases. The population in the city stays in the city, but they change their housing type from multi family housing (k = 2) to single family housing ($k = 1$). The rate of single family housing rent reduction in the city is larger than for multiple family housing.

On the other hand, when the road capacity decreases by 10%, congestion would increase, although the VMT would decrease, and this would act as a centrifugal force. In turn, the importance of public transportation would increase and this is the centripetal force. Jobs decrease by 84 in the CBD, decrease by 133 in the city and increase by 370 in the suburbs. The residential population increases by 854 in the CBD increases by 58 in the city, and decreases by 912 in the suburbs. When I separately look at the CBD and the other city zones the residential population becomes more centralized in the CBD. Total vacant land decreases by 1.1% in the CBD, by 0.6% in the city and by 0.6% in the suburbs.

4.2.4 Impact of the Fuel Price

The impact of increasing the fuel price, p_{FUEL}, is similar to the impact of decreasing the monetary cost of public transportation (MCPT) because both of these changes make travel by public transport relatively cheaper than by auto, but the difference is that the higher fuel price makes travel as a whole more expensive, but a lower MCPT makes travel as a whole cheaper.

When the fuel price increases by 10%, congestion decreases and this acts as a centripetal force. The locations near the center become more attractive because they can be accessed relatively cheaply by public transportation. This acts as a centripetal force. Hence both effects are centripetal centralization forces. Jobs and residential population increase by 1,441 and by 174 in the CBD, increase by 1,285 and by 3,137 in the city and decreases by 2,811 and by 3,310 in the suburbs. Vacant land increases by 0.1% in the CBD, by 0.1% in the city and by 0.2% in the suburbs. It appears again that vacant land increases because disposable income decreases due to the higher gas price, thus causing a reduction in housing demand which translates into a reduction in the demand for residential land.

In addition, there are indirect effects through other variables in the general equilibrium process. I observe that total travel time decreases and that the labor supply increases. Wage decreases. The travel cost increases, and full income decreases. Producers substitute land to labor, and rent decreases. All kinds of building stocks decreases in city and suburb excepting the single family residential building ($k = 1$) in the city.

When the fuel price decreases by 10%, approximately opposite results are obtained. Jobs and residential population decrease by 1,450 and by 178 in the CBD, they decrease by 1,326 and by 3,331 in the city and increase by 2,872 and by 3,509 in the suburbs. The vacant land decreases 0.2% in CBD, 0.2% in city and 0.3% in suburb.

4.2.5 Impact of the construction elasticity

When the dispersion coefficient of the construction probability, Φ_{i0} of construction, increases by 10%, the construction of high profitable buildings for the developer increases especially in the zones with more vacant land. Thus there is more suburbanization of residences and jobs. Jobs and residences decrease by 194 and by 197 in the CBD and decrease by 1,052 and by 3,552 in the city and increase by 1,240 and by 3,749 in the suburbs. The total vacant land increases by 2.6% in the CBD, increases by 0.4% in the city and decreases by 1.1% in the suburbs. The impact on the other variables through general equilibrium is more complex than other comparative statics. When construction becomes more elastic and the city is decentralized, the total travel time increases and that the labor supply decreases, and that the wage decreases. Hence the labor demand decreases. One of the reasons is that the rent decreases in all kinds of buildings. Producers substitute land for labor. The industrial stock ($k=3$) increases, but the commercial stock ($k=4$) decreases in both city and suburb. The multifamily housing stocks ($k=2$) in the city (zone 1-5) decreases, but single-family housing increases. With those effects and because the total travel cost increases, the disposable income of employed consumer decreases. The housing demand also decreases.

When the elasticity of construction decreases by 10%, I get approximately opposite results. Jobs and residential population increase by 231 and by 208 in the CBD, increase by 1,298 and by 4,123 in the city and decrease by 1,519 and by 4,331 in the suburbs, respectively. The vacant land decreases by 3.3% in the CBD, decreases by 0.4% in the city and increases by 1.2% in suburbs.

Appendix 4. The impact on stock, rent and value

In this appendix, the percent changes in the total stocks, the average rents and the average values found in the comparative statics exercise reported in section 4.2 is placed in Tables A4 (a), (b) and (c), respectively.

Table A4 (a) Percent change of stock.

			Single family housing (k=1)	Multiple family housing (k=2)	Industrial (k=3)	Commercial (k=4)
$ineff_c$ (inefficiency)	10%	City	0.293	-0.943	-0.362	-0.472
		Suburb	-0.977	-1.248	-0.331	-0.414
	-10%	City	-0.341	1.072	0.438	0.554
		Suburb	1.060	1.393	0.407	0.497
p_{FUEL} (Fuel price)	10%	City	0.068	-0.220	-0.078	-0.102
		Suburb	-0.291	-0.333	-0.098	-0.111
	-10%	City	-0.102	0.309	0.136	0.163
		Suburb	0.343	0.440	0.152	0.170
v_{2ijfc}^w (MCPT)	10%	City	0.014	-0.040	-0.016	-0.004
		Suburb	-0.027	-0.017	0.018	0.019
	-10%	City	-0.043	0.110	0.070	0.055
		Suburb	0.050	0.093	0.026	0.025
CAP_I and $ICAP_i$ (Capacity)	10%	City	0.249	-0.910	-0.182	-0.409
		Suburb	-0.627	-0.928	0.005	-0.169
	-10%	City	-0.357	1.286	0.309	0.576
		Suburb	0.805	1.272	0.055	0.270
Φ_{i0} (phiconv of con)	10%	City	0.118	-0.169	0.549	-1.197
		Suburb	1.420	0.002	0.734	-0.340
	-10%	City	-0.184	0.263	-0.565	1.521
		Suburb	-1.559	0.076	-0.837	0.412

Table A4 (b) Percent change of average rent.

			Single family housing (k=1)	Multiple family housing (k=2)	Industrial (k=3)	Commercial (k=4)
$ineff_c$ (inefficiency)	10%	City	-1.640	-0.895	-0.644	-0.752
		Suburb	-1.115	-0.836	-1.464	-1.521
	-10%	City	1.886	1.008	0.755	0.885
		Suburb	1.227	0.907	1.627	1.686
p_{FUEL} (Fuel price)	10%	City	-0.379	-0.216	-0.111	-0.177
		Suburb	-0.337	-0.249	-0.434	-0.463
	-10%	City	0.540	0.298	0.200	0.221
		Suburb	0.409	0.302	0.542	0.562
$v^w_{2ij\!fc}$ (MCPT)	10%	City	-0.066	-0.062	-0.067	-0.044
		Suburb	-0.016	-0.018	-0.036	-0.033
	-10%	City	0.190	0.123	0.133	0.088
		Suburb	0.072	0.053	0.090	0.099
CAP_i and $ICAP_i$ (Capacity)	10%	City	-1.412	-0.833	-0.621	-0.619
		Suburb	-0.706	-0.605	-0.922	-0.992
	-10%	City	2.057	1.162	0.932	0.885
		Suburb	0.930	0.783	1.211	1.289
Φ_{i0} (phiconv of con)	10%	City	-0.171	-0.010	-0.266	-0.088
		Suburb	-1.339	-0.329	-0.651	-0.198
	-10%	City	0.322	0.062	0.333	0.133
		Suburb	1.604	0.418	0.922	0.331

Table A4 (c) Percent change of average value.

			Vacant land (k=0)	Single family housing (k=1)	Multiple family housing (k=2)	Industrial (k=3)	Commercial (k=4)
$ineff_c$ (inefficiency)	10%	City	-1.517	-3.58	-2.956	-1.356	-1.633
		Suburb	-0.188	-3.202	-2.343	-4.776	-3.853
	-10%	City	1.824	4.145	3.38	1.585	1.917
		Suburb	0.209	3.548	2.567	5.411	4.367
p_{FUEL} (Fuel price)	10%	City	-0.298	-0.76	-0.65	-0.243	-0.333
		Suburb	-0.06	-0.921	-0.682	-1.398	-1.124
	-10%	City	0.522	1.127	0.954	0.421	0.544
		Suburb	0.072	1.152	0.851	1.793	1.456
v^w_{2ijlfc} (MCPT)	10%	City	-0.107	-0.093	-0.158	-0.073	-0.064
		Suburb	-0.008	-0.049	-0.007	-0.033	-0.03
	-10%	City	0.297	0.353	0.398	0.206	0.234
		Suburb	0.013	0.157	0.092	0.238	0.201
CAP_i and $ICAP_i$ (Capacity)	10%	City	-0.938	-3.063	-2.763	-1.221	-1.302
		Suburb	-0.096	-2.037	-1.483	-2.854	-2.275
	-10%	City	1.6	4.495	3.896	1.819	1.957
		Suburb	0.126	2.707	1.931	3.891	3.117
Φ_{i0} (phiconv of con)	10%	City	7.413	-0.148	-0.028	-0.624	0.21
		Suburb	-7.05	-4.035	-0.614	-0.91	-0.637
	-10%	City	-8.617	0.452	0.223	0.851	-0.101
		Suburb	8.723	4.76	0.843	1.416	1.035

Chapter 5. The Effects of Anti-Congestion Policies on Urban Sprawl, Gasoline Consumption and CO_2 Emissions

5.1 Introduction

As is studied in the early papers of urban economics, such as Wheaton (1974), the relationship between transportation cost and urban structure such as land use and residence location is center stage in the field. This relationship becomes more important and problematic when the externality of traffic congestion becomes more serious which is normally the case in larger cities. Pines and Sadka (1985) compare Pigouvian tolls as the first best policy, to the urban growth boundary as a second-best policy for improving efficiency in the presence of traffic congestion, but in a monocentric city.

Although some anti-congestion policies have also been studied by operations researchers in the transportation field[20], the general equilibrium models that link the urban land-use and transportation sector are constructed only by urban economists. The second-best policy of cordon pricing in the monocentric city in which urban density, traffic congestion and labor supply are endogenous is examined by Verhoef (2005). It is shown that cordon pricing captures 94% of the welfare gains from first-best pricing, and that residential population density increases inside the cordon around the CBD (central business district).

Since the early 1970s, urban economists recognized the importance of a general equilibrium model of the urban economy, but developed such

---
[20] There are a number of papers that study the issue purely as a transportation problem. These papers ignore the effects of the policies on land use or the urban economy. Akiyama et al. (2004) study a single-layered cordon, a multi-layered cordon, uniform pricing, and zone pricing in the network model of the Osaka metropolitan area. Cordon pricing is effective in reducing the total efficiency loss from traffic congestion. They show that the existing pricing reduces the efficiency loss of traffic congestion and the pricing on existing toll roads keeps the consumer surplus loss low to achieve the same efficiency gain as does the cordon pricing.

models only for monocentric cities in which all jobs are assumed to stay in a central business district or CBD. Although the analytical solution of the monocentric city model yielded many theoretical insights, its applicability remained limited because of its severe assumption about the concentration of jobs in just one place. These early contributions toward the general equilibrium model of a monocentric city included Dixit (1973), Mills (1972) and O'Sullivan (1983), who developed the most complete models all solved with numerical analysis, because they were too complex to be solved analytically. But these models were still theoretical, not empirical.

The general equilibrium modeling of a polycentric city with dispersed employment is getting more attention recently and again numerical analysis is even more necessary to solve these models. Such models have been developed for linearly shaped hypothetical cities, in which it is assumed that jobs can be endogenously located anywhere in the city. In such models, congestion tolls are studied in Anas and Xu (1999), tolls and the growth boundary are compared in Anas and Rhee (2006), and also in an extension by Ng (2007).

The earliest version of such models was by Anas and Kim (1996), and they included not only traffic congestion but also agglomeration economies which are the linkages and cost-savings that make firms locate near each other. They demonstrated that there is a trade-off between agglomeration economies and accessibility. The weaker are the agglomeration economies or the higher the traffic congestion, then the larger is the number of places where jobs concentrate in equilibrium. Tolling the congestion externality has two effects. One effect is that residences move closer to employment centers in order to reduce travel distances over which the toll must be paid. The other is that producers/jobs may decentralize in order to avoid paying higher wages to attract workers to congested job centers.

In Anas and Rhee (2006), the authors showed that unless consumers prefer to have a greenbelt around the city because they have a preference for open space or a natural amenity the urban boundary is harmful in the city with dispersed employment, since it distorts the land markets and leaves the congestion unpriced. In this book, the urban growth boundary will be examined in a new way in Chapter 6. But in this chapter I focus on policies directly aimed at traffic.

In Fujishima (2007), cordon and area tolls are examined in a model where travelers have car or railway choice. Cordon pricing is more efficient than is area pricing, if the longer-distance commuters are prevalent. Residents within the cordoned area increase the most under the area toll, less under first-best pricing and still increase but even less under the cordon toll. Production and employment, increase in the suburbs more than in the center under the cordon and area tolls, and the production is more centralized under the first-best Pigouvian pricing than under the cordon toll.

More recently, there has been attention paid not only to congestion, but also to greenhouse gas emissions from traffic. The anti-congestion policies work indirectly to mitigate the gasoline consumption and the CO_2 emissions[21]. The gasoline consumption and CO_2 emissions in the congested road are highly correlated with the amount of vehicle miles traveled, although this correlation turns negative at high speeds as explained in Chapter 2 (see Figure 2.3.2). When the emission is not mentioned in the papers, it is possible to read CO_2 emissions information if gasoline consumption is discussed, since the CO_2 emissions are proportionally related with gasoline consumption. In addition to the tolls and the gasoline tax, there are alternative policies such as the ones pointed out by Barth and Boriboonsomsin (2007). They estimated CO_2 emissions under real world driving conditions, and under steady-state driving conditions as functions of speed (See Figure 2.3.3). The difference in CO_2 emissions under real world versus steady state driving conditions is caused by the different smoothness of driving. By making traffic flow smoother, the CO_2 emissions could be reduced at each driving speed. Proost and Van Dender (2001) compare the impacts of several policies to reduce the gasoline consumption; an air quality policy (regulation of car emission technology), fuel-based policies (minimum fuel efficiency policy and fuel taxes) and alternative transport policies (fuel external cost pricing, cordon

---

21 Some other papers scopes the effect of emission on global worming and urban heat island phenomenon. Those papers study the relations of such phenomenon and emission from car (Saitoh et al. (1996)), building (Kikegawa et al. (2006)) and both (Ihara et al. (2008)). Not many papers study the relationship between transportation and heat island. One exception is Saito et al. (2005) that studies the impact of electric vehicle on emission and urban warming.

pricing, parking charges). The regulation of emission or fuel efficiency may reduce the emission, though congestion externalities are hardly affected. The transport policies reduce the congestion and create an environmental benefit at the same time. When the policies are compared, the policy which focuses on the inefficient transportation can lead to larger welfare gains. They summarize that an isolated policy may decrease welfare and an integrated policy is necessary.

Daniel and Bekka (2000) simulate the effects of congestion pricing on the highway network in New Castle County, Delaware. Congestion pricing reduces emissions, although the degree of reduction is depending on the demand elasticity. If the demand is elastic, then the emission reduces more. The optimal gasoline tax to improve welfare in Britain and United States is examined in Parry and Small (2005) who use a very aggregated and simple model. The total optimal tax is composed of congestion, accidents, air pollution and Ramsay taxes. The authors say that although the optimal gasoline tax in Britain is higher than in the United States, it is too high in Britain and too low in the United States. If the price elasticity of gasoline consumption is low, then the optimal gasoline tax would be high. The revenue usages including redistribution back to the public or subsidized or vehicle emissions equipment repairing, transit subsidies and so on are surveyed in Harrington et al. (2001). The most popular policy was HOT (high-occupancy toll). The reduction of other taxes is supported by the public, but alternative policies are not popular. The authors attribute this to the respondents not understanding how the taxes and the redistribution work.

Two very aggregated models that examine CO_2 emissions in Beijing, China and Sao Paulo, Brazil have been developed by Anas et al. (2008) for Beijing, and by Anas and Timilsina (2009) for and São Paulo. In the former paper, the revenue neutral Pigouvian toll and gasoline tax reduce travel time, cars owned, car trips, and car-kilometers, but the gas tax performs better than the toll in reducing emissions. In the latter paper, policies such as highway building, transit subsidies and changing the efficiency of vehicles have minor effects on aggregate CO_2, whereas raising the cost of car travel by tolling has a strong effect.

The purpose of this chapter of the book is to report on the empirical analysis of the effects of anti congestion policies in a general equilibrium setting. For this purpose, I will apply the RELU-TRAN2 model, the empirical calibration and testing of which was discussed in Chapters 3 and 4, to analyze the effects of Pigouvian congestion tolls, a cordon toll, a gasoline tax and a CBD parking fee.

In section 5.2, I will introduce the anti-congestion policies and explain their characteristics. In section 5.3, the equations for implementing those policies are shown. In section 5.4, I explain the differences between those policies. In section 5.5, I simulate the policies. At first I will compare the results of the different policies when they are revenue neutral with quasi-Pigouvian toll. Then I gradually increase the level of fuel tax rate, parking fee or cordon toll to observe how the results change.

5.2 Anti-congestion policies: congestion tolls, the cordon toll, the fuel tax and the parking tax

In this chapter, I will compare the effects of alternative policies to mitigate traffic congestion. All of the policies examined in this chapter directly or indirectly target the cost of driving. In particular, I will examine:

(a) a quasi-Pigouvian congestion toll (that varies by route of travel and type of road);
(b) the fuel tax (per gallon);
(c) a cordon toll paid by in-bound downtown traffic; and,
(d) a downtown parking fee.

The details of how these policies are designed and how they differ from one another are now explained in economic terms. The technical calculation of the fees, taxes and tolls will be described later in this chapter.

5.2.1 The quasi-Pigouvian congestion toll

It is well-known that the first-best optimal policy in the context of the traffic congestion externality is a Pigouvian toll. Since traffic congestion is a negative externality, drivers travel too much. The reason drivers travel too much is that there is no mechanism to make them pay the cost of the delays and other externalities such as fuel consumed, accidents or pollution that they impose on other drivers and on third parties. The Pigouvian toll on each car-mile should be equal to the marginal damage cost created by each mile of driving and would be different on each mile and vary by time of day, since the volume of traffic varies on different routes and by time of day.

The RELU-TRAN2 model does not calculate accident probabilities. Hence, it is an assumption that traffic in the model flows accident free. Although the model does calculate CO_2 emissions, it does not calculate other types of emissions. As well, the model does not calculate any damage costs from CO_2 emissions. The model calculates only two externalities: the first is the time delay caused by the volume of traffic (that is, congestion delay) and the other is the excess fuel consumption induced by the traffic, that is the fact that when traffic moves more slowly it needs to consume more gasoline per mile. The model calculates these two externalities on each mile of road for both major roads (links of the highway network) and local roads (intra-zonal travel), but the model does not distinguish between different times of the day, thus implying that all the travel occurs over a relatively wide "rush hour." Thus, the toll calculated by the model will be different on each highway link and for each set of local roads within the model zones but it will be uniform during the day.

The time delay and fuel consumption relationships that apply to the calculation of the two externalities were discussed in detail in Chapter 2. Figure 2.3.2 shows that the measured relationship between gasoline per car-mile and car-speed is roughly U-shaped. As speed decreases gasoline consumption per mile increases keeping the car's design fuel economy constant. At very high speeds per mile, gasoline consumption per mile again increases with speed, but is fairly flat between these two extremes. Therefore a first-best Pigouvian toll focused on the fuel externality alone would be dersigned as follows. If cars are traveling at very high speeds, the desired action is to decrease speeds and thus also decrease fuel consumption. Then, roads where cars are traveling that fast should be subsidized so that more drivers choose them and speed comes down bringing fuel consumption down with it. On such roads, therefore, the Pigouvian toll should be negative. If cars are traveling at quite low speeds, the fuel consumption can be lowered by increasing speed and this can be done by a positive Pigouvian toll that discourages driving, reduced car volume and thus increases speed and reduces fuel consumption. In this region of the curve of Figure 2.3.2, the fuel externality and the time-delay externality are responding similarly to the quasi-Pigouvian toll. As the toll per mile increases, traffic is reduced less fuel is burned and delays are lower as well. Because less fuel is burned CO_2 emissions per mile are also lower. It should be noted that in the model, drivers do not choose their travel speeds but speed is determined by the traffic congestion relationship that is the inverse of speed (travel time) per mile that is a strictly increasing and strictly convex function of travel volume on that mile. Therefore, the only way to influence the level of the two externalities is by lowering speed, which can only happen by the toll causing a diversion of car trips to other modes or to less congested routes.

There are reasons why first-best Pigouvian tolls cannot be easily calculated. One such reason is the fact that on every mile of road, travelers with different values of time are traveling at the same time. The first-best Pigouvian toll could only be calculated accurately by knowing the marginal rate of substitution between travel time and other goods for each traveler, because the first-best toll would be in monetary units. This toll would be obtained by taking the marginal time delay experienced by the travelers on that mile of road and multiplying this by the mentioned MRS and then adding up the results over all travelers so delayed. This is an extremely difficult and complex calculation that would require much more time consuming runs of RELU-TRAN2. It is also unrealistic that road authorities could distinguish each drivers value of time, VOT. In stead, I assume that the road authorities know the average VOT of drivers on each road.

Another reason why my congestion tolls are quasi-Pigouvian is that in the model the consumers can save fuel not only by switching to faster routes but also by switching to vehicles with higher design fuel economy. The first-best policy would vary the part of the Pigouvian toll aimed to capture the fuel externality, not only according to route but also according to vehicle type. Again, I assume that road authorities do not tax different price for different vehicle type, but road authorities know the average vehicle type on each road and set the toll common for any type of vehicle. When I calculate congestion tolls I ignore variation by vehicle type.

The above non-trivial qualifications aside, the quasi-Pigouvian tolls I calculate aim to logically capture the time and fuel savings that would come about from congestion tolling. That is, the tolls I calculate, measure the excess time delay imposed by each car-trip on all other car-trips plus the excess fuel consumption imposed by each car-trip on all other car-trips. Precisely how these tolls are calculated from the equations of the model will be described later in this chapter.

5.2.2 The fuel tax

Under this policy, all car-traffic pays the same tax per gallon of gasoline consumed. Such a fuel tax would be a lower-best policy when compared to true Pigouvian tolling per mile of travel. As explained in the discussion of quasi-Pigouvian tolling, the tolls ignore the fact that a car's fuel economy affects the fuel externality it causes. The gasoline tax, to the contrary, takes the fuel externality by car-type into account because cars with lower fuel economy would consume more gasoline and thus pay higher fuel taxes. Thus, on the one hand, the gasoline tax does a better job than the quasi-Pigouvian toll of creating an incentive for trips to be made with vehicles that have higher fuel efficiency. On the other hand, the gasoline tax does a poorer job of internalizing the delay externality of congestion. It affects congestion only indirectly by raising the monetary cost of travel and thus reducing travel volume and improving speed. In contrast, the quasi-Pigouvian toll is directly proportional to the delay caused by congestion and does a much better job of reducing the time-delay externality.

5.2.3 The cordon toll

In practice, congestion tolling has been implemented by tolling only the most congested places in an urban area, that is traffic incoming into the CBD or downtown. For example, the policies implemented for downtown London and the City of Stockholm have done the congestion charging scheme. Such a scheme in London is examined by Beevers and Carslaw (2005a, 2005b) and Leape (2006), and that in Stockholm by Eliasson and Mattsson (2006). Beevers and Carslaw (2005a, 2005b) examine the London's congestion charging scheme (CCS) to see the relationship between speed and emissions. The charged zone is the central part of inner London. They observe the speed increasing in the zone that is charged by the CCS. Although emissions are decreased inside the charged zone, the effect is weaker in the inner ring road which is outside the charged area, or emissions may even increase there (Leape (2006)). The CCS policy was imposed in 2003 on the vehicles driving through or parking in central London between 7:00 am and 6:30 pm of work days. This leads to reduced congestion.

The equity effects of road pricing using the proposed congestion-charging scheme for Stockholm are discussed by Eliasson and Mattsson (2006). Results show, for example, that high income group and residents in the central area are affected the most, since they pay often. But, by using the toll revenues to improve public transportation, women and low income groups benefits the most. The initial travel patterns and revenue usage are important factors in the formulation of an appropriate congestion policy.

My cordon toll policy is similar. The most congested area in Chicago is the CBD that corresponds roughly to the model zone 3. I select the major roads that allow entry into the CBD and calculate a uniform toll that all car traffic will pay when entering (but not when exiting) zone 3. I can optimize this cordon toll by maximizing an appropriate welfare measure or calculate it to get revenue equivalence with another policy. Comparing the welfare effects of this toll to other policies will be of interest especially since this policy has been applied in reality.

5.2.4 The parking fee

The parking fee policy is similar to the cordon toll policy in the sense that both policies target the CBD, the most congested zone. In the parking fee policy, it is assumed that all trips terminating within the CBD pay a parking fee, whereas in the cordon toll policy through traffic passing through the CBD also pays the cordon toll. Thus, the parking fee reduces congestion by discouraging trips that terminate in the CBD but by reducing congestion in this way, the parking fee actually encourages more through traffic. It therefore has an ambiguous effect on congestion in the CBD. On the other hand, the intra-zonal trips in the CBD are discouraged by the parking fee but not by cordon toll.

5.3 Technical calculation of the anti-congestion policy instruments

I will now explain how the policy instruments that are used in the above mentioned anti-congestion policies are calculated by modifying the model's equations.

5.3.1 The fuel tax

The fuel tax is universal in that it is paid at the pump, for each gallon of gasoline purchased. It therefore affects all trips whether they happen on major roads or local roads. Suppose that the rate of the fuel tax per gallon is τ_{FUEL}, then the after tax of gasoline per gallon is $(1+\tau_{FUEL}) \times p_{FUEL}$. The relevant calculations are all made in TRAN and affect the monetary costs of travel which are then passed to RELU. Recall that $ineff_c$ refers to the fuel diseconomy level of a car type c, $lfuel_z$ and $fuel_\ell$ refer to the fuel per mile (which is a function of speed and shown in general shape in Figure 2.3.2) on local roads and major roads respectively, and Io_z, o_ℓ are other than fuel monetary costs per unit vehicle inefficiency on local roads and major roads. Given all this, the following equations give the monetary cost per mile by car-type c on major roads and local roads respectively:

$$IUCOST_{z|c} = (1 + \tau_{FUEL}) \times p_{FUEL} \times Ifuel_z \times ineff_c + Io_z \times ineff_c,$$

$$UCOST_{\ell|c} = (1 + \tau_{FUEL}) \times p_{FUEL} \times fuel_\ell \times ineff_c + o_\ell \times ineff_c.$$

Once these costs are calculated by car-type per mile, they affect all route and intra-zonal costs of travel per mile by car type and feed up from TRAN to RELU via the mode choice equations and the composite monetary costs associated with all zone pairs.

5.3.2 Quasi-Pigouvian tolls

A quasi-Pigouvian toll can be calculated to quasi-internalize the time delay externality of congestion or the excess fuel consumption externality of congestion. I discuss the calculation involved in these two cases, separately.

The quasi-Pigouvian toll on time delay

As explained earlier the time-delay must be calculated in units of time and then converted to monetary units. The toll, so calculated, is independent of car-type since in the model it is assumed that car-types (according to fuel economy) create the same delay on other cars. The monetary toll is calculated per car and divided by the exogenous and fixed car occupancy rate, $\tilde{\eta}$, in person-trips per car. It is a limitation of the model that it cannot treat car-pooling behavior. Such behavior would mean that consumers can increase the value of $\tilde{\eta}$, thus reducing the burden of the congestion toll by sharing it. The monetary cost of a person-trip by car including the qusi-Pigouvian toll $IQPTOLL_z$ and $QPTOLL_l$ is then the following for local roads and major roads respectively.

$$IMCOST_{z|c} = IUCOST_{z|c} \times ILENGTH_z \times \frac{1}{\tilde{\eta}} + IQPTOLL_z \times \frac{1}{\tilde{\eta}},$$

$$MCOST_{\ell|c} = UCOST_{\ell|c} \times ILENGTH_\ell \times \frac{1}{\tilde{\eta}} + QPTOLL_l \times \frac{1}{\tilde{\eta}}.$$

The quasi-Pigouvian toll of time delay is the difference of marginal social time cost and average private time cost of travel. To see how this is calculated, recall that the congestion function that gives travel time (in minutes) on a road link is, from equation (2.2.4a):

$$TIME_\ell = ALPHA_\ell \times LENGTH_\ell \left(1 + BETA_\ell \left[\frac{FLOW_\ell}{CAP_l}\right]^{CEXP}\right).$$

The total time traveled on the link roads are gain by multiplying $TIME_\ell$ and $FLOW_\ell$. The marginal social time-cost, $MSTC_l$, of additional $FLOW_\ell$ is,

$$MSTC_l = ALPHA_\ell \times LENGTH_\ell \left(BETA_\ell \times CEXP\left[\frac{FLOW_\ell}{CAP_l}\right]^{CEXP}\right) + TIME_\ell.$$

Then subtract the average private time to get the marginal time-delay damage cost.

$$ALPHA_\ell \times LENGTH_\ell \left(BETA_\ell \times CEXP\left[\frac{FLOW_\ell}{CAP_l}\right]^{CEXP}\right).$$

By adjusting time to hour and multiplying the link specific average value of time the toll price is found, and similar for the zone roads.

$$IQPTOLL_i^{time}$$
$$= \left(IALPHA_i \times ILENGTH_i \times IBETA_i \times ICEXP \times \left[\frac{IFLOW_i}{ICAP_i}\right]^{ICEXP} / 60\right)$$
$$\times IAveVOT_i,$$

$$QPTOLL_l^{time}$$
$$= \left(ALPHA_\ell \times LENGTH_\ell \times BETA_\ell \times CEXP \times \left[\frac{FLOW_\ell}{CAP_\ell}\right]^{CEXP} / 60\right)$$
$$\times AveVOT_l.$$

Here $IAveVOT_i$ and $IAveVOT_l$ are the zone and link road specific average values of time over all of the flow types (f, c) on each zone i and link l. That is they are the average values of time calculated according to who is using the roads, but keeping in mind that the underlying values of time vary only by income level f, and are the values of time that are assumed to hold at the zone and link road level in TRAN, as explained earlier.

$$IAveVOT_i = \frac{\sum_{fc}(IFLOW_{ifc} \times VOT_f)}{\sum_{fc} IFLOW_{ifc}}$$

and

$$AveVOT_l = \frac{\sum_{fc}(FLOW_{lfc} \times VOT_f)}{\sum_{fc} FLOW_{lfc}}.$$

These quasi-Pigouvian tolls of time delay are defined as the gap between the marginal social time cost and the average private time cost but do not account for the gap between the marginal social monetary cost and average private monetary cost that arises from the fuel consumption externality. This point would not be important if I had assumed that fuel consumption per mile is constant regardless of driving speed, but since the fuel consumption differs according to the driving speed, the fuel consumption differs by congestion. But, this externality from fuel consumption is not large relatively to the time externality, although I will see how it is calculated next.

The quasi-Pigouvian toll on time delay and fuel consumption

To derive the quasi-Pigouvian toll that quasi-internalizes the fuel consumption externality, I use the average vehicle inefficiencies on major and local roads: *IAveIneff$_i$* and *AveIneff$_l$*.

$$IAveIneff_i = \frac{\sum_{fc}(IFLOW_{ifc} \times Ineff_c)}{\sum_{fc} IFLOW_{ifc}}$$

and

$$AveIneff_l = \frac{\sum_{fc}(FLOW_{lfc} \times Ineff_c)}{\sum_{fc} FLOW_{lfc}}.$$

The quasi-Pigouvian toll of fuel consumption ($QPToll_l^{fuel}$) on major roads is the difference between the marginal social monetary cost and average private monetary cost, calculated as follows (where the details of the differentiation are suppressed):

$$\begin{aligned} QPToll_l^{fuel} &= FLOW_l \times \\ &= -p_{FUEL} \times AveIneff_l^{link} \\ &\times \left(\begin{array}{l} -0.0117211 + 0.0012826\,\text{speed}_\ell - 5.6196E-05\text{speed}_\ell^2 \\ +1.20E-06\text{speed}_\ell^3 - 1.2359E-08\text{speed}_\ell^4 \\ +4.93986E-11\text{speed}_\ell^5 \end{array} \right) \\ &\times \frac{(\text{speed}_\ell)^2}{60} \times \left[ALPHA_\ell \times LENGTH_\ell \left(BETA_\ell \times CEXP \left[\frac{FLOW_\ell}{CAP_l} \right]^{CEXP} \right) \right]. \end{aligned}$$

The quasi-Pigouvian toll of fuel consumption on local roads is similarly calculated. Here the average monetary cost on each zone and link roads, $IAMCOST_i$ and $AMCOST_l$, are calculated the same way as $IMCOST_{i|c}$ and $MCOST_{l|c}$ were calculated in the case of the quasi-Pigouvian toll on time delay only. But in this case I use as weights the average fuel economy levels $IAveIneff_i$ and $AveIneff_l$ instead of the car-type specific fuel economy levels $Ineff_c$, because the fuel consumption externality suffered does depend on car-type and to get the total externality suffered one must weight by the average fuel inefficiency that holds on the relevant road.

The quasi-Pigouvian toll that quasi-internalizes both the time delay and the fuel consumption externalities ($QPToll_l^{time-fuel}$), is sum of quasi-Pigouvian toll on time delay ($QPToll_l^{time}$) and the quasi-Pigouvian toll on the fuel consumption ($QPToll_l^{fuel}$).

$$QPToll_i^{time\text{-}fuel} = QPToll_i^{time} + QPToll_i^{fuel},$$
$$IQPToll_i^{time\text{-}fuel} = IQPToll_i^{time} + IQPToll_i^{fuel}.$$

5.3.3 The cordon toll

When there is cordon toll applied to selected links, the monetary cost is replaced by,

$$MCOST_{\ell|c} = UCOST_{\ell|c} \times LENGTH_\ell \times \frac{1}{\eta} + CTOLL_\ell \times \frac{1}{\eta}.$$

In the model there are three network links that represent the major roads entering the CBD. Any car-trip entering the CBD must use one of these roads and pays the same $CTOLL_\ell$.

5.3.4 The parking fee

As explained earlier, while the cordon toll is paid only by all incoming trips including those passing through the CBD, the CBD parking fee is paid by all trips terminating inside the CBD. When there is parking fee, the generalized cost for the round trip to zone 3 becomes:

$$C_{1ij|fc}^w = \tilde{c}_{1ij|fc}^w + \tilde{c}_{1ji|fc}^w + parkfee_j^w \times NWR_j^w \times \frac{1}{\eta}$$

and

$$g_{ij|fc}^w = \pi_{1ij|fc}^w \left[v_{1ij|fc}^w + v_{1ji|fc}^w + parkfee_j^w \times NWR_j^w \times \frac{1}{\eta} \right] + \sum_{m=2,3} \pi_{mij|fc}^w (v_{mij|fc}^w + v_{mji|fc}^w).$$

$NWR_i^w = 1$ if $w = 1$ (work trip) and $NWR_i^w > 0$ if $w \neq 1$ (non – work trip) are defined to express the ratio of average travel distance over the local roads for non-work trips relative to work trips. I apply this ratio to the parking fee so that the parking for non-work trips and work trips are different. If

$NWR_i^{non\text{-}work}$ >1, it could be interpreted that the non-work traveler would stop at more than one place.

The auto travelers who come to the CBD zone ($j = 3$), including those traveling intra-zonally by car within the CBD zone, are charged the parking fee. But the travelers who reside in the CBD and come back to their home in the zone j from other zones do not pay parking fee on the assumption that they have access to private parking.

5.4 Differences and similarities among the policies according to their expected impacts

Now that the way the alternative anti-congestion policies are treated by the model has been reviewed, it is important to also consider how these policies might differ as to their impacts on the general equilibrium of the simulated urban economy. The policies will impact different groups by income, residence location, job location etc. differently. Some of these differences in impacts are now discussed. Superficially, the quasi-Pigouvian toll and the gasoline tax may be expected to have similar effects, while the CBD cordon toll and the CBD parking tax may also be expected to have similar effects.

5.4.1 The CBD cordon toll versus the CBD parking fee
The Impact on Travelers who travel into the CBD

Both policies have some similar effects on this group of trips. The cordon toll or the parking fee are paid once per round trip and have a congestion ameliorating effect by inducing similar tax avoidance behavior. Incoming trips can avoid the tax by switching to the transit mode.

Another tax avoidance response would be to switch some non-working trips to destinations other than the CBD, or to change one's job location to a place outside the CBD. In this regard also the two policies have similar effects.

The difference is that parking fee could be different for work and non-work trips by NWR_j^w. This could be made by different parking time length or frequency of parking in a trip.

The impact on travelers who travel within the CBD

For intra-zonal trips within the CBD, the cordon toll is not charged but the parking fee is charged. Obviously, by changing mode from auto to other modes, within-CBD travelers can still avoid paying the parking fee. Intra-CBD travelers would also prefer to change the destinations of their trips to other zones outside the CBD and thus avoid paying the parking fee. Under the cordon toll policy, however, the intra-zone travelers are not affected directly. Since the congestion decreases in CBD because the travel by auto from outside zone decreases, the intra-zonal auto travel would increase.

The impact on travelers who travel out of the CBD

The cordon toll is charged to those who live in the CBD when they travel back from other zones. But the parking fee is not charged since parking at home is assumed to be free. Under the parking fee policy, therefore, if there are two choices to live in CBD and commute out to other zones, and to work in the CBD and commute in from other zones, the parking fee promotes to former, if other conditions are the same.

Impact on through trips

The cordon toll is charged on through traffic crossing the CBD. In response, some through-drivers can change their mode from auto to transit. This will decrease the congestion in the tolled link. Some of the other drivers might make a detour to avoid paying the cordon toll. Those drivers prefer to pay additional driving time and monetary cost caused by detouring than to pay the cordon toll. Because of this detouring behavior, the links near the tolled link could become more congested, harming those travelers, while the tolled links are becoming less congested.

At the same time, while the cordon toll increases the monetary cost, some drivers would enjoy the reduced congestion. Thus it is possible that some travelers who want to save time would switch their mode to auto and choose to pay the cordon toll to travel on the less congested roads.

Although the parking fee reduces congestion for those entering the CBD, it is not paid by though traffic. In fact, the parking fee serves to speed up through traffic.

Impact on firms' locations

Since both the cordon toll and the parking fee increase the cost of traveling into the CBD, they make the CBD a less attractive place for firm location. Firms would be motivated to move out of the cordon. Note that in the model, firms are not directly impacted by these taxes or tolls, but only indirectly because of their workers.

Impact on residence locations

The impact of the cordon toll and the parking fee on residence in CBD is ambiguous. Under both policies, CBD becomes less attractive location. Under the cordon toll and the parking fee, CBD the intra-zonal commuting could increase in CBD although the inter-zonal commuting decreases, and under the parking fee the intra-zonal commuting decreases although inter zonal commuting from CBD would increase.

Impact on development

Because of the foregoing observations, I would expect real estate inside the cordon to be converted in the margin from business floor space to residential floor space.

5.4.2 The quasi-Pigouvian toll and the fuel tax

An important feature of congestion tolling in practice is that it might be infeasible to toll all roads. In most realistic proposals only the major roads are proposed for tolling and local roads would remain untolled. If the quasi-Pigouvian toll (regardless of whether it is a toll time delay only, or whether it is a toll on both time delay and fuel consumption) is levied on major roads only, the differences between quasi-Pigouvian tolling and gasoline taxation are magnified, because drivers on local roads (i.e. traveling intra-zonally in the model) would not be charged under quasi-Pigouvian tolling but would pay the fuel tax. Under such quasi-Pigouvian tolling, the inter-zonal travel would decrease while intra-zonal trips would increase.

If the quasi-Pigouvian toll is levy both on links and in zones, it is similar to fuel tax in a sense because both policies cause drivers additional cost in any auto travel. Aside from the above, the quasi-Pigouvian toll will be higher than would be the fuel tax on highly congested roads that take longer time to go through. On the other hand, the fuel tax would be expensive where drives consume more fuel. Hence drivers would feel that the fuel tax is too high on long distance and on slower routes (except very high speed road where fuel consumption is inefficient). Under both policies, it is not very helpful for drivers to make detours since all roads would be impacted.

The most important difference between the two policies is that the quasi-Pigouvian toll removes the externality of congested roads, but that the fuel tax does not. A second important difference is that, the quasi-Pigouvian toll is the same for any types of vehicle on the same road, but the fuel tax paid is proportional to the vehicle inefficiency for vehicles traveling on the same road.

5.4.3 The quasi-Pigouvian toll on all roads versus the limited quasi-Pigouvian toll

I start by defining the limited quasi-Pigouvian toll. That is derived in the same way as the quasi-Pigouvian toll but charged only on specific major or local roads. In some of the simulations, a limited quasi-Pigouvian toll is charged on the links that enter the CBD. This policy is a close substitute of the cordon toll policy with the difference that the toll charged varies by link as opposed to the uniform cordon toll that was the same for all roads entering the CBD. The differences between the two will be discussed in the next subsection.

In the case of Pigouvian tolling I can compare (i) the quasi-Pigouvian toll on the time delay externality only, and the limited quasi-Pigouvian toll on the time delay externality only; and (ii) the quasi-Pigouvian toll on the time delay and fuel consumption externalities, and the limited quasi-Pigouvian toll on the time delay and fuel consumption externalities.

In both comparisons, on the roads tolled by limited the quasi-Pigouvian toll, the toll under limited quasi-Pigouvian tolling is higher than the quasi-Pigouvian toll when all roads are tolled. But as I charge more links under limited quasi-Pigouvian tolling, travel by car decreases, and the average level of the toll comes down also.

In other words, the toll itself causes a pecuniary externality. Since the toll reduces car travel, the congestion on the non-tolled road is also reduced. Thus I would say there is a positive pecuniary externality from tolling. But I should not forget that when there is a toll, some travelers make detour or change trip origins and destinations. This could increase congestion in the other roads. If this effect is strong, the toll would cause a negative pecuniary externality.

5.4.4 The difference between the limited quasi-Pigouvian toll and the cordon Toll

The limited quasi-Pigouvian toll quasi-optimizes the travel cost on each road. Since the purpose is to remove the externality on each specific road, the toll on each road is different. Because of this, the limited quasi-Pigouvian toll optimizes only the tolled road. Even if the congestion increases in other roads because of detours, limited quasi-Pigouvian tolling does not take this into account.

The cordon toll is the same for all the tolled roads, and so the externality on each tolled road is not optimized. For this reason, the cordon toll may be considered a lower-best alternative to the limited quasi-Pigouvian tolling.

5.4.5 Mode changes

An important margin through which the policies work is the travel mode choice decision. For example, because the cordon toll increases after-toll monetary cost but decreases the time delay of congestion, travelers whose value of time is high relative to monetary cost (higher income group) might change from other modes to auto. The parking fee can also cause mode changes, as already mentioned.

5.5 Simulating the impacts of the policies

In this section I examine the impacts of policies on consumer's utility, population location and fuel consumption related variables. To compare the policies to each other, I have settled on the revenue-neutral comparison. That is the level of tolling is adjusted so that after all markets have adjusted to the simulated policy, the tax, fee or toll revenue raised by the policy is the same. The aggregate revenue of each policy is not redistributed.

5.5.1 Revenue-neutral comparison of the policies
Revenue Neutrality

Quasi-Pigouvian tolls are endogenously determined so that the marginal social cost and the average private cost plus the marginal damage cost are equalized on each road.

For the other policies there is no equivalent formula that can be used to find the right level of the policy instrument. Instead there are many different ways these policies could be optimized by varying the level of the cordon toll or the parking fee. For example, one could maximize the sum of consumer utilities weighted by arbitrary weights assigned to each income group. This sounds good, but the weights are arbitrary and can affect the results. Alternatively, one could maximize a monetary measure of consumer surplus that is the aggregation of the consumer surplus of all the consumers. The problem with this approach is that in RELU the utility function is not quasilinear. Therefore, the consumer surplus measure is not uniquely determined. Approximate measures of consumer surplus can be computed by dividing the consumer surplus of each consumer with the consumer's marginal utility of income, but since this marginal utility is not constant, thus the constructed consumer surplus is not a reliable measure. In large part also, the results depend on how each policy's aggregate revenue is redistributed or recycled. For example, alternative Pareto efficient outcomes can be calculated depending on how this redistribution is made.

To avoid these pitfalls, I decided to make revenue neutral comparison of the policies discussed above. More precisely, I proceeded as follows. I change the policy instrument (fuel tax rate, parking fee or cordon toll) gradually from more moderate to more intense. I stop when the revenue from each policy is equalized to the revenue from the corresponding quasi-Pigouvian tolling. Such a specification of revenue neutral policy levels is used by Anas, Timilsina and Zheng (2008). They compare the impacts of congestion tolling

(Pigouvian toll) and fuel taxation in Beijing, where the fuel tax level is set to be revenue neutral fuel tax with the revenue from congestion toll.

I tested three kinds of quasi-Pigouvian tolls. (i) the quasi-Pigouvian toll for time delay and fuel consumption on all major roads only; (ii) the quasi-Pigouvian toll for time delay and fuel consumption on all roads; and (iii) the limited quasi-Pigouvian toll for time delay and fuel consumption on the major roads entering the CBD. Under (iii) the same roads are tolled as under the uniform cordon toll. The annual revenue per capita (RELU consumers) from the three quasi-Pigouvian tolling policies are: (i) $277.60, (ii) $1,173.11[22] and (iii) $25.67.

I set two revenue neutral fuel tax levels so that the revenue from the fuel tax is equalized with the revenue from the quasi-Pigouvian tolls (i) and (ii). Revenue from the cordon toll and the parking fee cannot achieve the level of revenue neutrality with the quasi-Pigouvian toll (i) and (ii). As the cordon toll or the parking fee increase, the revenue increases and then decreases after reaching a peak. But even the highest revenue at the peak is less than revenue from the quasi-Pigouvian toll (i) and (ii). I use the revenue of the limited quasi-Pigouvian toll (iii), to define the revenue neutral level of the cordon toll and the parking fee. The two fuel tax rates that are revenue neutral with the quasi-Pigouvian tolls (i) and (ii) are 146% and 227%, respectively. The cordon toll and the parking fee that are revenue neutral with the limited quasi-Pigouvian toll (iii) are $1.49 and $2.24, respectively[23].

As policies increase from moderate to intense, the revenue increases at first but starts to decreases later. Hence there are two other points of interest in addition to the revenue neutral points. These are the revenue peak and the second revenue neutral point that lies on the other side of the peak. Those two points for the cordon toll are $11 (at the peak, the revenue is $93.76 per capita), and $29.39 (second revenue neutral point, the revenue per capita is $ 25.67). For the parking fee the corresponding numbers are $11 (at the peak, the revenue is $64.93 per capita) and $24.76 (second revenue neutral

---

[22] The quasi-Pigouvian toll on time delay only has a similar result, since the fuel externality is small relative to the time externality. The annual revenue per person from the quasi-Pigouvian toll on time delay on major roads is $ 281.90 and that from time delay only on all roads is $1,110.40.
[23] I find those revenue neutral policies by linear approximation form the closest results.

point, the revenue per capia being $ 25.67). The revenue peak of the fuel tax is 1,100% ($2,709.01 per cap), but I could not find the other revenue neutral tax rate within the range I examined (from 0% to 1,500%). Since the fuel price elasticity of fuel consumption is small, even if the fuel tax rate increases greatly, the fuel consumption decrease only moderately. Within the two revenue neutral points of each policy, the first revenue neutral point (on the ascending portion of the revenue curve) is closer to the quasi-Pigouvian toll than is the second revenue neutral point (on the descending portion of the revenue curve).

Quasi-Pigouvian tolling of major roads and the fuel tax

In table 5.5.1 (a), the fourth and third columns from the right show the results of the quasi-Pigouvian toll (i) and the corresponding revenue neutral fuel tax rate. The annual revenue par capita (RELU consumers) is $277.60 and the revenue neutral fuel tax rate is 145.9%. The most important difference between the two policies is the cost of traveling intra-zonally since those travelers pay the fuel tax but not the quasi-Pigouvian toll since they travel on local roads only.

In both policies, the unemployed consumers benefit and the employed consumers are harmed as measured by the expected utility levels. As it might be expected both policies decrease travel times and increase the monetary cost of travel including the charges. The travel time decreases by 5.0% under the quasi-Pigouvian tolling, and by 8.2% under the fuel tax, and the monetary cost of travel increases by 15.6% and 50.4%, respectively. The increased travel money cost harms all consumers and decreased travel time benefits employed consumers.

In addition, there are other effects from RELU variables. But to analyze the effect of policies on these other RELU variables is difficult because those variables have circular effects on each other in the general equilibrium process. Under the quasi-Pigouvian toll (i), Wages ($f = 1,...,4$) decrease from 5.6% to 5.6% and this harms employed consumers. Consumption good prices ($r = 4$) decrease by 0.2% and housing rents ($k = 1,2$) decrease by 2.9% and 2.2%, and these changes benefit both the employed and the unemployed consumers. Under the fuel tax, wages ($f = 1,...,4$) decrease from 11.3% to 11.3% and this harms the employed consumers. Consumption good prices ($r=4$) decrease by 3.2% and housing rents ($k=1,2$) decrease 6.0% and 4.1%, and these changes benefit both employed and unemployed consumers.

Under the quasi-Pgiouvian toll (i) and the corresponding revenue neutral fuel tax, the annual gain from total stock value per capita (RELU consumer) decreases by $605.92 and by $1,188.73, respectively. The stock value is correlated with rent and floor space demand. The location choice, the decreased wage and the increased travel cost cause the reduction in the demand of housing space. The vacant land increases in all locations. As the demand for housing shrinks somewhat, the vacant land stock increases. The total land demand in each zone is related with sum of the demand of housing space and the demand of office space. The demand of housing space is affected by the number of residents and land demand per capita. The demand of office space is affected by the size of industries and the land demand per industry.

The two policies have opposite impacts on job locations and similar impacts on resident locations. Under the quasi-Pigouvian toll (i), jobs decrease by 5,228 in the city and increase by 4,607 in the suburbs[24], and residents increase by 6,544 in the city and decrease by 6,544 in the suburbs. On the other hand, under the fuel tax, jobs increase by 36,120 in the city and decrease by 37,570 in the suburbs. Residents increase by 53,033 in the city and decrease by 53,033 in the suburbs. Under the quasi-Pigouvian toll (i), in which local roads are not charged, commuters can avoid paying the toll if they reside and work in the same zone thus using only local roads, or by moving to the less congested suburbs where the tolls paid would be lower. Jobs move to the suburbs where is easy to access labor, and residents move to the city where is easy to access jobs. When the travel cost by auto increases, the most important factor in location choices is the fact that public transport becomes

---

[24] The total number of residences must be the same, but the number of jobs can be different before and after the policies, because consumers can choose to be employed and unemployed. Parry and Bento (2001) point out that the congestion tax discourages labor force participation because it increases the commuting cost. By using the revenue from the congestion tax to reduce the labor tax, they show that the impact on the labor supply becomes positive. In my case, all taxes other than the efficiency-improving taxes of the policies have been set to zero.

more attractive relative to car. This is one of the reasons that both jobs and residents are centralized in the city and CBD under the fuel tax: switching to transit to avoid the high fuel charges induces city dependence because transit is more plentiful in the city.

Both policies show similar and reasonable results for fuel consumption related variables. Fuel consumption and CO_2 emissions decrease by 7.0% and 12.3%, VMT decreases by 5.6% and by 10.2%, and MPG increases by 1.6% and 2.4%, respectively. As I have noted, the quasi-Pigouvian toll is the same amount for any type of vehicle on the same road, but tax on fuel increases with the vehicle's fuel inefficiency. Consumer can avoid a part of the fuel tax if they have a more efficient vehicle, but cannot avoid the quasi-Pigouvian by having a more efficient vehicle. Thus under the fuel tax, consumers can chose more efficient vehicles than under the quasi-Pigouvian toll. Indirectly, consumers also improve their MPG under the quasi-Pigouvian toll. That is because the quasi-Pigouvian toll increases the monetary cost of travel and this causes income and substitution effects in favor of more efficient cars.

Quasi-Pigouvian toll on all roads and the fuel tax

In table 5.5.1 (a), the two columns from the right are the results of the quasi-Pigouvian toll (ii) and the corresponding revenue neutral fuel tax. The annual revenue per capita (RELU consumers) is $1,173.11 and the revenue neutral fuel tax rate is 226.8%.

Although the unemployed consumers benefit and the employed consumers are harmed by both policies, the quasi-Pigouvian toll (ii) performs better than does the fuel tax for all types of consumers. Total travel time decreases by 11.2% and 11.3%, and total travel cost increases by 74.8% and 73.1%, respectively. Through the general equilibrium process, wages, rents and prices decrease. Under the quasi-Pigouvian toll (ii), wages ($f=1,...,4$) decrease from 15.7% to 15.8%. Consumption goods prices ($r=4$) decrease 5.7% and housing rents ($k=1,2$) decrease 8.4% and 6.2%. Under the fuel tax, wages ($f=1,...,4$) decrease about 15.1%. Consumption goods prices ($r=4$) decrease 4.5% and housing rent ($k=1,2$) decrease 8.2% and 5.6%. The annual gain from total stock value per capita decreases by $1,712.67 and $1,589.73, respectively.

150 Simulation Analysis of Urban Economy

Table 5.5.1 (a). Effects of the quasi-Pigouvian toll (i) on major roads, and its revenue neutral fuel tax; and the quasi-Pigouvian toll (ii) on all roads and its revenue neutral fuel tax.

			QPT(i)	Fuel tax145.9%	QPT(ii)	Fuel tax226.8%
Revenue per cap ($)			277.60	277.60	1,173.11	1,173.11
UExpU	% change	f = 1	-0.457	-0.983	-1.367	-1.373
(CU of emp)		f = 2	-0.393	-0.798	-1.099	-1.114
		f = 3	-0.333	-0.671	-0.907	-0.937
		f = 4	-0.230	-0.466	-0.599	-0.644
UExpUUOL	% change	f = 1	0.054	0.244	0.443	0.334
(CU of unemp)		f = 2	0.049	0.206	0.386	0.278
		f = 3	0.042	0.194	0.365	0.260
		f = 4	0.031	0.167	0.313	0.223
wage	% change	f = 1	-5.590	-11.316	-15.667	-15.112
		f = 2	-5.627	-11.303	-15.711	-15.098
		f = 3	-5.630	-11.325	-15.750	-15.140
		f = 4	-5.591	-11.305	-15.736	-15.119
rent	% change	k = 1	-2.931	-5.998	-8.426	-8.179
		k = 2	-2.203	-4.136	-6.247	-5.619
		k = 3	-2.531	-5.826	-8.295	-7.803
		k = 4	-2.710	-6.212	-8.596	-8.321
price	% change	r = 1	-2.685	-6.489	-9.384	-8.787
		r = 2	-1.877	-5.081	-7.653	-6.923
		r = 3	-1.933	-5.199	-7.863	-7.093
		r = 4	-0.226	-3.203	-5.693	-4.502
Total Value	change		-15,754	-30,907	-44,529	-41,333
Annual gain fromtotal value per cap ($)	change		-605.92	-1,188.73	-1,712.67	-1,589.73
Gallon and Emission	% change		-7.031	-12.265	-17.112	-18.084
VMT	% change		-5.579	-10.200	-13.633	-15.312
MPG	% change		1.562	2.354	4.198	3.383
Speed	% change		4.726	6.469	10.763	9.683
Ineff	% change		-0.064	-0.207	-0.056	-0.309
TTT (total travel time)	% change		-4.997	-8.187	-11.208	-11.325
TTC (total travel cost)	% change		15.560	50.358	74.776	73.081
Jobs	change	CBD	-289	19,041	12,484	27,071
		City ex-CBD	-4,939	17,079	5,112	23,388
		City	-5,228	36,120	17,596	50,459
		Suburb	4,607	-37,570	-19,721	-52,469
Residence	change	CBD	622	2,930	3,885	4,590
		City ex-CBD	5,833	50,103	40,343	73,876
		City	6,455	53,033	44,228	78,466
		Suburb	-6,455	-53,033	-44,228	-78,466
Vacant Land (acar)	change	CBD	29.125	44.020	80.211	58.472
		City	231.423	352.041	602.260	474.440
		City ex-CBD	260.548	396.060	682.471	532.912
		Suburb	15,440.941	42,695.448	53,209.797	57,232.927

Both policies centralize jobs and residents. Under the quasi-Pigouvian toll (ii), jobs increase by 17,596 in the city and decrease 19,721 in the suburbs, and residents increase by 44,228 in the city and decrease by 44,228 in the suburbs[25]. Under the fuel tax, jobs increase by 50,459 in the city and decrease by 52,469 in the suburbs and residents increase by 78,466 in the city and decrease by 78,466 in the suburbs. Thus the population is centralized more by the fuel tax than by the quasi-Pigouvia toll (ii). The quasi-Pigouvian toll is higher near the center (where there is more congestion) relative to the suburbs. The fuel tax should also be higher near the center than in the suburbs, but the variation from the city to the suburbs should be lower than that of the quasi-Pigouvian toll. Thus less is gained by locating in the suburbs under the fuel tax and the degree of centralization under the fuel tax is stronger than it is under the quasi-Pigouvian toll (ii).

The quasi-Pigouvian toll (ii) and the fuel tax reduce fuel consumption and CO_2 emissions by 17.1% and 18.1%, respectively. Similarly, the VMT decreases by 13.6% and 15.3%, and the MPG increases by 4.2% and 3.4%, respectively. Since consumer can avoid some of the fuel tax by driving more efficient vehicles, but cannot equally well avoid the quasi-Pigouvian toll, fuel economy improves more under the fuel tax.

Limited quasi-Pigouvian toll on time and fuel for links to enter CBD, cordon toll and parking fee.

Table 5.5.1 (b) shows the results of the limited quasi-Pigouvian toll (iii) and the corresponding revenue neutral cordon toll and parking fee. The annual revenue per capita (RELU consumers) is $25.67 and the revenue neutral cordon toll is $1.49 and the parking fee is $2.24. All the policies benefit the unemployed and harm the employed. The exception is that the employed of the highest income group benefit from the parking fee. Under the limited quasi-Pitouvian toll (iii), and the revenue equivalent cordon toll and parking fee, the total travel time decreases by 0.6%, 0.6% and 0.5%, and total monetary travel cost increases by 1.5%, 1.5% and 2.2%,

---

[25] It is also interesting to compare the impact on job by quasi-Pigouvian toll on link roads and that on both link and zone roads. Commuter can avoid former if they reside and work in the same zones, but cannot avoid later. This is important factor why job are suburbanized in former and centralized in latter.

Table 5.5.1 (b). The results of the limited quasi-Pgouvian toll, its revenue neutral cordon toll, and its revenue neutral parking fee.

			Limited QPT (iii)	CT$1.494	PF$2.235
Revenue per cap ($)			$25.67	$25.67	$25.67
UExpU	% change	f = 1	-0.037	-0.038	-0.022
(CU of employed)		f = 2	-0.030	-0.031	-0.014
		f = 3	-0.023	-0.023	-0.007
		f = 4	-0.012	-0.012	0.003
UExpUUOLF	% change	f = 1	0.010	0.011	0.011
(CU of unemployed)		f = 2	0.009	0.010	0.012
		f = 3	0.008	0.010	0.011
		f = 4	0.007	0.008	0.009
Wage	% change	f = 1	-0.543	-0.567	-0.373
		f = 2	-0.565	-0.589	-0.378
		f = 3	-0.544	-0.566	-0.372
		f = 4	-0.513	-0.534	-0.352
Rent	% change	k = 1	-0.209	-0.222	-0.139
		k = 2	-0.201	-0.212	-0.105
		k = 3	-0.312	-0.335	-0.098
		k = 4	-0.131	-0.145	-0.129
Price	% change	r = 1	-0.214	-0.230	-0.167
		r = 2	-0.176	-0.192	-0.128
		r = 3	-0.199	-0.214	-0.121
		r = 4	-0.045	-0.057	-0.021
Total value	change		-1,169	-1,230	-558
Annual gain from total value per cap ($)	change		-44.97	-47.32	-21.44
Gallon and Emission	% change		-0.716	-0.722	-0.863
VMT	% change		-0.413	-0.416	-0.534
MPG	% change		0.306	0.308	0.332
Speed	% change		0.426	0.427	0.539
Ineff	% change		-0.008	-0.009	0.009
TTT (total travel time)	% change		-0.576	-0.585	-0.503
TTC (total travel cost)	% change		1.471	1.469	2.208
Jobs	change	CBD	-7,337	-7,648	-449
		City ex-CBD	1,067	1,247	599
		City	-6,270	-6,401	151
		Suburb	6,217	6,346	-182
Residents	change	CBD	-229	-245	89
		City ex-CBD	-1,329	-1,321	182
		City	-1,559	-1,566	271
		Suburb	1,559	1,566	-271
Vacant Land (acar)	change	CBD	11.307	11.865	-3.562
		City	19.865	19.547	3.302
		City ex-CBD	31.171	31.412	-0.260
		Suburb	832.108	870.918	900.446

respectively. Through the general equilibrium process, wages, rents and prices are decreased. Under the limited quasi-Pigouvian toll (iii), wage ($f=1,...,4$) decreases from 0.5% to 0.6%, consumption good price ($r=4$) decreases by 0.05%, and housing rent ($k=1,2$) decreases by 0.2% and 0.2%. Under the cordon toll, wage ($f=1,...,4$) decreases from 0.5% to 0.6%, and the consumption good price ($r=4$) decreases by 0.06%, housing rent ($k=1,2$) decreases by 0.2% and 0.2%. Under the parking fee, wage ($f=1,...,4$) decreases about 0.4%, consumption good price ($r=4$) decreases by 0.02% and the housing rent ($k=1,2$) decreases by 0.1% and 0.1%. The annual gain from total value per capita decreases by $44.97, $47.32 and $21.44, respectively.

The population distribution shows different results for the downtown parking fee policy than for the other policies. Under the limited quasi-Pigouvian toll (iii), jobs decreased by 7,337 in the CBD, increased by 1,067 in the city, and increased by 6,217 in the suburbs, the residences decreased by 229 in the CBD, decreased by 1,329 in the city and increased by 1,559 in the suburbs. Under the cordon toll, the jobs decreased by 7,648 in the CBD, increased by 1,247 in the city, increased by 6,346 in the suburbs, and the residents decreased by 245 in the CBD, decreased by 1,321 in the city and increased by 1,566 in the suburbs. Under the parking fee, the changes were smaller. Jobs decreased by 499 in the CBD, increased by 599 in the city, and decreased 182 in the suburbs. Residents increased by 89 in the CBD, increased by 182 in the city and decreased by 271 in the suburbs. Thus the metropolitan area becomes more suburbanized by the limited quasi-Pigouvian toll (iii) and the cordon toll, but becomes more centralized by the parking fee. The important differences between the parking fee and the other policies is that the through traffic does not pay the parking fee. The other difference is that intra-CBD auto travelers need to pay the parking fee. But the limited quasi-Pigouvian toll (iii) and the cordon toll do not require the intra-CBD drivers to pay a toll while though traffic pays. There is a trade off under the parking fee that the congestion near the center decreases and travel by auto becomes convenient, but the travel to the CBD becomes more expensive. If the former effect is more attractive, the metropolitan area would be centralized. The trade off under the cordon toll and the limited quasi-

Pigouvian toll (iii) is that the travel cost near the CBD becomes expensive, although less congested, but intra-zonal travel in CBD becomes cheaper. If the former effect is stronger, the city would be suburbanized.

The vacant land increases in any locations under the limited quasi-Pigouvian toll and the cordon toll, and under the parking fee, it decreases in the CBD, and increases in the city and in the suburbs.

The fuel consumption related variables have similar results under all policies. Under the limited quasi-Pigouvian toll (iii), the cordon toll and the parking fee, fuel consumption and CO_2 emissions decrease by 0.7%, 0.7% and 0.9%, VMT decreases by 0.4%, 0.4% and 0.5%, and MPG increases by 0.3%, 0.3% and 0.3%, respectively. It is only a tiny difference, but speed increases more under the parking fee than other policies.

5.5.2 Population and job shifts caused by the anti-congestion policies

In this section, I will examine, in more detail, the impacts of selected anti-congestion policies on the job location and residential location pattern of the population, and in particular the concentration of jobs and residences inside the CBD. The policies examined for this purpose are the CBD cordon toll, the CBD parking fee and the fuel tax. I will gradually increase the instruments of these policies observing how targeted variables are changing.

The cordon toll

The commuters to the CBD can avoid paying the cordon toll by residing in the CBD or by switching to other modes of travel. Some trough traffic could also change mode or could make detours around the CBD. It is not impossible that link roads that are not subject to the cordon toll could become more congested.

Figure 5.5.2 (a-1) shows the impact of the cordon toll on the job distribution. When the cordon toll is low, jobs decrease in the CBD and increase in the other zones. The reason is that since the cost traveling into the CBD increases, some jobs move out. The results also show that when the cordon toll is high, these effects on jobs get reversed. Jobs come back to the CBD and decrease in other zones. Why is this reversal observed at high levels of the cordon toll? In order to understand the reason for the reversal, it is

Change of jobs by Cordon toll

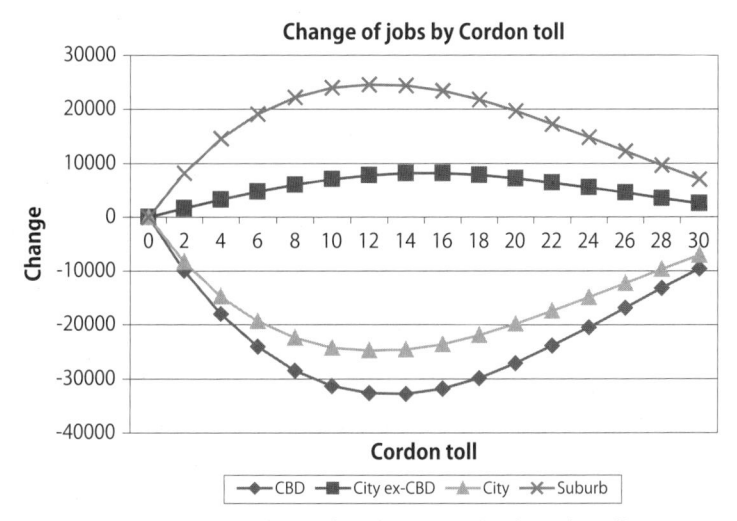

Figure 5.5.2 (a-1) Change of jobs locations under the cordon toll.

Change of residential population

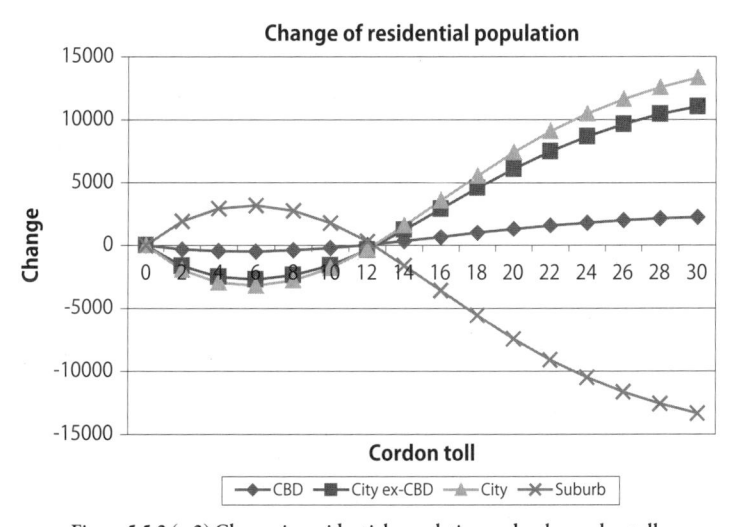

Figure 5.5.2 (a-2) Change in residential population under the cordon toll.

useful to first understand the effect of the cordon toll on residential locations.

Figure 5.5.2 (a-2) shows the impact of the cordon toll on the distribution of the residential population. When the cordon toll is low, the residential population increases in the suburbs and decreases in the CBD

156　Simulation Analysis of Urban Economy

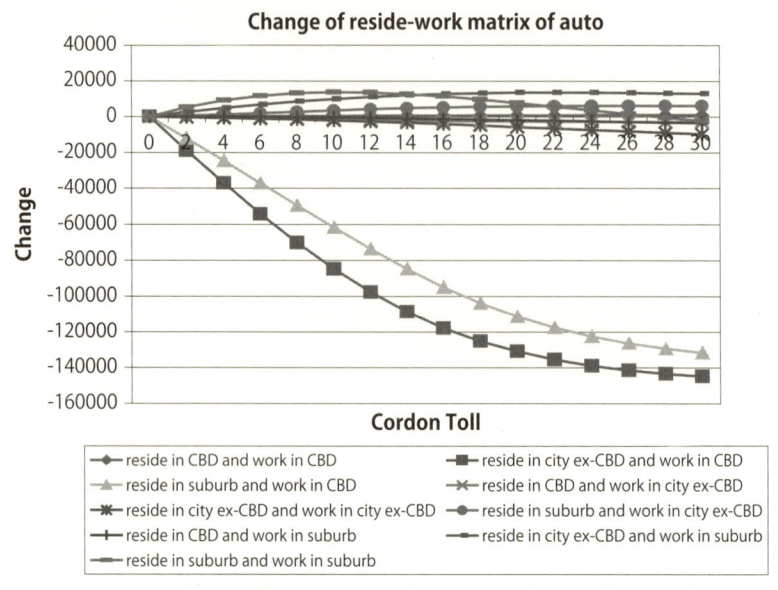

Change of reside-work matrix of auto

Legend:
- reside in CBD and work in CBD
- reside in city ex-CBD and work in CBD
- reside in suburb and work in CBD
- reside in CBD and work in city ex-CBD
- reside in city ex-CBD and work in city ex-CBD
- reside in suburb and work in city ex-CBD
- reside in CBD and work in suburb
- reside in city ex-CBD and work in suburb
- reside in suburb and work in suburb

Figure 5.5.2 (a-3) Change in the residence to work trip matrix by car under the cordon toll.

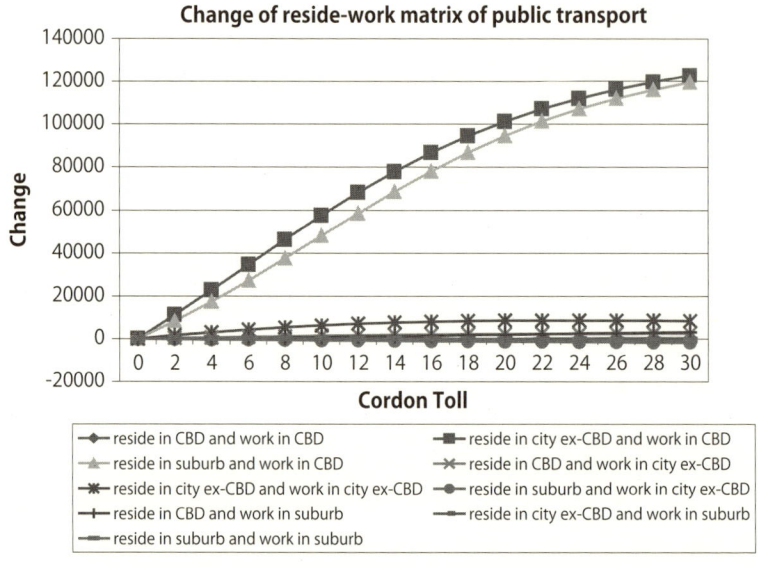

Change of reside-work matrix of public transport

Legend:
- reside in CBD and work in CBD
- reside in city ex-CBD and work in CBD
- reside in suburb and work in CBD
- reside in CBD and work in city ex-CBD
- reside in city ex-CBD and work in city ex-CBD
- reside in suburb and work in city ex-CBD
- reside in CBD and work in suburb
- reside in city ex-CBD and work in suburb
- reside in suburb and work in suburb

Figure 5.5.2 (a-4) Change in the residence to work matrix by pubic transport under the cordon toll.

Change of reside-work matrix of other

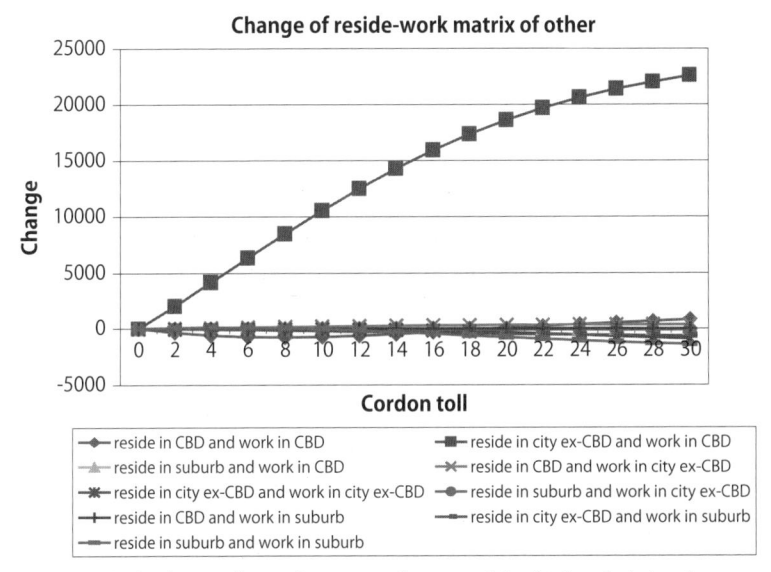

[Chart showing Change vs Cordon toll, with legend:
- reside in CBD and work in CBD
- reside in city ex-CBD and work in CBD
- reside in suburb and work in CBD
- reside in CBD and work in city ex-CBD
- reside in city ex-CBD and work in city ex-CBD
- reside in suburb and work in city ex-CBD
- reside in CBD and work in suburb
- reside in city ex-CBD and work in suburb
- reside in suburb and work in suburb]

Figure 5.5.2 (a-5) Chage in the residence-to-work matrix of the third mode (other than car or transit) under the cordon toll.

and in the city. Since not only drivers to CBD but also through traffic drivers need to pay the cordon toll, travel cost in the city becomes expensive. But when the cordon toll becomes high enough, the results reverse. The residential population increases inside the CBD and in the city and decreases in the suburbs. They can choose a job inside the CBD and commute into the CBD by switching from car to transit. The city residential population increases and that of the suburbs decreases, because the very high cordon toll causes switches to CBD oriented transit which means that some suburban residents move to the city to be closer to transit. As well, those who do not switch mode, move to the city shortening their car commuting distance to the CBD to make up for the higher cordon toll.

Figures 5.5.2 (a-3), (a-4) and (a-5) show the impact of the cordon toll on the residence-workplace matrix of each mode, (a-3) auto, (a-4) public transport and (a-5) other. The impacts are that, with high enough cordon tolls, commuters by auto from the city and the suburb to the CBD decrease, while the commuters by public transport from the city and the suburban

Change of vacant land by cordon toll

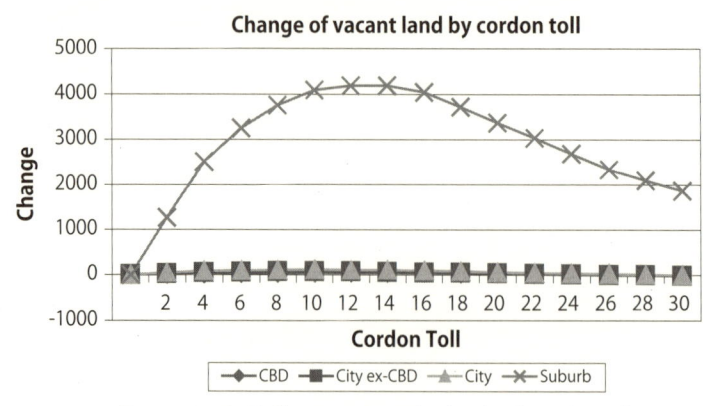

[Chart with x-axis "Cordon Toll" from 2 to 30, y-axis "Change" from -1000 to 5000, showing series: CBD, City ex-CBD, City, Suburb. The Suburb series rises from ~1000 at toll 2 to a peak of ~4200 around toll 12-14, then declines to ~1800 at toll 30. Other series remain near zero.]

Figure 5.5.2 (a-6) Changes in vacant land under the cordon toll.

zones to the CBD increase, and the commuters by other modes from the city to the CBD also increase. Thus the impact of Cordon toll on the job and residential population could be explained. When cordon toll is low, the reduction of commuters by auto from city and suburb to CBD is faster than the increment of commuters by public transport from city and suburb to CBD and the commuters by other from city to CBD. When cordon toll becomes expensive this relation become opposite.

Figure 5.5.2 (a-6) shows the impact of the cordon toll on vacant land. When the cordon toll is low the vacant land in the suburbs increases, but when the cordon toll is high, the vacant land in suburbs decreases.

This tendency is inconsistent with the job and residential population, although not only the size of industries and number of residents but also the floor demands by each industry and each resident affect the size of vacant land in the suburbs. The effect of vacant land in the CBD and city is similar but smaller because there is much less vacant land to begin with. As cordon toll becomes higher, the amount of money paid for cordon toll increase and then decreases. Thus the consumer's income spent on other goods decreases and increases, keeping other variables constant.

Actually other variables change, and there are side effects through those variables. In the suburbs, the labor supply increases when the cordon toll is low. This would explain that the wage decreases and employed consumer's full income decreases, since residents in the suburbs work relatively more in the suburbs than in the city. Thus the housing demand decreases. Producers would substitute labor for land since wages decrease, although the total office demand increases. As a result the vacant land increases and the floor space rent decreases. This tendency becomes opposite when the cordon toll is higher.

In the CBD, jobs and labor supply decrease. Even so, the wage decreases and the full income of employed consumers decreases. Behind this, rent decreases, especially office rent decreases more than housing rent in percentage. Producers might substitute land for labor although the stock of offices decreases. On the other hand, the housing stock increases but residents decrease. As a whole, the vacant land increases. When the cordon toll becomes higher, the effects are reversed.

The city excluding the CBD is affected in ways that are mostly similar to how the suburbs were affected, but some variables in the city are affected in ways similar to how the CBD was affected. When the cordon toll is low, the labor supply increases, the wage decreases and the full income of employed consumers decreases. Rent decreases. The single-family housing stock increases but multi-family housing stock decreases. These changes become opposite when the cordon toll is higher. The office stocks decrease, increase and decrease again as the cordon toll becomes higher. As a result, the vacant land increases and then decreases.

The parking fee

The parking fee is levied on drivers whose destination is the CBD. Through traffic does not pay the parking fee. Hence those drivers enjoy less congested roads.

Figure 5.5.2 (b-1) shows the impact of the parking fee on the job distribution. When the parking fee is low, jobs increase in the city and decrease in the CBD and the suburbs. But when the parking fee becomes high enough, jobs decrease in the city and start to increase in the and in the suburbs.

Figure 5.5.2 (b-2) shows the impact of the parking fee on the residential population distribution. The residential population increases in the CBD

160 Simulation Analysis of Urban Economy

and the city and decreases in the suburbs.

Figure 5.5.2 (b-3), (b-4) and (b-5) show the impact of the parking fee on the residence-to-work commuting matrix by each mode. The parking fee makes attractive commuting by public transit and by the third mode to the

Figure 5.5.2 (b-1) Change in jobs under the parking fee.

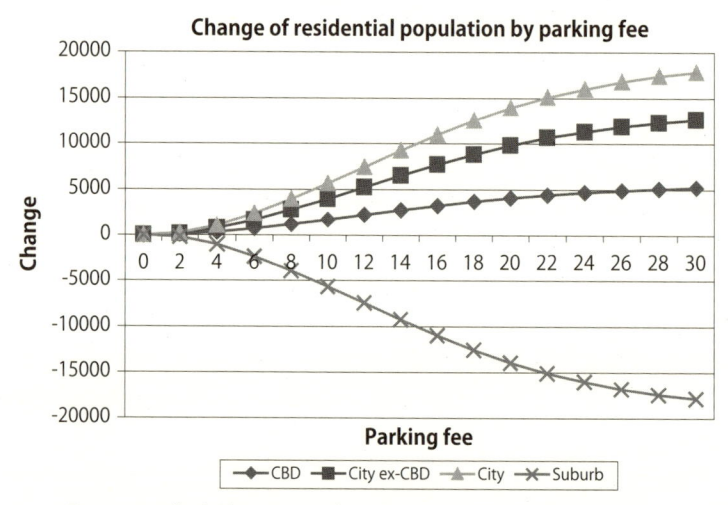

Figure 5.5.2 (b-2) Change in residential population under the parking fee.

city and the CBD. As a result, the increase of commuters to the CBD by public transit and other modes is more than the reduction of commuters to the CBD by car.

Figure 5.5.2 (b-6) shows the impact of the parking fee on the vacant land. In the suburbs, as the parking fee increases, vacant land initially increases and then decreases. Under the parking fee, vacant land in the CBD decreases, although the amount is very small. The movement of residents and jobs mostly explains the effect on the vacant land.

In addition, there are effects through other variables. As the parking fee becomes higher, the amount spent on parking increases and then decreases. Thus the disposable income for consumers decreases, and the housing demand would decrease, keeping other variables constant.

Those other variables change the effect on land use. In the suburbs, when the parking fee is low, the labor supply increases, although jobs decrease. Wage decreases and full income decreases. Since residents also decrease, housing stock decreases. Housing rent decreases. The producer would substitute labor for land and the office stock also decreases and office

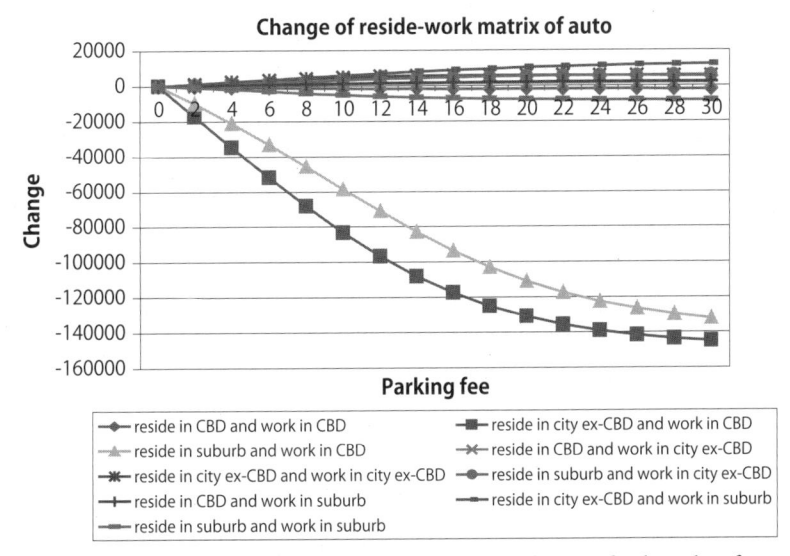

Figure 5.5.2 (b-3) Change in the residence-to-workplace matrix by car under the parking fee.

162   Simulation Analysis of Urban Economy

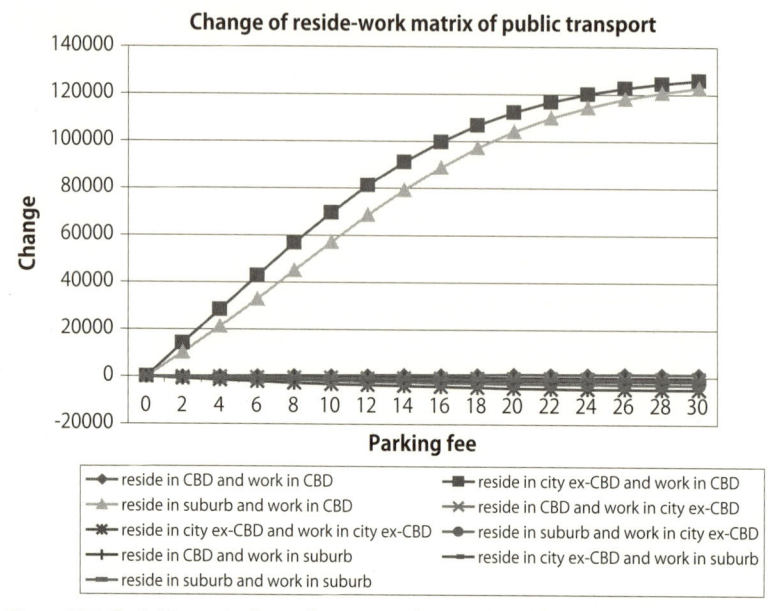

Change of reside-work matrix of public transport

Figure 5.5.2 (b-4) Change in the residence-to-work matrix by public transit under the parking fee.

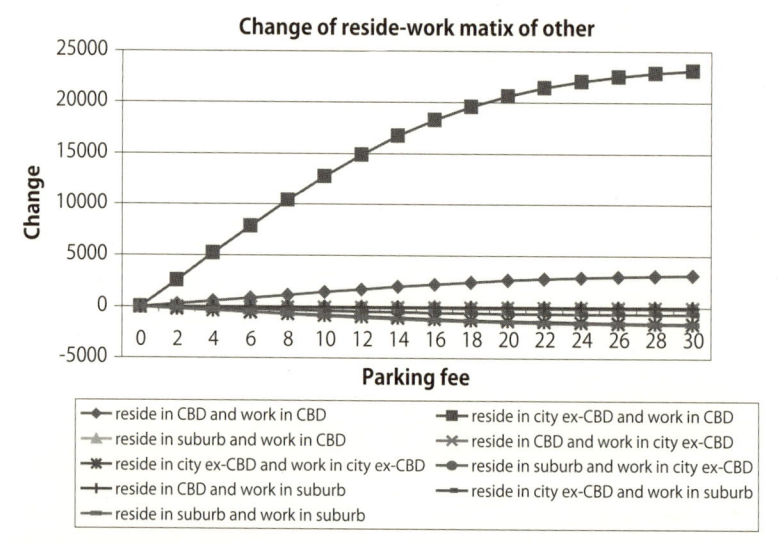

Change of reside-work matix of other

Figure 5.5.2 (b-5) Changes in the residence-to-work matrix of the third mode (other) under the parking fee policy.

Change of vacant land by parking fee

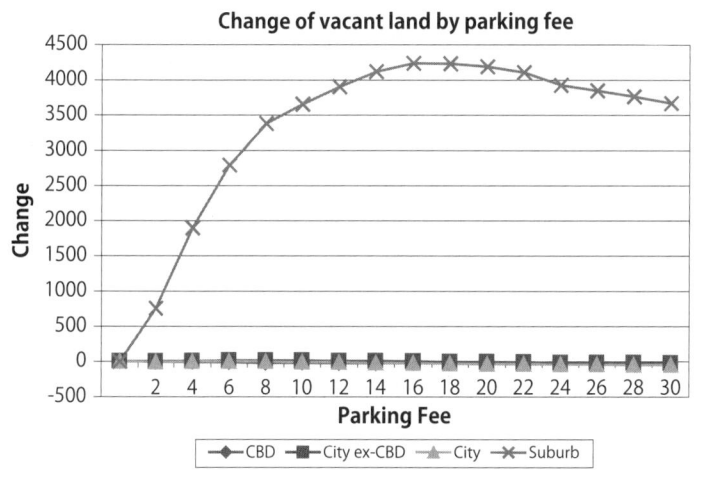

Figure 5.5.2 (b-6) Changes in vacant land under the parking fee.

rent decreases. When the parking fee becomes higher, although residents keep decreasing and labor supply increases because jobs increase, other effects become opposite. Thus vacant land increases and then decreases.

In the CBD, when the parking fee is low, the labor supply increases although jobs decrease, and wage decreases. The full income also decreases. The housing demand per person decreases, but since the residents increase, the housing demand as a whole could increase. The single-family housing decreases and multiple-housing stock increases. The housing rent increases and office rent does not have big change. Since wage decrease, producers would substitute land for labor, and the office building stock slightly increases. Thus the vacant land decreases. When the parking fee becomes expensive, jobs, labor supply, and wages, show the opposite result, but since the residents keep increasing, the multiple-family housing keeps increasing and single-family housing decreases. The office buildings decrease. Housing rent increases, but office rent does not change. Thus vacant land increases and then decreases.

In the city excluding the CBD, when the parking fee is low, jobs and the labor supply increase. Wage and full income decrease. But since residents increase, single-family housing increases and multiple-family housing decreases. The rents of all buildings decrease. But the industrial building stock does not change and commercial building stock decreases. Thus vacant land increases. When the parking fee becomes higher, most of the effects are reversed, although residents keep increasing and commercial buildings keep decreasing.

The fuel Tax

When the fuel tax is levied and the monetary transportation cost by car increases accordingly, some residences and jobs would locate in zones with easy access to public transit to avoid consuming the the now more expensive fuel.

Figure 5.5.2 (c-1) shows the impact of the fuel tax on jobs. When the fuel cost is low, jobs increase in the CBD and in the city and decrease in the suburbs. When the fuel tax becomes higher, the jobs increase in the suburbs and decrease in the CBD and in the city. Jobs move to suburbs to have better access to labor.

Figure 5.5.2 (c-2) shows the impact of the fuel tax on the residential population. The residential populaiton in the CBD changes only moderately. The residential population in the city increases and then deacreases and in the suburbs decreases and then increases in the similar pattern as that is seen for jobs.

Thus as the fuel tax becomes higher, jobs and residential population become more centralized and then more decentralized. Again it is easiyer to understand this irregular impact of the fuel tax on jobs and residiential populaiton location if I watch the impact of the fuel tax on the residence-to-workplace matrix of each mode, as shown in Figures 5.5.2 (c-3), (c-4) and (c-5). Drivers cannot avoid paying the fuel tax unless they change mode. Thus the commuters by auto decrease, while commuters by public transport and by the other mode increase throughout the region. The fuel tax affects many of the residence-to-work place pairs by each mode. The most notable changes are observd in the suburbs. The commuters from suburb to suburb by auto decrease and those by public transport and by the other mode increase.

Figure 5.5.2 (c-6) shows the impact of fuel tax on vacant land. As the fuel tax increases, the vacant land in suburbs first increases and then

Change of jobs by fuel tax

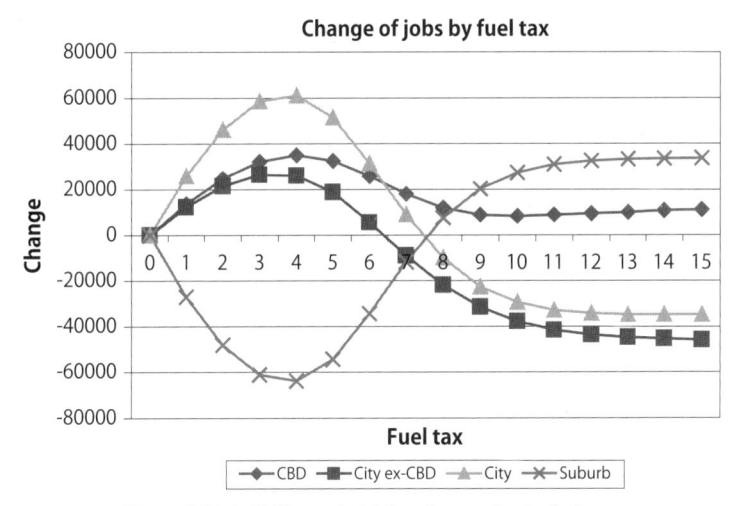

Figure 5.5.2 (c-1) Change in job locations under the fuel tax.

Change of residential population by fuel tax

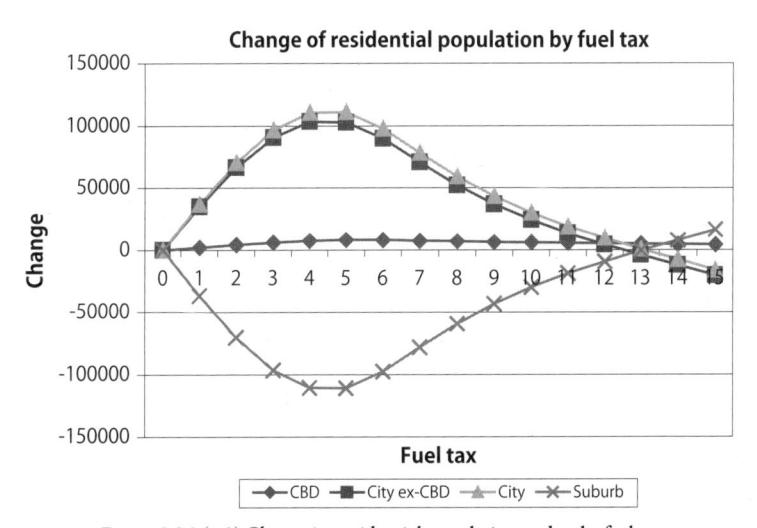

Figure 5.5.2 (c-2) Change in residential population under the fuel tax.

decreases. This is consistent with the patterns of the centralization and the suburbanization of jobs and of the residential population as shown earlier.

Since the fuel consumption does not vary a great deal among zones, its

Change of reside-work matrix of auto by fuel tax

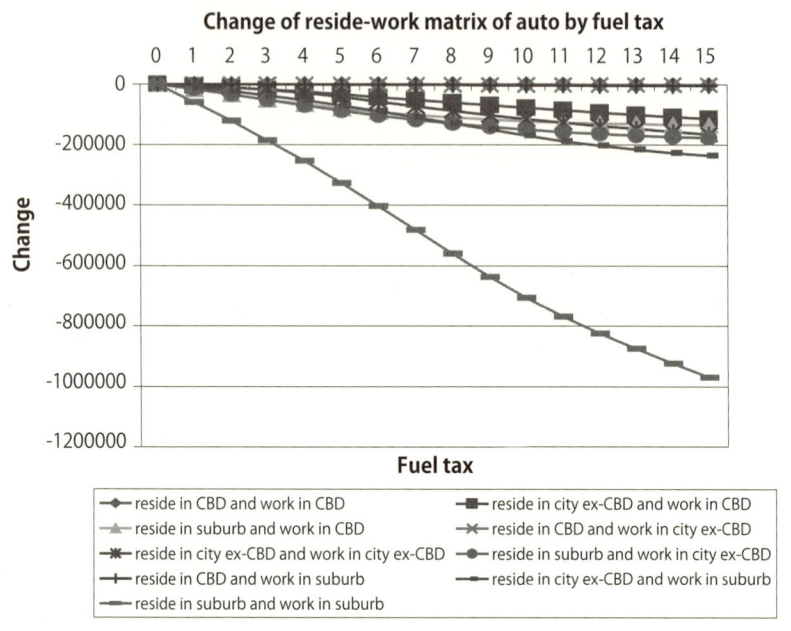

[Chart with x-axis "Fuel tax" ranging 0–15, y-axis "Change" ranging 0 to −1,200,000]

Legend:
- reside in CBD and work in CBD
- reside in city ex-CBD and work in CBD
- reside in suburb and work in CBD
- reside in CBD and work in city ex-CBD
- reside in city ex-CBD and work in city ex-CBD
- reside in suburb and work in city ex-CBD
- reside in CBD and work in suburb
- reside in city ex-CBD and work in suburb
- reside in suburb and work in suburb

Figure 5.5.2 (c-3) Changes in residence-to-work trips by car under the fuel tax.

effects on other variables is simpler than the cordon toll's or the parking fee's. The disposable income decreases and then increases since the amount paid for fuel tax increases and then decreases. In addition, there are side effects through the other variables.

In the suburbs, when the fuel tax is low, labor supply increases, although jobs decrease, and wages decrease. Full income decreases, and since residents decrease, the housing stock and housing rent also decrease. The office stock also decreases because the producers would substitute labor for land, and office rent decreases. Thus the vacant land increases. When the fuel tax is high, the effect becomes the opposite.

In the CBD, when the fuel tax is low, jobs and labor supply increase, and wages decrease. Full income decreases. But since residents increase, single-family housing increases and multi-family housing decreases. Housing rent decreases. Producers would substitute labor for land, and the office building decreases. Thus the vacant land increases. When the fuel tax becomes higher,

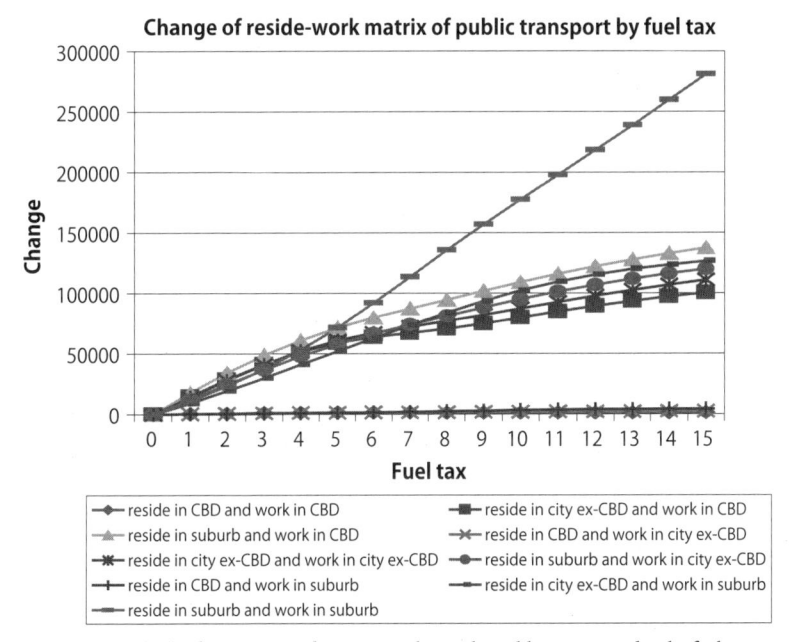

Change of reside-work matrix of public transport by fuel tax

Figure 5.5.2 (c-4) Changes in residence-to-work trips by public transit under the fuel tax.

the effects are reversed, but in the case of multi-family housing, its stock first increases, and then it again decreases when the fuel tax becomes even higher.

In the city excluding the CBD, when the fuel tax is low, jobs and labor supply increase and wages decrease. Full income decreases, but since residents increase, the single family housing stock increases and the multi-family housing stock decreases. Housing rent decreases. The producers substitute labor for land, and the office stocks decrease. Office rent decreases. Thus the vacant land increases. When the fuel tax becomes higher, the effects reverse.

168 Simulation Analysis of Urban Economy

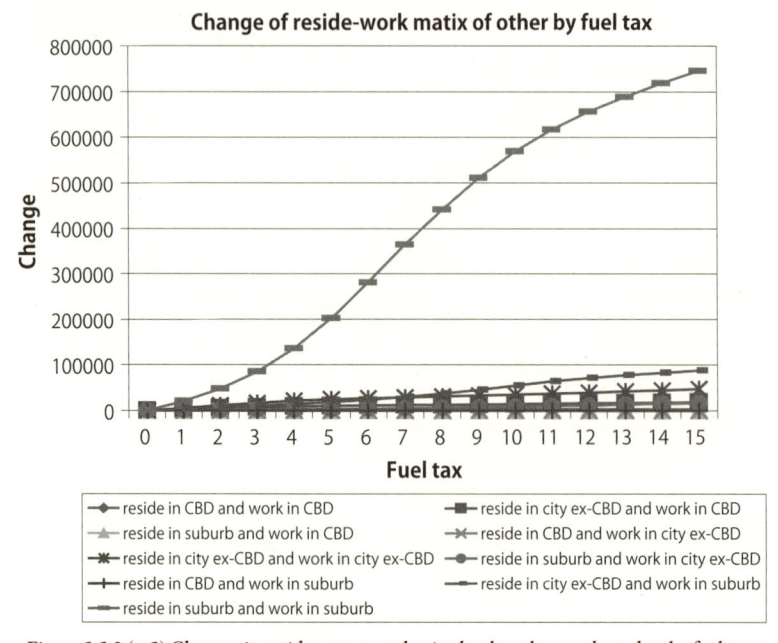

Change of reside-work matix of other by fuel tax

- reside in CBD and work in CBD
- reside in city ex-CBD and work in CBD
- reside in suburb and work in CBD
- reside in CBD and work in city ex-CBD
- reside in city ex-CBD and work in city ex-CBD
- reside in suburb and work in city ex-CBD
- reside in CBD and work in suburb
- reside in city ex-CBD and work in suburb
- reside in suburb and work in suburb

Figure 5.5.2 (c-5) Changes in residence-to-work trips by the other mode under the fuel tax.

Chagne of vacant land by fuel tax

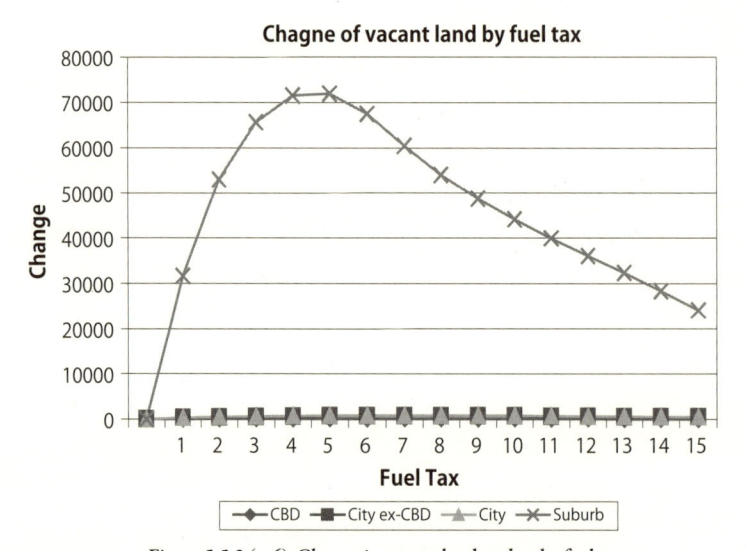

- CBD
- City ex-CBD
- City
- Suburb

Figure 5.5.2 (c-6) Change in vacant land under the fuel tax.

5.5.3 Impact of the policies on fuel consumption and related variables

In this section, we will see the impact of the anti-congestion policies on variables that are related to fuel consumption and CO_2 emissions. I limit my attention to the cordon toll, the parking fee and the fuel tax. Although only the fuel tax aims directly to reduce fuel consumption and CO_2 emissions, it is expected that the other policies will also reduce fuel consumption and CO_2 emissions.

Figure 5.5.3 (a)-(c) shows the impact of these three anti-congestion policies on aggregate fuel consumption and CO_2 emissions, and on aggregate VMT, average fuel economy (MPG), average driving speed and average vehicle inefficiency.

Fuel consumption and CO_2 emissions

As the policies become more intense, fuel consumption and CO_2 emissions are increasingly mitigated. The aggregate fuel consumption is mostly determined by the average MPG in the intensive margin of travel and by the aggregate VMT in the extensive margin of travel. The CO_2 emissions and the fuel consumption are proportional to each other.

VMT

All three policies indirectly remedy congestion by increasing the monetary travel cost by car. As auto travel cost is increased under any policy, aggregate VMT decreases. There are several ways for travelers to reduce VMT. Traveler can drive on shorter routes, or switch to other modes in work and non-work travel. For non-work travel, drivers can shop in zones that are closer to home. Employed consumers can change their residence-workplace pair so that work travel would be monetarily cheaper if longer in time. Employed consumer even could choose to be unemployed in response to very high cost increases under the policies. In addition, all these responses become even more complex because consumers can react to any policy that makes driving more expensive, by switching to more fuel efficient cars.

Average MPG

Average MPG increases smoothly under the fuel tax and parking fee policies. Under the cordon toll average MPG first increases but it decreases eventually when the cordon toll becomes high enough as shown in Figure

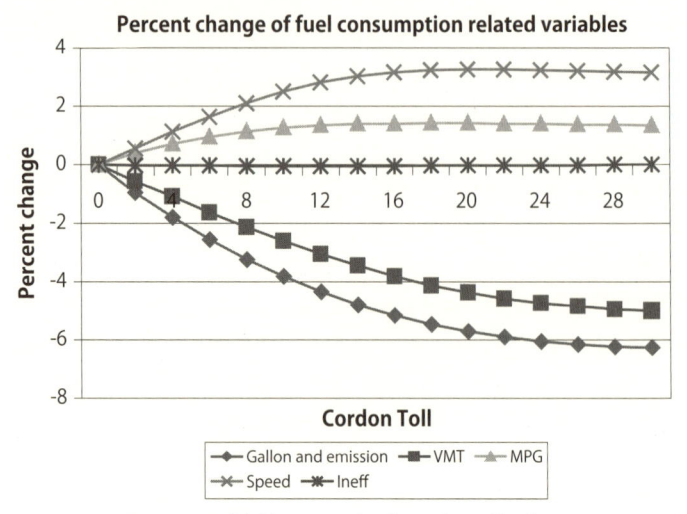

Percent change of fuel consumption related variables

Figure 5.5.3 (a) Changes under the cordon toll policy.

5.5.3 (a). Vehicle fuel economy and travel speed are the two most important factors that decide the average MPG. MPG is low on both slow speed roads and very high speed roads (see Figure 2.3.2). In addition, shifting traffic from a high MPG road to a low MPG road, makes average MPG lower. This can be the case and average MPG can decrease even if the MPG is improved on all the roads. Hence it is possible that because of higher travel cost by auto, travelers prefer shorter distance trips such as intra-zone trips, driving on local roads relative to major roads increases, and average MPG decreases.

Average speed

Average speed increases under the cordon toll or the parking fee. Average speed increases under a relatively low fuel tax but decreases as the fuel tax becomes sufficiently higher as shown in Figure 5.5.3 (c). Because the cost of auto trips increases, congestion decreases. Speeding up of traffic occurs on each link. It is not impossible under the cordon toll that the detours to avoid an expensive road make other roads more congested, to the point that the average speed on such roads can decrease. Suppose that the fuel tax becomes too high. Drivers can change their trips from inter-zonal to intra-zonal, to save on travel cost. Since the local road speed is slower than the major road

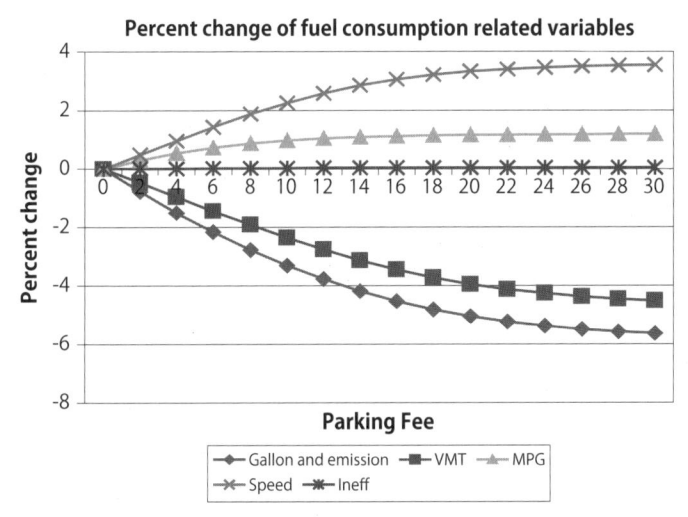

Percent change of fuel consumption related variables

Figure 5.5.3 (b) Changes under the parking fee.

speed, average speed can decrease.

Inefficiency

I assume that there is no technological progress. Therefore, the only way that vehicle inefficiency can change is by the consumers changing their vehicle types. There are several factors that can affect a consumer's choice of vehicle type. One is that if a policy decreases a consumer's disposable income, it could induce that consumer to prefer a more efficient vehicle, since in the model a vehicle's inefficiency is associated with higher vehicle comfort and safety, regarded as a normal good. A second important factor is, of course, the fuel price. An increase in the price of fuel raises the operating cost of any vehicle, thus making more efficient vehicles more desirable. In summary, the income and substitution effects of an increase in the fuel tax are aligned in the direction of inducing consumers to choose more fuel efficient vehicles. But against the above intuition, under a high fuel tax, the average vehicle inefficiency increases as shown in Figure 5.5.3 (c). I also observe that the cordon toll and the parking fee affect vehicle inefficiency very slightly. This is not surprising, since the cordon toll and the parking fee are equal for vehicles of different fuel economy.

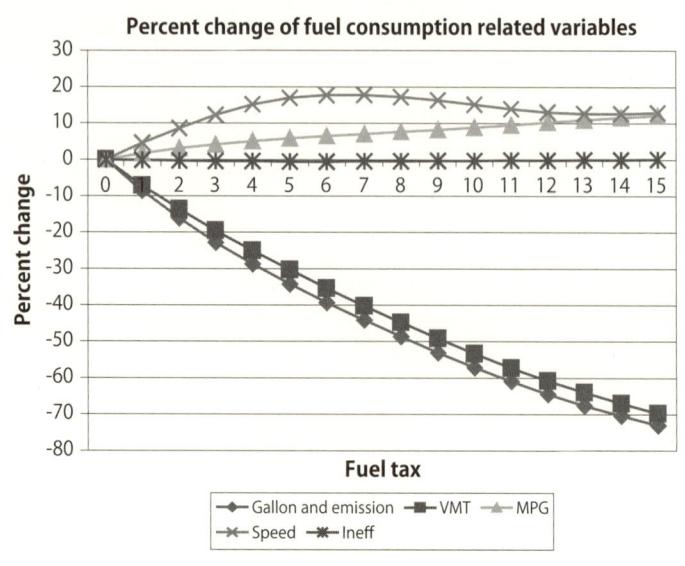

Percent change of fuel consumption related variables

[Chart showing percent change (y-axis from -80 to 30) vs Fuel tax (x-axis from 0 to 15) with series: Gallon and emission, VMT, MPG, Speed, Ineff]

Figure 5.5.3 (c) Changes under the fuel tax.

Since drivers who consume more fuel prefer more efficient vehicles, the driving distance (or VMT) affects a driver's vehicle inefficiency choice. This implies, for example, that if a policy induces urban sprawl that results in long distance travels, then such urban sprawl has the potential of resulting in lower vehicle inefficiency. Another type of urban sprawl, that is one that shortens the average drive distance, would have the opposite effect and would result in higher vehicle inefficiency, which is what happens in the results shown in Figure 5.5.3 (c).

Finally, congestion makes the driving speed slower and the fuel consumption (or MPG) more inefficient, increasing fuel consumption. Hence, the travelers who drive on the more congested roads will prefer more efficient vehicles.

In the model, consumers make a trade-off between high vehicle maintenance cost and travel cost. A person who seldom drives would prefer a more inefficient vehicle, since this inefficient vehicle is more comfortable and safer, but is not affected by the small amount of driving.

Appendix 5. Short-run simulations (without Stock Conversion)

I examine the shorter run results. In this shorter run, the building are not constructed or demolished and so the stock of real estate remains the same in each zone.

Table A5 compares the impact of the long-run and short-run quasi-Pigouvian toll on both the time-delay and fuel externalities on all roads. The employed consumer's utility in the short-run is harmed less and the unemployed consumer's utility benefits more. Thus consumers get better outcomes in the short-run.

Although wage, price, rent and value decrease more in the short-run, the larger differences are observed in rents and values. This is not surprising since those are the variables that are most closely related to the building stocks that are being kept constant. Hosing rent ($r = 1,2$) decreases by 8.4% and by 6.2% in the long run simulation, but it decreases by 14.6% and 13.3% in the short-run. The annual gain from total value per capita decreases by $1,712.67 and $2,732.09, respectively. Since the stock cannot adjust in the short-run, those variables must adjust more instead of the stocks. In RELU-TRAN2 and shorter-run, Total travel time decreases by 11.2% in the long run and by 1.1% in the short run, and total travel cost increases by 74.8% and 75.3%, respectively. So I can see that some variables adjust to almost their long run values in the short run. On the contrary, jobs and residence location changes are less pronounced in the short run, being limited by the constant stock of buildings.

There are only small differences between the long run and the short run, in fuel consumption and related variables. Most of the reductions in VMT, speed, fuel consumption and CO_2 are achieved in the short-run. MPG and inefficiency are improved more in short-run and then become moderated when stocks are adjusted in the long run.

Table A5 Results of the long run versus the short run.

			QPT_IQPT(time&fuel) (RELU-TRAN2)	QPT_IQPT(time&fuel) (short-run)
Revenue per capita ($)			1,173.11	1,179.19
UExpU (Employed Consumer's Utility)	% change	f = 1	-1.367	-1.277
		f = 2	-1.099	-1.009
		f = 3	-0.907	-0.820
		f = 4	-0.599	-0.518
UExpUUOLF (Unemployed Consumer's Utility)	% change	f = 1	0.443	0.733
		f = 2	0.386	0.652
		f = 3	0.365	0.611
		f = 4	0.313	0.523
wage	% change	f = 1	-15.667	-17.007
		f = 2	-15.711	-17.043
		f = 3	-15.750	-17.079
		f = 4	-15.736	-17.052
rent	% change	k = 1	-8.426	-14.646
		k = 2	-6.247	-13.283
		k = 3	-8.295	-11.457
		k = 4	-8.596	-11.748
price	% change	r = 1	-9.384	-10.544
		r = 2	-7.653	-9.145
		r = 3	-7.863	-9.116
		r = 4	-5.693	-7.179
Annual gain from total value per cap ($)	change		-1,712.67	-2,732.09
Gallon and Emission	% change		-17.112	-16.929
VMT	% change		-13.633	-13.434
MPG	% change		4.198	4.208
Speed	% change		10.763	10.657
Ineff	% change		-0.056	-0.068
TTT (total travel time)	%change		-11.208	-11.140
TTC (total travel cost)	%change		74.776	75.313
jobs	change	CBD(3)	12,484	10,291
		City(1,2,4,5)	5,112	3,214
		City(1-5)	17,596	13,504
		Sub(6-14)	-19,721	-15,870
Residence	change	CBD(3)	3,885	2,459
		City(1,2,4,5)	40,343	25,194
		City(1-5)	44,228	27,653
		Sub(6-14)	-44,228	-27,653
Vacant Land (acer)	change	CBD(3)	80.21	0
		City(1,2,3,4)	602.26	0
		City(1-5)	682.47	0
		Sub(1-14)	53,209.80	0

Chapter 6. The Urban Growth Boundary and Congestion Toll as the Energy Saving Policy and Its Side Effects

6.1 Introduction

Although urban sprawl has been an issue for a long time in urban economics, the environmental aspects, such as the air pollution from traffic and open space reduction, were not the main aspects of interest until recently. What used to get more attention about urban sprawl were the urban land-use, population densities, housing rent, commuting time aspects.

Brueckner (2000) pointed out that the urban sprawl problem may be serious since cities are subject to traffic congestion take too much. He concluded that land is allocated to urban use excessively, a resource misallocation resulting from the fact that traffic congestion is not priced. In principle, the scarcer agriculture land that remains after urban expansion and any benefit form open spaces, could be reduced by urban sprawl. Also, excessive urban expansion could cause too much time to be spent in urban travel and commuting. Excessive urban expansion could also cause excessive fuel use and so also excessive air pollution. Urban economists have known it for a long time and Brueckner (2000) summarizes it well that remedying urban sprawl by correctly pricing traffic congestion would cause higher land price and a reduction of housing space per person.

Glaeser and Kahn (2008) estimate the carbon dioxide emissions from driving, public transit, home heating and household electricity usage associated with different locations across the country. In addition to the effect of locational factors such as weather, they find that the land use regulations have negative correlation with total emissions. Central cities have lower emissions than suburban areas. Brownstone and Golob (2009) estimate the impacts of residential density on vehicle annual mileage and fuel consumption. If two households are identical but located in different density residential areas, the household in the denser area drives fewer miles, chooses a higher fuel economy vehicle and consumes less fuel. Wellisch (1995) studies the policies such as emission tax or rights for the efficient location of mobile firms that emit the pollution. Although this is not aiming to mitigate the environmental problem, he finds that the compact city is more environmentally friendly than sprawled city, in general[26].

The most intuitive anti-sprawl policy is the UGB (urban growth boundary). By regulating the aggregate land availability in the suburbs, the economic activities are limited to locate only inside the UGB. Although the literature referred to below does not emphasize the environmental effects of the UGB, it still provided important insights. It has been considerd true by urban economists since the late 1970s, that the first best policy is congestion tolling and the second best policy is the UGB, zoning or land use including the proper amount of land allocated to roads. In several pioneering articles, such consideration is confirmed by Kanemoto (1977), Arnott (1979) and Pines and Sadka (1985), in the monocentric city model, thanks to an origonal insight provided by Solow (1972). In the monocentric city, the jobs location is fixed in the CBD and residents choose their residential location distance from the CBD.

In a more recent study, the relative efficiency of development taxes, urban growth boundaries, property taxes and gasoline taxes in the monocentric city are analyzed by Bento, Franco and Kaffine (2006). The authors concluded that from an efficiency point of view, development taxes and urban growth boundaries are the most effective anti-sprawl policies. If distributional consideration is the basis of choice of the anti-sprawl instruments, it is not clear which policy is the most-socially-preferred.

---

26   This is not always true. Suppose there are two cites. One is a decentralized city with several job subcenters and the other is centralized city with only one CBD. In the former city, although the city area is broadly sprawled, residences lives nearer the sub-centers on average. It is possible that commuting travel distances and air pollution levels are lower than those in the centralized city on average. In addition, it is reasonable that congestion tolls can make the city compact in a monocentric model, but there is no reason to believe this will be true in a polycentric city. Anas and Xu (1999) demonstrated that the congestion toll can make the jobs more dispersed and in Anas and Kim (1996) congestion tolls could make the number of subcenters increase.

Brueckner (2007) shows that the welfare gains of the urban growth boundary in the monocentric city are not large relative to congestion tolls, and the UGB may not be a useful second best-policy instrument in a congested monocentric city.

In Anas-Rhee (2007) (similar but simpler than Anas-Rhee (2006) which, as mentioned in earlier chapters, is a non-monocentric model in which jobs can locate anywhere and in which there is cross-commuting and reverse commuting), results are totally reversing of the traditional beliefs of the urban economists which are all based on the monocentric city model. This was the first article that demonstrated the inefficiency of a UGB. In such a case the UGB is not always second best because by the UGB the population can be forced to be located to a more congested area, whereas with congestion tolls that are first best, it may be optimal to locate more jobs and population to less congested areas such as the suburbs. They provide a good summary when the UGB is not the second best in the simplified polycentric city. In their polycentric city, there are two business districts: one in the central city (CBD) and the other in the suburbs (SBD). Under the toll, workers tend to reside and work more in the same region since to commute between the center and the suburbs is costly. If at the first-best optimum (that is under congestion tolls), more workers reside and work in the suburbs, then the UGB is not the second best policy, because the tolls make the city larger, but the UGB makes the city smaller. If more consumers reside and work in the city at the optimum, then the result would be similar to the results one would get for a monocentric city and then there would be a restrictive UGB that would be second-best efficient. In this case, there is still the possibility that the UGB is only a poor second best policy, because the UGB does not make commuting cost expensive enough compared to first-best tolls, and the commuters between the two regions do not decrease as much as in the case of the toll.

Anas and Rhee (2006) and Ng (2007) also show that the urban boundary is harmful in the case of the polycentric linearly shaped city model. The UGB distorts the land markets and leaves the congestion unpriced. Preferences for open space and agglomeration economics are introduced. Households and firms can locate anywhere. In the model, congestion pricing and an urban growth boundary are examined. Congestion policies may decrease welfare if agglomeration economies are high. An urban growth boundary improves welfare only if open space (greenbelt) preferences are strong. Anas and Pines (2008) distinguish between urban sprawl as geographic sprawl that is urban area expansion, and economic sprawl measured by aggregate commuting costs. They compare tolls and UGB in the model where there are two cities with different amenity levels. When those cities are monocentric, tolls alleviate economic sprawl but increase geographic sprawl. A UGB policy in both cities makes both cities in aggregate, more sprawled when the elasticity of substitution is zero. When those cities have two areas, core and periphery, that are connected with congested bridges, the toll and the UGB policy make their two cities geographically more sprawled if the elasticity of substitution is small enough.

Congestion pricing is the popular anti-sprawl policy for economists, because it is the first-best policy. Tolls make travel more expensive and the prices just right so they should reduce not just congestion but also emissions and this was demonstrated in the simulations of the previous chapter. For more information, see chapter 5.

In this Chapter, I examine the effectiveness of an urban growth boundary (UGB) policy as an alternative anti-congestion policy. Economists know that externalities are best internalized by imposing Pigouvian taxes (or subsidies) in the margins across which the externalities exist. Thus, since congestion is a negative externality of car travel, the Pigouvian congestion toll is the first-best solution. This policy was evaluated in approximate form in the previous chapter together with closely related policies such as the cordon toll, the parking fee and the fuel tax. Urban planners, however, have not hesitated to propose policies that work in unrelated markets as a way of creating more compact and more densely populated urban forms. Such policies are aimed at controlling the total amount of suburban land that is developed. They are typically referred to as "urban growth boundary" policies. By restricting this amount, a distortion is caused in the land markets, but frequently such a policy is defended by arguing that it limits urban sprawl, encourages more intensive use of public transit.

My UGB regulates the development of vacant land in the suburban zone. By reducing the available land for development in the suburbs, it is expected that the urban form will become more centralized, that is the same population will be squeezed into a smaller total urban land area. Is it true that an urban area regulated by such a UGB will be less congested? Without an increase in the road capacity within the area restricted by the urban growth boundary, I would expect that congestion per mile would increase assuming little switching of trips to other modes. At the same time, however, the UGB could indirectly reduce travel distances by causing trip origins and destinations to be closer to each other. So the answer as to what would happen to average congestion, total fuel use and total emissions is not clear. It is possible that a city not restricted by a UGB would be more sprawled and spread out and that in such a city jobs and residences would cluster near each other on average, resulting in shorter travel distances and less congestion, fuel consumption and emissions.

The simulations of RELU-TRAN2, reported in the previous chapter had the common feature that the total undeveloped (or vacant) land available in the suburban zones was entirely available for development. This corresponds to a policy of free land development. In this chapter the concept of an UGB is introduced by assuming that less than the full amount of undeveloped land is actually available for urban development. I define a variable called UGB that can obtain any value between zero and one. If the value is zero, that would mean that all of the currently undeveloped land is kept out of development. This means that subsequent development cannot occur on new (previously undeveloped land). It does not mean, however, that no development occurs. In fact under a policy designated as UGB = 0, two types of development can still takes place. One of these is "infill development" which means that vacant land areas within the city can be developed and will be more likely to be developed since suburban vacant land is not available. The second type is "redevelopment," which means that as the urban area adjusts to a new general equilibrium (in response to the UGB), buildings within the UGB can be demolished and new buildings can be constructed on the vacant land thus freed. The tightness of the UGB can be simulated by varying the value of the variable UGB gradually from zero towards 1. For example, a value of UGB = 0.2 would mean that 80% of the vacant land in the urban area is kept out of development and only 20% of the vacant land in each suburban zone is allowed to be developed.

In section 6.2, the UGB policy is implemented in suburban zones. In section 6.3, the UGB is applied to the land in only one zone. In section 6.4, I compare the UGB of suburban zones and the quasi-Pigouvian toll. I also test the effect of distributing the revenue from the quasi-Pigouvian toll.

6.2 Impacts of the UGB

6.2.1 Impacts of the UGB on jobs and residential location

Figure 6.2.1 (a) shows the impact of the UGB on jobs and residential population location. As the UGB becomes tighter, both jobs and residential population increase inside the city and decrease in the suburbs. The number of residents that move from the suburbs to the city is larger than the number of jobs that move from the suburbs to the city. Figure 6.2.1 (b) shows the impact of the UGB's tightness on the residence-to-work commuting matrix by all three modes. The number of city-to-city commutes increases. The city-to-suburb and suburb-to-city commutes also increase but more moderately. Suburb-to-suburb commuting decreases. Thus jobs and residential population become more centralized.

Figure 6.2.1 (c) shows the impact of the UGB on commuting patterns by car. As the UGB becomes tighter, the suburb-to-suburb commuting by car sharply decreases, while the city-to-city commuting and the city-to-suburb commuting increase, and the suburb-to-city commuting decreases very moderately. Thus the car commuters show qualitatively the similar changes, as do the residence-to-work commuters as a whole in Figure 6.2.1 (b). The largest part of the reduction in the suburb-to-suburb commuting is explained by the reduction of suburb-to-suburb commuting by car. This is because the most used suburb-to-suburb commuting mode is the car. On the other hand, the increase in city-to-city commuters by car explains only a

Change of jobs and residents

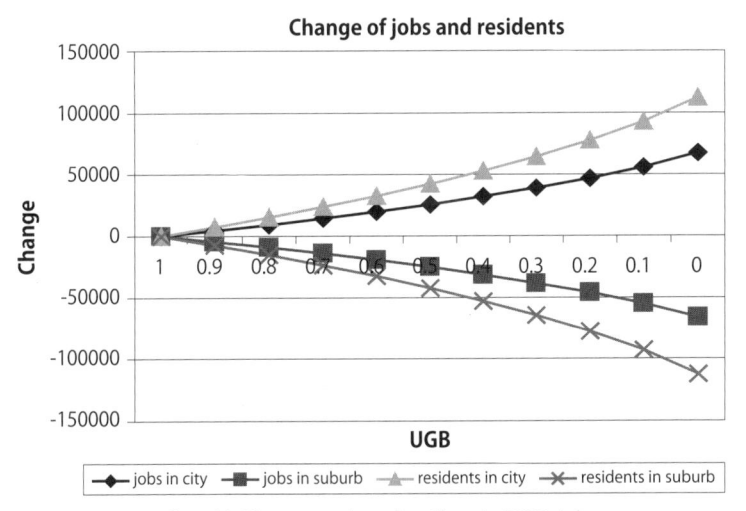

Figure 6.2.1 (a) Changes in jobs and residents by UGB tightness.

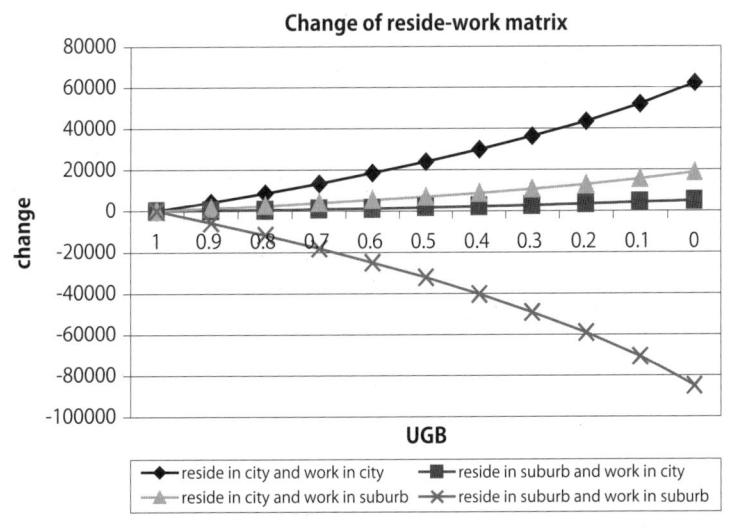

Change of reside-work matrix

Figure 6.2.1 (b) Changes in commuting by all modes under the UGB policy.

182   Simulation Analysis of Urban Economy

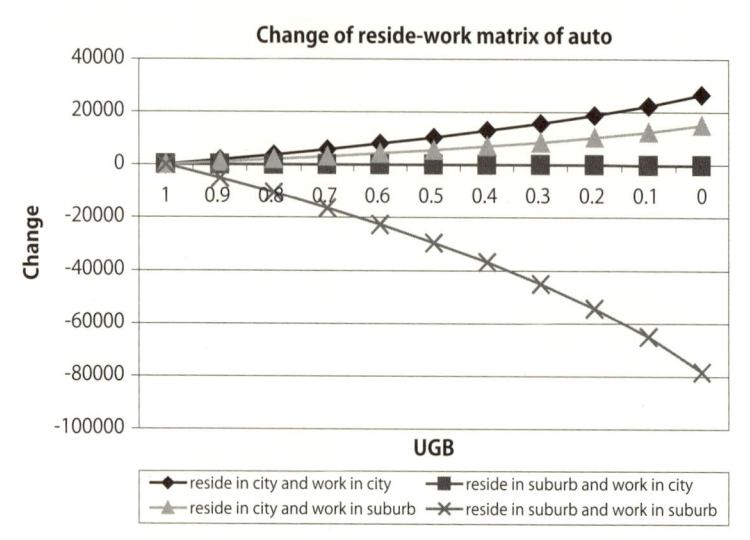

Change of reside-work matrix of auto

[Chart showing changes plotted against UGB from 1 to 0, with four series: reside in city and work in city; reside in suburb and work in city; reside in city and work in suburb; reside in suburb and work in suburb]

Figure 6.2.1 (c) Changes in commuting by car under the UGB policy.

part of the increment of city-to-city commuters as a whole. This is because not a small portion of the city-to-city commuting is by public transportation or the other mode, since it is convenient to use public transportation or the other mode for city-to-city commuting. When commuters switch their residence-workplace pair to the city-to-city pair from the other pairs, many of them do not choose car as their commuting mode. In other words, many suburb-to-suburb car commuters become city-to-city commuters by the non-auto modes. Hence, although the auto commuters increase in the city and decrease in the suburbs, auto commuting as a whole, decreases. Figures 6.2.1 (d) and 6.2.1 (e) show the impact of the UGB on commuting by public transportation and by the other mode, respectively. In both cases, only the suburb-to-suburb commuting decreases. The commuters of the other pairs increase, especially the city-to-city commuters by those modes increase more than do commuters on the other arrangements.

Figure 6.2.1 (f) shows the impact of the UGB on the average commuting time for each residence-to-work pair. As the UGB becomes tighter, the average commuting time increases in the city and decreases in the suburbs

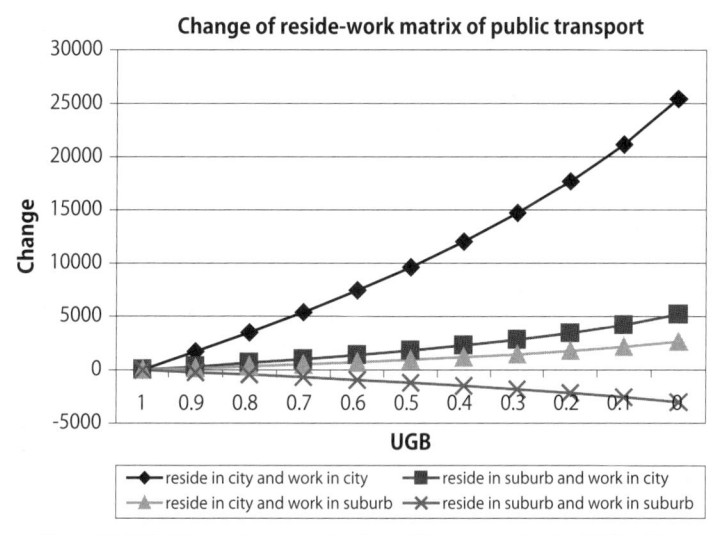

Figure 6.2.1 (d) Changes in commuting by public transit under the UGB policy.

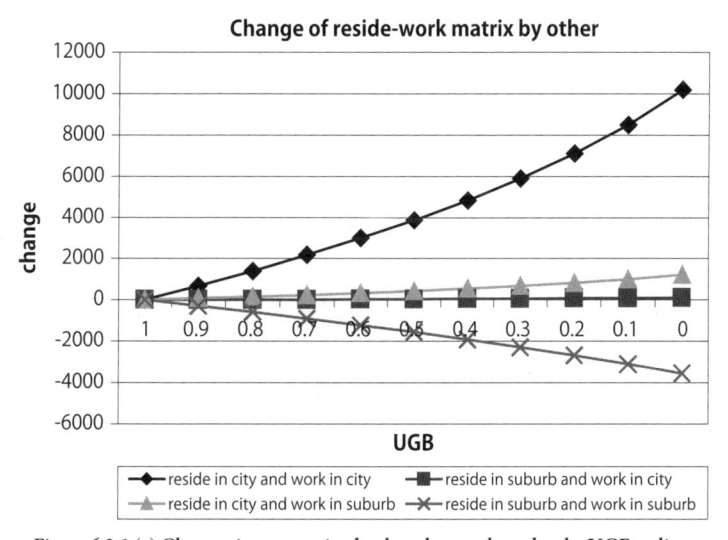

Figure 6.2.1 (e) Changes in commuting by the other mode under the UGB policy.

184   Simulation Analysis of Urban Economy

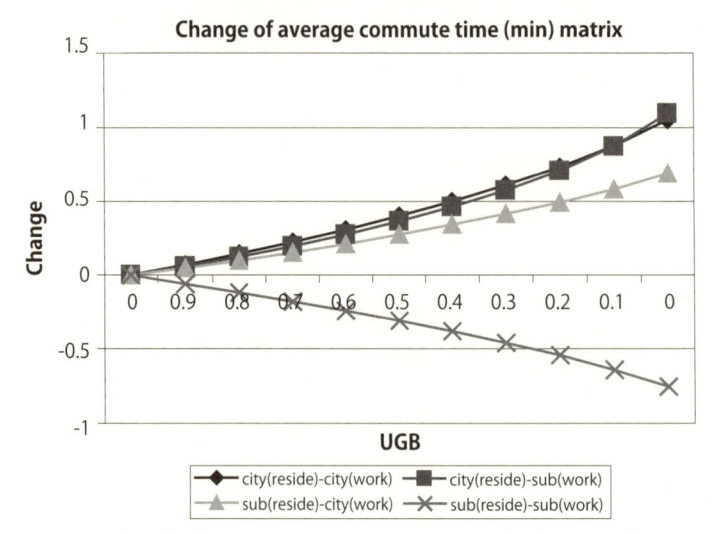

Figure 6.2.1(f) Changes in average commuting time under the UGB policy.

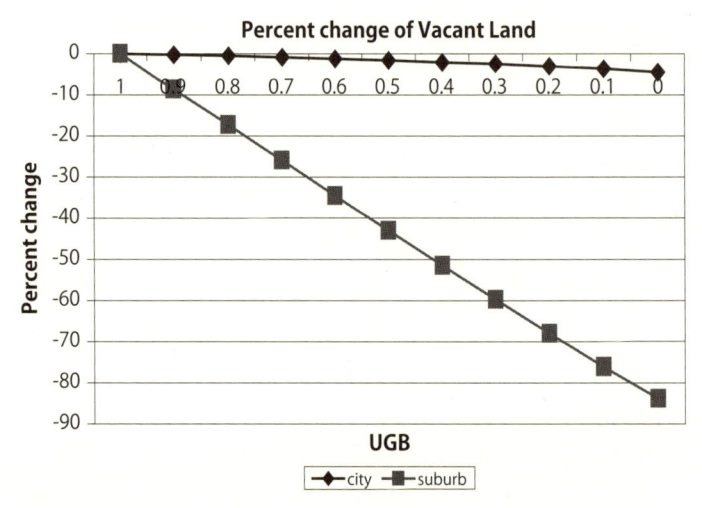

Figure 6.2.1(g) Percent change in available vacant land under the UGB policy.

although the change is not more than a maximum average of a minute or so. There are several reasons why the average commuting travel time in the city increases when jobs and population become more centralized in the city, by the UGB. The first is driving speed. As economic activities increase in the city, the roads become more congested and the driving speed decreases. The second reason is mode choice. Since the roads in city become more congested, the mode share of auto would decrease. As I have seen, in the RELU-TRAN2 model it is assumed that the travel time by public transportation and by the other mode, between the same zone pair are not subject to congestion and therefore remain constant. Travel by public transportation between most pairs of zones takes a longer time than the time it takes by auto. If the share of commuters by public transportation in the city increases because of the UGB, the average travel time increases. The third reason is the adjustment of the commuting patterns within the city. If the share of longer residence-workplace pairs increases, travel time would increase. If, for example, keeping the other variables constant, suppose that a CBD-to-CBD commuter becomes a CBD-to-City commuter by switching his job location to a city zone that is outside the CBD, then obviously, this could increase average travel time.

Figure 6.2.1 (g) shows the impact of the UGB on the available vacant land. The vacant land decreases in both the city and the suburbs. However, the decrease in the suburban vacant land is slower than the amount that would be implied by the UGB regulation. For example, when the UGB is 0.5 (that is 50% of the originally vacant land of the base case is available for new development), the available vacant land decreases by less than 50%. This is because, as the UGB restriction causes shifts in job and residence location demands, some of the existing buildings are demolished and become newly created vacant land. The vacant land decreases in the city, by infill and by redevelopment, as economic activities move from the suburbs to the city. Since the amount of vacant land in the city is limited, the decrease of vacant land in the city is small. In addition to the number of residents and the size of industries, the floor space demand by each resident and industry also affects the amount of vacant land. For example, when rent increases, the floor space demand per person decreases. Thus even if the population in a zone increases, the floor space demand in the zone would not increase as much. It is not impossible that the total floor space demand would decrease.

6.2.2 Impact of the UGB on fuel consumption and related variables

Figure 6.2.2 shows the impact of the UGB on fuel consumption and related variables. As more land in the suburbs is kept out of development by the UGB, more economic activity becomes centralized. The VMT, fuel consumption and CO_2 emissions decrease. Although I get this intuitive result, the opposite result could still occur an urban area where are suburban employment sub-centers. In such an urban area workers would commute to the sub-centers that are close to their home. The result on VMT, fuel and CO_2 would then depend on how the UGB restruction would affect such an urban arrangement. If the UGB caused everyone to squeeze closer in to their job location, VMT, fuel and CO_2 should decerease, but if the UGB makes this urban area more centralized by causing many suburban residents to move to the city and commute longer distances to suburban jobs, then the commuting distance possibly increases. In the result, the average car speed increased. Since, under the UGB, the congestion increases in the city

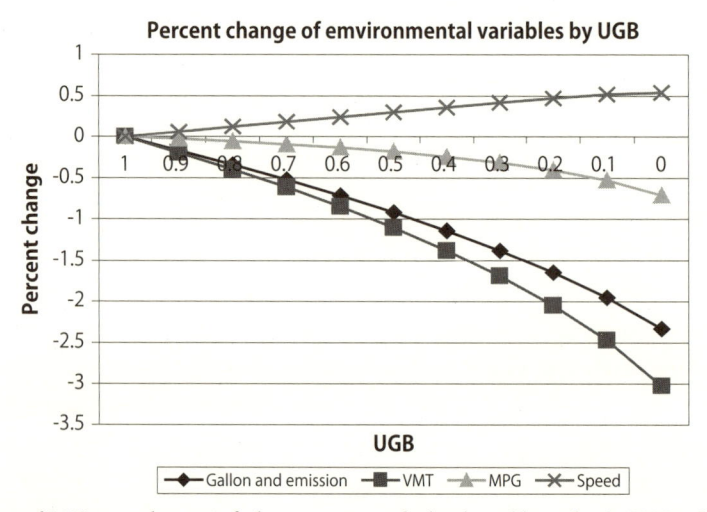

Figure 6.2.2 Percent changes in fuel consumption and related variables under the UGB policy.

(speed down), but decreases in the suburubs (speed up), the average speed could either increase or decrease. In this case, even though the average car speed increases, the MPG decreases because VMT decreases more than fuel consumption. One of the reasons is that the weight of traveling on more congested (low MPG) roads in city increases relatively to the weight of traveling on less congested (high MPG) roads in the suburbs. On some major suburban roads, MPG decreases as driving speed increases because the centralization of jobs and residences under the UGB reduces the suburban travel. On other suburban roads, MPG increases when congestion is reduced by the UGB. Nevertheless, the main reason for the reduction in fuel use and in related variables is due to the switching to transit that comes about, as shown earlier, because jobs and residences move to the city from the suburbs.

6.2.3. Impact of the UGB on the consumer's utility

To evaluate the welfare effects of a UGB policy, I observe sepratey the expected welfare of each income group and the changes in real estate values outside the UGB and in various areas and for building types, as needed, inside the CBD.

Impacts on the consumer's utility

Table 6.2.3 shows the impact of UGB tightness on some variables. UGB harms both the employed and the unemployed consumer's utility for all f types. Because the UGB stimulates the centralization population and jobs which encourages switching to public transit, as the UGB becomes tighter, the total travel time and the total travel money cost decrease. Since the UGB regulates the development of the vacant land, the available land becomes scearcer and floor rent increases. The percentage change of rent is faster in the suburbs where the UGB is implemented than it is in the city. Since rent increases, the producers substitute other inputs for floor space (and thus, indirectly, for land). Thus, labor demand would increase. On the labor supply side, the number of employed consumers increases slightly because travel time and cost decrease as shown. As Parry and Bento (2001) pointed out, higher commuting cost discourages consumers' labor force participation. In current model, the labor supply of each employed worker is asumed to be

Table 6.2.3 Impacts of the UGB on selected variables.

UGB tightness			0.9	0.8	0.7	0.6	0.5	0.4	0.3	0.2	0.1	0
UExpU (CU of employed)	% change	f=1	-0.023	-0.043	-0.062	-0.083	-0.105	-0.128	-0.153	-0.18	-0.211	-0.248
		f=2	-0.021	-0.039	-0.057	-0.077	-0.098	-0.119	-0.142	-0.168	-0.197	-0.232
		f=3	-0.02	-0.037	-0.055	-0.074	-0.093	-0.114	-0.137	-0.162	-0.19	-0.224
		f=4	-0.018	-0.034	-0.05	-0.068	-0.086	-0.105	-0.127	-0.15	-0.177	-0.21
UExpUUOLF (CU of unemployed)	% change	f=1	-0.062	-0.141	-0.226	-0.317	-0.415	-0.522	-0.64	-0.773	-0.927	-1.115
		f=2	-0.057	-0.13	-0.209	-0.293	-0.384	-0.482	-0.592	-0.715	-0.857	-1.031
		f=3	-0.053	-0.12	-0.193	-0.27	-0.354	-0.445	-0.546	-0.66	-0.791	-0.951
		f=4	-0.046	-0.104	-0.166	-0.233	-0.305	-0.384	-0.471	-0.569	-0.682	-0.82
Wage	% change	f=1	0.292	0.785	1.331	1.916	2.57	3.297	4.118	5.062	6.177	6.589
		f=2	0.303	0.803	1.356	1.948	2.61	3.346	4.175	5.129	6.254	6.677
		f=3	0.301	0.797	1.345	1.934	2.591	3.322	4.145	5.093	6.212	6.628
		f=4	0.298	0.79	1.333	1.916	2.568	3.292	4.108	5.049	6.159	6.567
wage (city)	% change	f=1	0.293	0.8	1.36	1.955	2.613	3.351	4.177	5.12	6.213	6.59
		f=2	0.328	0.858	1.448	2.067	2.764	3.532	4.396	5.385	6.535	6.976
		f=3	0.349	0.9	1.509	2.158	2.881	3.68	4.571	5.595	6.79	8.281
		f=4	0.372	0.947	1.579	2.253	3.002	3.83	4.757	5.817	6.056	8.605
wage (suburb)	% change	f=1	0.29	0.775	1.32	1.901	2.553	3.283	4.111	5.061	6.188	6.631
		f=2	0.288	0.768	1.295	1.871	2.506	3.22	4.024	4.953	6.056	6.465
		f=3	0.275	0.737	1.251	1.806	2.428	3.115	3.897	4.797	5.871	6.234
		f=4	0.262	0.712	1.212	1.749	2.352	3.023	3.783	4.661	5.703	6.035
Rent	% change	k=1	1.48	3.14	4.928	6.859	8.98	11.325	13.939	16.931	20.455	24.822
		k=2	0.731	1.563	2.441	3.384	4.403	5.508	6.718	8.078	9.637	11.515
		k=3	1.445	3.059	4.763	6.581	8.521	10.606	12.874	15.358	18.134	21.346
		k=4	1.439	3.04	4.727	6.517	8.433	10.484	12.704	15.14	16.86	21.001
rent (in city)	% change	k=1	0.711	1.573	2.521	3.545	4.682	5.943	6.364	9.013	10.956	13.421
		k=2	0.391	0.874	1.389	1.934	2.551	3.209	3.95	4.793	5.781	6.005
		k=3	0.422	0.954	1.531	2.153	2.818	3.573	4.394	5.326	6.414	6.767
		k=4	0.442	0.973	1.593	2.212	2.92	3.673	4.513	5.487	6.593	8.009
rent (suburb)	% change	k=1	1.708	3.616	5.669	6.898	10.352	13.078	16.133	19.646	23.807	28.995
		k=2	1.076	2.285	3.557	4.936	6.421	8.048	9.835	11.845	14.157	16.941
		k=3	2.115	4.465	6.996	9.725	12.672	15.907	19.469	23.427	26.928	33.207
		k=4	2.116	4.529	6.074	9.818	12.826	16.099	19.702	23.736	28.298	33.686
price	% change	r=1	0.24	0.646	1.089	1.562	2.078	2.639	3.269	3.984	4.813	5.841
		r=2	0.514	1.2	1.94	2.73	3.589	4.52	5.555	6.72	8.058	9.685
		r=3	0.351	0.872	1.438	2.047	2.714	3.441	4.259	5.19	6.273	6.615
		r=4	0.44	1.066	1.744	2.473	3.271	4.14	5.116	6.226	6.515	9.109
price (city)	% change	r=1	0.274	0.75	1.269	1.827	2.441	3.108	3.862	4.722	5.72	6.956
		r=2	0.282	0.729	1.214	1.736	2.309	2.93	3.631	4.427	5.351	6.492
		r=3	0.251	0.674	1.134	1.629	2.174	2.765	3.433	4.193	5.074	6.165
		r=4	0.356	0.899	1.488	2.12	2.813	3.565	4.411	5.372	6.484	6.855
price (Suburb)	% change	r=1	0.234	0.629	1.059	1.518	2.018	2.561	3.171	3.863	4.664	5.659
		r=2	0.606	1.391	2.237	3.145	4.133	5.209	6.407	6.759	9.317	11.217
		r=3	0.405	0.98	1.604	2.276	3.013	3.817	4.722	5.754	6.956	8.451
		r=4	0.486	1.156	1.883	2.666	3.522	4.457	5.507	6.702	8.094	9.818
TTT (total travel time)	% change		-0.09	-0.178	-0.264	-0.354	-0.444	-0.53	-0.622	-0.714	-0.802	-0.88
TTC (total travel cost)	% change		-0.119	-0.238	-0.363	-0.497	-0.64	-0.792	-0.961	-1.153	-1.377	-1.66

the time left over after subtracting total traveling time from the consumer's full time endowment. Thus, as the UGB in the model decreases total travel time the labor supply increaes somewhat. But the impact from labor demand is stronger than is the impact from the labor supply in the result, and the equilibrium wage increases. The price of the retail good also increases because input prices, that is wages and rents, increase. As a result of these effects, the UGB harms the consumer's utility, because although the higher wage and the lower travel time benefit the employed consumers, the other negarive effects, primarily the higher rents, are more powerful.

An important variation of the UGB policy that has been studies in the literature, treats the UGB policy in a context in which consumers have a positive preference for the additional open space created by the UGB. Anas and Rhee (2006), Bento et al. (2006), and Ng (2007) have examined a UGB in their models which incorporated a preference for open space. It is shown by Bento et al. (2006) that the UGB, coupled with the property tax is a welfare-improving policy if consumers have preferences for the open space created by the UGB. Anas and Rhee (2006) and Ng (2007) show that a welfare loss is caused by UGB, if the consumers do not value the open space[27].

Impact on real estate values

Since the UGB prohibits the development of vacant land, thus keeping those lands vacant in perpetuity, there are two very different effects of the UGB on land asset values. On the one hand, as shown the floor rents inside the UGB increase and obviously the land inside the UGB which can continue to be developed or redeveloped, gains value. On the other hand, the land outside the UGB permanently loses value because the option to develop that land in the future has been made worthless by the UGB. Therefore, for vacant land situated inside the UGB I continue to use the land asset price equation of Chapter 3 in valuing it. Thus,

---

[27] The possible importance of agglomeration economics in production should also should be noted. In Ng (2007), in addition to the preferences for open space, the presence of agglomeraiton economics in the production function are also treated. If the economy has such agglomeration economics, the UGB can increase consumer utility if it causes jobs to centralize in the city which would enhance the positive externality due to agglomeration.

$$V_{i0} = \frac{1}{\Phi_{i0}} \ln\left(\exp\left(\Phi_{i0}\tilde{\Pi}_{i00}\right) + \sum_{s=1...\aleph} \exp\left(\Phi_{i0}\tilde{\Pi}_{i0s}\right)\right) + \sum_{y=1}^{year} \left(\left(\frac{1}{1+\rho}\right)^{y-1} R_{i0}\right).$$

For the land situated outside the UGB, the post-UGB probability of developing it into any kind of building is zero, while the probability of keeping it vacant land becomes unity, under the assumption that the UGB is policy is permanent and all market agents understand that.

$$Q_{i0k}^{UGB}(V_{i0}^{UGB}, V_{i1}, ..., V_{i\aleph}) = \begin{cases} \dfrac{0}{\exp\left(\Phi_{i0}\tilde{\Pi}_{i0}^{UGB}\right) + 0} = 0 & \text{if } k > 0 \\ \dfrac{\exp\left(\Phi_{i0}\tilde{\Pi}_{i0}^{UGB}\right)}{\exp\left(\Phi_{i0}\tilde{\Pi}_{i0}^{UGB}\right) + 0} = 1 & \text{if } k = 0 \end{cases}$$

where $\Pi_{i00}^{UGB} = \tilde{\Pi}_{i00}^{UGB} + \varsigma_{i00} = \left(\frac{1}{1+\rho}\right)^5 V_{i0}^{UGB} - \mathbb{C}_{i00} + \varsigma_{i00}$. For investors in vacant land, the expected economic profit known from the logit calculus and which I had derived in Chapter 2, is

$$E\left[\max\left(\Pi_{i00}, \Pi_{i0k}; k=1...\aleph\right)\right] = \frac{1}{\Phi_{i0}} \ln\left(\exp\left(\Phi_{i0}\tilde{\Pi}_{i00}\right)\right) = \tilde{\Pi}_{i00}.$$

The economic profit discounted to the beginning of the model's 5-year development period is as follows, (where the annual rent and the 5-year period's end value are discounted to the present and the period's maintenance cost is subtracted):

$$V_{i0}^{UGB} = \tilde{\Pi}_{i00} + \sum_{y=1}^{5}\left(\left(\frac{1}{1+\rho}\right)^{y-1} R_{i0}\right)$$

$$= \left(\frac{1}{1+\rho}\right)^5 V_{i0}^{UGB} - \mathbb{C}_{i00} + \sum_{y=1}^{5}\left(\left(\frac{1}{1+\rho}\right)^{y-1} R_{i0}\right).$$

By solving this, the stationary-state value of the vacant land that is kept out of development by the UGB is

$$V_{i0}^{UGB} = \frac{-\mathbb{C}_{i00} + \sum_{y=1}^{5}\left(\left(\frac{1}{1+\rho}\right)^{y-1} R_{i0}\right)}{1-\left(\frac{1}{1+\rho}\right)^{5}}.$$

Thus, by denoting that the stock of vacant land excluded from development under the UGB as S_{i0}^{UGB}, and the stock of land (vacant plus built-up) not excluded under the UGB as S_{i0}, the total value is $\sum_{i=1}^{I}\left(V_{i0}^{UGB} S_{i0}^{UGB} + \sum_{k=0}^{K} V_{ik} S_{ik}\right)$. Since excluding the vacant land from development reduces its value, $V_{i0}^{UGB} < V_{i0}$. Thus if nothing else changed, the total value of vacant land would be decreased by any UGB. But since the available land becomes scarce, the building space inside the UGB decreases and the value of the building space increases. In the new stationary equilibrium that will hold after the UGB is implemented, the construction and the demolition flows of each building type will be equal. When the available land decreases, construction decreases keeping other variables (especially, the construction probability) constant. Summing up those two effects, total value could be decreased or increased by the UGB.

The Figures 6.2.3 (a) and (b) show the impact of the UGB on the average value of k type stock in the city and the suburbs, respectively. All types of building values in both the city and the suburb increase as the UGB's tightness increases. The value of the vacant land not excluded by the UGB also increases in all zones. As noted, the value of all the land that is excluded by the UGB must decrease. Thus each suburban zone's vacant land has two parts: a constant amount that is excluded by the UGB and loses its option value and a part that is not excluded by the UGB and still remains vacant post-UGB, that gains value. The avergae or aggregate vacant land value in

Percent change of average value in city

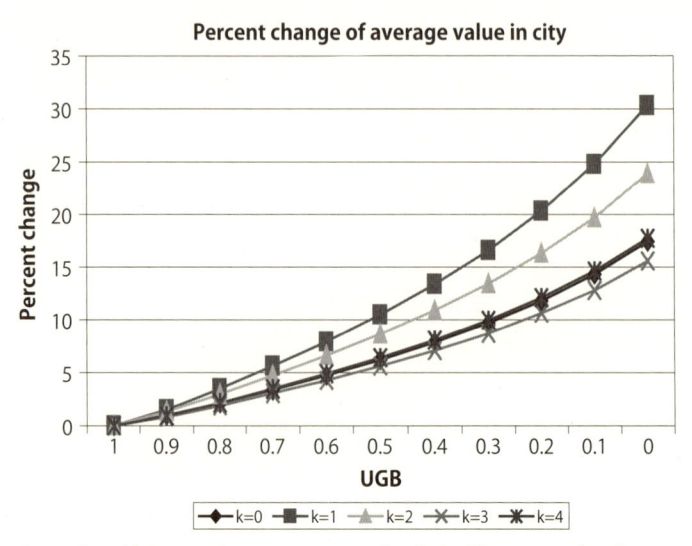

[Chart showing percent change curves for k=0, k=1, k=2, k=3, k=4 across UGB values from 1 to 0]

Figure 6.2.3 (a) Percent changes in average values by building type within the city.

a zone can therefore increase or decrease. It turns out that the average value of vacant land in the suburbs decreases. This is because the available vacant land that has relatively higher value in some suburban zones becomes more developed than the available vacant land that has relatively lower value in other suburban zones. When the vacant land is excluded by the UGB, its aggregate value decreases by 66.9%. More residents than jobs move into the city, and so the value of housing space increase more than the value of business office space, while in the suburbs the value of business office space increases faster than the value of housing space.

Figures 6.2.3 (c) and (d) show these impacts of the UGB on total value, in percent changes and in dollar amount changes, respectively. These impacts are shown for the city and for the suburbs, and in the case of the latter they are shown by including or not the vacant land excluded from development by the UGB.

The total value of the vacant land excluded by the UGB increases as the UGB becomes tighter. Since the value of the vacant land excluded by the UGB is constant, the total value of this vacant land increases proportionaly

Chapter 6 193

Percent change of average value in suburb

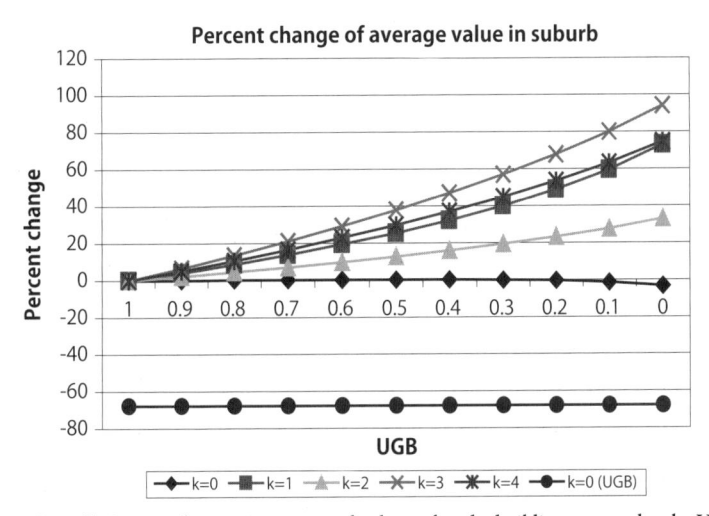

Figure 6.2.3 (b) Percent changes in average suburban values by building type under the UGB policy.

Percent change of total value

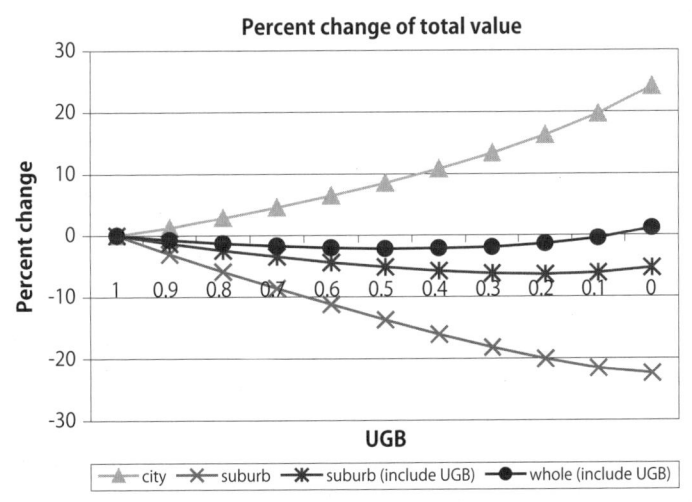

Figure 6.2.3 (c) Percent change in total real estate values under the UGB policy.

Change of total value

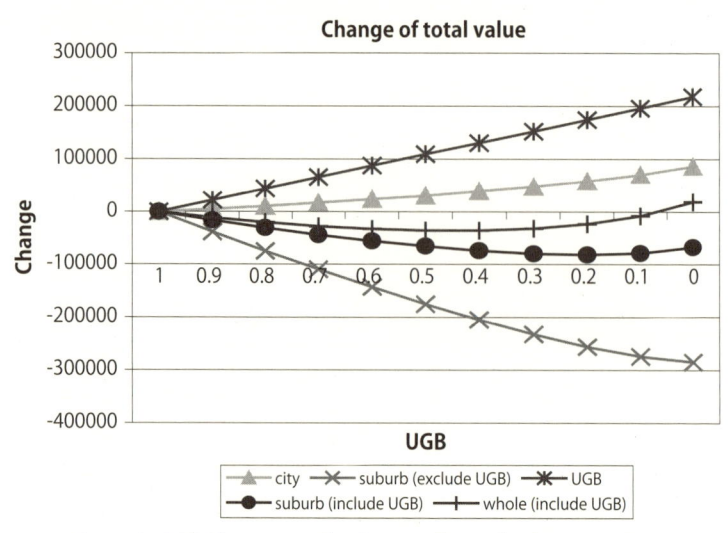

[Chart showing change in total value across UGB values from 1 to 0, with five series: city, suburb (exclude UGB), UGB, suburb (include UGB), whole (include UGB). Y-axis labeled "Change" ranges from -400000 to 300000.]

Figure 6.2.3 (d) Change in total real estate values under the UGB policy.

to the UGB's tightness. Although the value of each building type increases per unit floor space, the total avairable land used by that building decreases as the UGB becomes tighter. The total value of all land decreases and then increases as the UGB becomes tighter. The reason for this is that since the same population and production must be accommodated on less and less land as the UGB becomes tighter, eventually the land not excluded by the UGB becomes extremely scarce and valuable and the increase in its value outweighs the loss of option value for the land that remains outside the UGB.

6.3 Local growth controls

The UGB such as that in Portland, Oregon is a device that is applied at the metropolitan level. But since the metropolitan areas are composed of communities and townships, or counties that normally control land use within their jurisdictions, policies similar to the UGB can exist at those lower levels. A particular county or township could decide to exclude additional development. This type of policy is known as a "local growth control." It is, equivalently, a UGB policy that affects only some parts of the metropolitan land market but not the whole. I will refer to this as a local-UGB. It is possible to examine the impact of a local-UGB that could be imposed in any one of suburban zones. I pick zone 10 and examine the impacts of imposing a UGB only on this zone. Zone 10 has the highest concentration of jobs in the suburbs and includes the well-known city of Schaumburg, Illinois a famous edge city or suburban jobs center. After the CBD, zone 10 is the second highest job zone in the modeled region. Zone 10 also has the highest residential population in the suburbs and the second highest in the region after zone 1 which is in the city.

When the local-UGB is imposed on zone 10, both jobs and residential population decrease in zone 10. Residence decrease more rapidly than do jobs and the difference between jobs and residents becomes smaller as a result. The jobs and the residential population that leave zone 10, moves to both the city and to the other suburban zones. Thus I can observe the partial centralization of jobs and population in the city, even when imposing a local-UGB on a suburban zone.

Figure 6.3 (a) shows the impact of the local-UGB on zone 10 on the

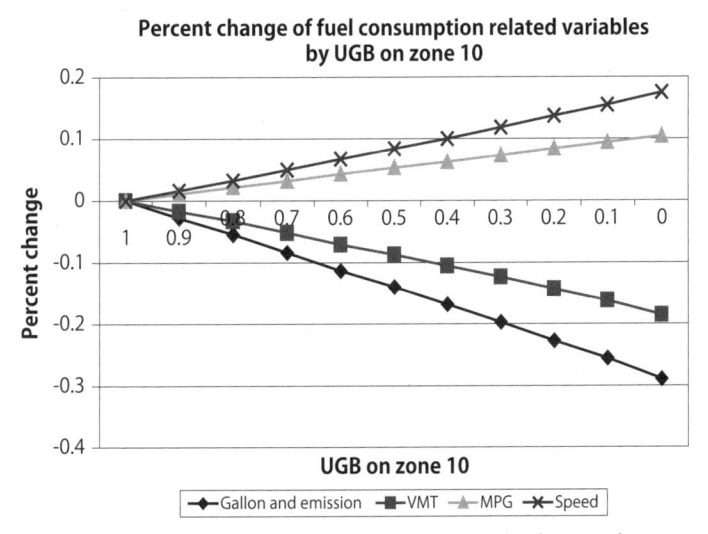

Figure 6.3 (a) Percent change in fuel and related variables under the local-UGB policy in zone 10.

Table 6.3 (a) Effects of the local-UGB in zone 10 on residents and jobs.

	UGB in zone 10		0.8	0.6	0.4	0.2	0
Jobs	change	CBD	465	1,019	1,593	2,225	2,915
		City ex-CBD	893	1,935	3,041	4,249	5,581
		City	1,357	2,954	4,635	6,474	8,496
		Suburb	-1,348	-2,926	-4,581	-6,390	-8,376
		zone 10	-3,397	-7,506	-11,810	-16,550	-21,770
Residents	change	CBD	76	157	245	342	451
		City ex-CBD	2,167	4,463	6,910	9,609	12,620
		City	2,242	4,620	7,156	9,951	13,071
		Suburb	-2,242	-4,620	-7,156	-9,951	-13,071
		zone 10	-6,658	-13,973	-21,803	-30,575	-40,368

fuel consumption related variables. As the local-UGB on zone 10 becomes tighter and the city is draws in more jobs and population, and VMT, fuel consumption and CO_2 emissions decrease. Speed and MPG increase.

Table 6.3 (a) and (b) shows the impact of the local-UGB on zone 10 on residents and jobs, and selected variables, respectively. All consumers' utilities decrease with a tighter UGB. Total travel time and money cost decreases. Rent increases in the city, in the suburbs, especially in zone 10, because of scarceness of the local available land. Figure 6.3 (b) shows the impact on the wage in zone 10. Because of the UGB, some jobs move out and the labor demand and supply both decrease. At the same time, the producers in zone 10 substitute land for labor. In the city and the suburbs, the wage increases. In zone 10, the impact of the local-UGB on wage is different by labor's type f. Output price increases in the city, the suburbs and zone 10, reflecting the higher input prices. Although the wages increase or decrease by different f in zone 10, the effect of increment of rent is stronger and reduce utility.

Figures 6.3 (c) and (d) shows the impact of the UGB in zone 10 on average and total value, respectively. When the vacant land is restricted by UGB in zone 10, it's value decreases by 53.6%. The value of all kinds of buildings ($k=0,1,...,4$) increase, excluding the vacant land under local-UGB. The total value across all zones increases. The exception is the total value of zone 10 when it excludes the restricted vacant land.

Table 6.3 (b) Effects of the local-UGB in zone 10 on selected variables.

UGB in zone 10			0.8	0.6	0.4	0.2	0
UExpU	% change	f = 1	-0.008	-0.015	-0.021	-0.027	-0.033
(CU of employed)		f = 2	-0.007	-0.014	-0.019	-0.025	-0.031
		f = 3	-0.007	-0.014	-0.019	-0.026	-0.032
		f = 4	-0.007	-0.013	-0.019	-0.026	-0.033
UExpUUOLF	% change	f = 1	-0.015	-0.036	-0.061	-0.091	-0.124
(CU of unemployed)		f = 2	-0.014	-0.034	-0.058	-0.086	-0.118
		f = 3	-0.014	-0.033	-0.056	-0.083	-0.113
		f = 4	-0.013	-0.031	-0.051	-0.076	-0.104
wage	% change	f = 1	0.043	0.150	0.312	0.510	0.747
		f = 2	0.048	0.161	0.327	0.529	0.769
		f = 3	0.045	0.154	0.316	0.512	0.747
		f = 4	0.040	0.141	0.295	0.483	0.708
Wage (city)	% change	f = 1	0.053	0.169	0.347	0.560	0.809
		f = 2	0.060	0.191	0.369	0.590	0.846
		f = 3	0.062	0.199	0.384	0.609	0.874
		f = 4	0.069	0.208	0.400	0.627	0.895
Wage (suburb)	% change	f = 1	0.035	0.141	0.290	0.484	0.713
		f = 2	0.042	0.144	0.300	0.492	0.720
		f = 3	0.036	0.129	0.280	0.457	0.679
		f = 4	0.026	0.109	0.245	0.413	0.616
wage (zone 10)	% change	f = 1	0.010	0.050	0.140	0.270	0.440
		f = 2	-0.030	-0.040	0.000	0.070	0.170
		f = 3	-0.080	-0.140	-0.150	-0.140	-0.110
		f = 4	-0.120	-0.240	-0.310	-0.370	-0.400
Rent	% change	k = 1	0.474	1.006	1.596	2.254	2.982
		k = 2	0.263	0.559	0.892	1.261	1.675
		k = 3	0.291	0.610	0.984	1.384	1.826
		k = 4	0.300	0.619	0.987	1.382	1.815
Rent (city)	% change	k = 1	0.171	0.417	0.711	1.052	1.450
		k = 2	0.103	0.237	0.401	0.586	0.802
		k = 3	0.111	0.266	0.466	0.688	0.932
		k = 4	0.133	0.265	0.487	0.708	0.929
Rent (suburb)	% change	k = 1	0.561	1.179	1.852	2.606	3.440
		k = 2	0.418	0.880	1.387	1.948	2.570
		k = 3	0.398	0.850	1.338	1.880	2.458
		k = 4	0.397	0.860	1.388	1.917	2.512
Rent (zone 10)	% change	k = 1	2.299	4.895	6.843	11.311	15.411
		k = 2	1.521	3.220	5.112	6.289	9.785
		k = 3	3.036	6.471	10.345	14.820	20.015
		k = 4	3.200	6.821	10.905	15.628	21.119
price	% change	r = 1	0.049	0.150	0.288	0.457	0.654
		r = 2	0.136	0.340	0.579	0.858	1.173
		r = 3	0.084	0.226	0.406	0.622	0.873
		r = 4	0.108	0.283	0.498	0.754	1.050
Price (city)	% change	r = 1	0.047	0.160	0.314	0.503	0.727
		r = 2	0.057	0.170	0.317	0.497	0.706
		r = 3	0.046	0.149	0.287	0.457	0.656
		r = 4	0.077	0.219	0.400	0.617	0.870
Price (suburb)	% change	r = 1	0.049	0.149	0.284	0.449	0.642
		r = 2	0.168	0.407	0.683	1.002	1.361
		r = 3	0.104	0.268	0.470	0.712	0.991
		r = 4	0.125	0.318	0.552	0.829	1.148
price (zone 10)	% change	r = 1	0.100	0.200	0.330	0.480	0.640
		r = 2	0.560	1.250	2.020	2.900	3.900
		r = 3	0.280	0.620	1.020	1.480	2.010
		r = 4	0.260	0.580	0.960	1.400	1.910

198　Simulation Analysis of Urban Economy

Percent change of wage in zone 10

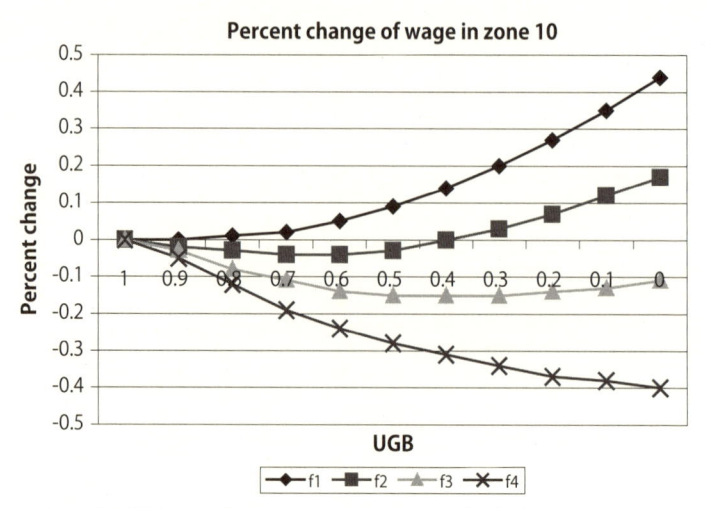

Figure 6.3 (b) Percent change in wages in zone 10 under the local-UGB policy.

Percent change of value (zone 10)

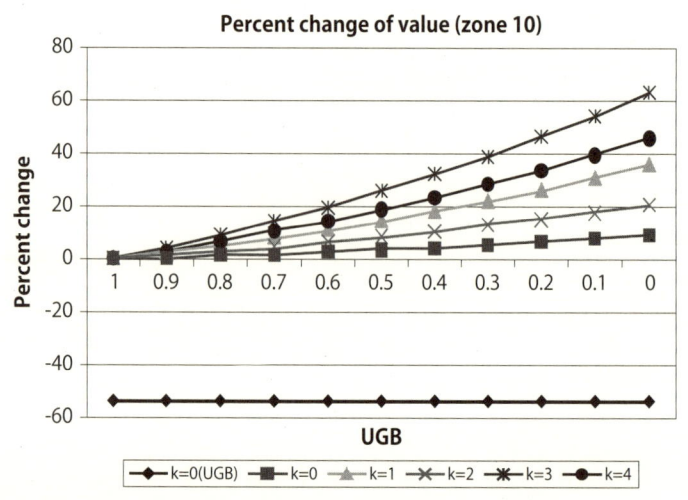

Figure 6.3 (c) Percent changes in the real estate values of zone 10 under the local-UGB policy.

Percent change of total value

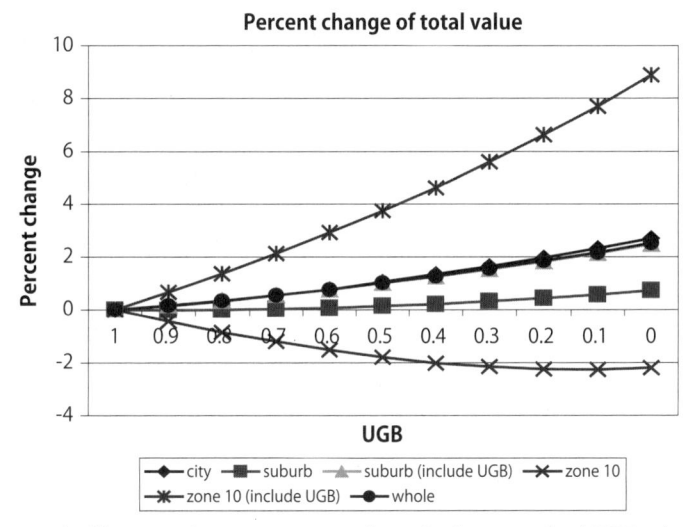

[Chart showing percent change vs UGB (from 1 to 0) with series: city, suburb, suburb (include UGB), zone 10, zone 10 (include UGB), whole]

Figure 6.3 (d) Percent changes in aggregate value under the zone 10 local-UGB policy.

6.4 Comparing the effects of quasi-Pigouvian congestion tolling and the UGB

I compare the effects of the UGB to the effects of the quasi-Pigouvian congestion toll that was studied in Chapter 5. Throughout this comparison, I focus on a UGB that is imposed in all the suburbs, and the quasi-Pigouvian toll that quasi-internalizes both the time delay and the fuel consumption externalities and that is imposed on all roads.

The UGB does not directly increase the monetary cost of car trips but the quasi-Pigouvian toll does. If the travel monetary cost of a particular car-trip arrangement is increased by the UGB, it is because congestion increases in the city and fuel consumption becomes less efficient. In the result, the centralization that is caused by UGB makes trips shorter and total travel cost decreases. Although the UGB leads to centralization, it does not aim to reduce congestion. The UGB makes people moves to the congested area (Anas and Rhee, 2007). As a result the congestion increases inside the UGB in the zones that were congested, but the congestion decreases inside the UGB in the zones that were not congested. The travel time would decrease because travel distances become shorter on average, as centralization of jobs and residences occurs.

The table 6.4 (a), (b) and (c) show the impacts of the UGB and the quasi-Pigouvian toll on jobs, residents and vacant land, fuel consumption related variables and selected variables when not be distributed. The quasi-Pigouvian toll removes the externality of congestion and the congestion becomes close to the first-best optimal level in all the roads. Under the quasi-Pigouvian toll, the travel time becomes shorter as expected. Centralization also works toward the reduction of travel time. The UGB reduces the available land but the quasi-Pigouvian toll takes money from drivers. Under the UGB, since available land becomes scarce, rent increases. Producers would substitute labor for land thus increasing their demands for labor. Wage could increase even though the labor supply increases. Labor supply increases, because travel time decreases and the number of employed consumers increases. Since rents and wages increase, output prices increase. Under the quasi-Pigouvian toll, the labor supply increases even though employed consumers decrease, because the travel time decreases as consumers react to the tolls by economizing on travel. Producers substitute labor for land and this would cause rent to decrease. Since input prices decreases, the output prices to decrease.

The employed consumer's utility decreases under both the UGB and the quasi-Pigouvian toll, but the unemployed consumer's utility decreases under the UGB and increases under the quasi-Pigouvian toll. Available vacant land decreases under the UGB and increases under the quasi-Pigouvian toll. The total real estate value shows a different result only when the UGB is very tight than when it is looser. Value falls under the quasi-Pigouvian toll and under the loose UGB, but increases under the tight UGB. When the land becomes very scarce, the value of available land increases by more than the reduction in the value of the land excluded from development. VMT, fuel consumption and CO_2 emissions decrease and speed increases under both policies. Under the UGB, MPG would decrease in the city and increase in the suburbs. Overall, average MPG decreases. More importantly, travel increases in the city where the MPG is low and decreases in the suburbs where the MPG is high. The

Table 6.4 (a) Effects of the UGB and quasi-Pigouvian toll (revenue non-distribution and distribution) on jobs, residents and vacant land.

			UGB 0.8	0.6	0.4	0.2	0	QPT (non dist)	QPT (dist)
Jobs	change	CBD	3,303	7,089	11,448	16,769	23,999	12,484	12,503
		City ex CBD	5,934	12,722	20,598	30,176	43,235	5,112	5,893
		City	9,237	19,810	32,045	46,945	67,235	17,596	18,396
		Suburb	-9,113	-19,515	-31,547	-46,195	-66,138	-19,721	-19,723
Residents	change	CBD	534	1,131	1,822	2,667	3,835	3,885	3,773
		City ex CBD	14,837	31,534	51,049	75,017	108,377	40,343	32,494
		City	15,371	32,665	52,871	77,684	112,211	44,228	36,268
		Suburb	-15,371	-32,665	-52,871	-77,684	-112,211	-44,228	-36,268
Vacant Land	change	CBD	-12.604	-28.745	-48.065	-72.166	-105.957	80.211	21.624
(acer)		City ex CBD	-80.443	-181.112	-301.417	-452.316	-663.893	602.260	228.798
		City	-93.047	-209.857	-349.482	-524.482	-769.85	682.471	250.422
		Suburb	-203,908	-406,666	-606,859	-802,620	-989,049	53,210	22,894
Vacant Land	%change	CBD	-0.692	-1.578	-2.638	-3.961	-5.816	4.403	1.187
(acer)		City ex CBD	-0.527	-1.187	-1.975	-2.964	-4.351	3.947	1.499
		City	-0.545	-1.229	-2.046	-3.07	-4.507	3.995	1.466
		Suburb	-16.297	-34.496	-51.477	-68.083	-83.897	4.514	1.942

Table 6.4 (b) Effects of the UGB and quasi-Pigouvian toll (revenue non-distribution and distribution) on fuel consumption related variables.

		UGB 0.8	0.6	0.4	0.2	0	QPT (non dist)	QPT (dist)
Gallon and Emission	% change	-0.343	-0.715	-1.137	-1.645	-2.329	-17.112	-14.793
VMT	% change	-0.399	-0.849	-1.378	-2.044	-3.025	-13.633	-11.643
MPG	% change	-0.057	-0.135	-0.244	-0.406	-0.712	4.198	3.697
Speed	% change	0.121	0.241	0.359	0.473	0.541	10.763	9.420
Ineff	% change	0.013	0.028	0.045	0.066	0.092	-0.056	0.018
TTT (total travel time)	% change	-0.178	-0.354	-0.530	-0.714	-0.880	-11.208	-6.844
TTC (total trael cost)	% change	-0.238	-0.497	-0.792	-1.153	-1.660	74.776	82.722

fuel externality part of the quasi-Pigouvian toll works toward improving MPG, while the time-delay externality part of the quasi-Pigouvian toll also works toward improving MPG in most cases. As the result, average MPG increases, although excessive centralization could decrease average MPG. The total real estate value is affected by changes in rents and stocks. Under the

202 Simulation Analysis of Urban Economy

Table 6.4 (c) Effects of the UGB and quasi-Pigouvian toll (revenue non-distribution and distribution) on selected variables.

			UGB					QPT No dist	QPT dist
			0.8	0.6	0.4	0.2	0		
Revenue per cap								1,173.11	1,246.748
UExpU	% change	f = 1	-0.043	-0.083	-0.128	-0.180	-0.248	-1.367	-0.518
(CU of employed)		f = 2	-0.039	-0.077	-0.119	-0.168	-0.232	-1.099	-0.506
		f = 3	-0.037	-0.074	-0.114	-0.162	-0.224	-0.907	-0.457
		f = 4	-0.034	-0.068	-0.105	-0.150	-0.210	-0.599	-0.333
UExpUUOLF	% change	f = 1	-0.141	-0.317	-0.522	-0.773	-1.115	0.443	0.802
(CU of unemployed)		f = 2	-0.130	-0.293	-0.482	-0.715	-1.031	0.386	0.455
		f = 3	-0.120	-0.270	-0.445	-0.660	-0.951	0.365	0.296
		f = 4	-0.104	-0.233	-0.384	-0.569	-0.820	0.313	0.088
wage	% change	f = 1	0.785	1.916	3.297	5.062	6.589	-15.667	-8.551
		f = 2	0.803	1.948	3.346	5.129	6.677	-15.711	-8.64
		f = 3	0.797	1.934	3.322	5.093	6.628	-15.750	-8.719
		f = 4	0.790	1.916	3.292	5.049	6.567	-15.736	-8.772
wage (city)	% change	f = 1	0.800	1.955	3.351	5.120	6.590	-16.194	-9.048
		f = 2	0.858	2.067	3.532	5.385	6.976	-16.084	-8.947
		f = 3	0.900	2.158	3.680	5.595	8.281	-15.963	-8.873
		f = 4	0.947	2.253	3.830	5.817	8.605	-15.853	-8.823
wage (suburb)	% change	f = 1	0.775	1.901	3.283	5.061	6.631	-15.377	-8.283
		f = 2	0.768	1.871	3.220	4.953	6.465	-15.494	-8.467
		f = 3	0.737	1.806	3.115	4.797	6.234	-15.639	-8.636
		f = 4	0.712	1.749	3.023	4.661	6.035	-15.684	-8.752
Rent	% change	k = 1	3.140	6.859	11.325	16.931	24.822	-8.426	-3.516
		k = 2	1.563	3.384	5.508	8.078	11.515	-6.247	-2.375
		k = 3	3.059	6.581	10.606	15.358	21.346	-8.295	-3.771
		k = 4	3.040	6.517	10.484	15.140	21.001	-8.596	-3.983
rent (city)	% change	k = 1	1.573	3.545	5.943	9.013	13.421	-11.809	-4.009
		k = 2	0.874	1.934	3.209	4.793	6.005	-6.706	-2.098
		k = 3	0.954	2.153	3.573	5.326	6.767	-6.125	-2.219
		k = 4	0.973	2.212	3.673	5.487	8.009	-6.726	-2.876
rent (suburb)	% change	k = 1	3.616	6.898	13.078	19.646	28.995	-6.281	-3.264
		k = 2	2.285	4.936	8.048	11.845	16.941	-5.585	-2.401
		k = 3	4.465	9.725	15.907	23.427	33.207	-9.418	-4.519
		k = 4	4.529	9.818	16.099	23.736	33.686	-9.686	-4.595
Price	% change	r = 1	0.646	1.562	2.639	3.984	5.841	-9.384	-4.18
		r = 2	1.200	2.730	4.520	6.720	9.685	-6.653	-2.92
		r = 3	0.872	2.047	3.441	5.190	6.615	-6.863	-3.057
		r = 4	1.066	2.473	4.140	6.226	9.109	-5.693	-0.397
price (city)	% change	r = 1	0.750	1.827	3.108	4.722	6.956	-10.189	-4.696
		r = 2	0.729	1.736	2.930	4.427	6.492	-6.729	-3.084
		r = 3	0.674	1.629	2.765	4.193	6.165	-8.188	-3.44
		r = 4	0.899	2.120	3.565	5.372	6.855	-6.459	-1.296
price (Suburb)	% change	r = 1	0.629	1.518	2.561	3.863	5.659	-9.247	-4.094
		r = 2	1.391	3.145	5.209	6.759	11.217	-6.623	-2.855
		r = 3	0.980	2.276	3.817	5.754	8.451	-6.685	-2.847
		r = 4	1.156	2.666	4.457	6.702	9.818	-5.266	0.107
Total value per cap									
(exclude UGB)	change		-64,301	-119,864	-165,935	-197,453	-198,811	-44,529	-20,523
(include UGB)	change		-20,750	-32,762	-35,282	-23,249	18,944	-44,529	-20,523
Annual gain from total value per capita									
(exclude UGB)	change		-526.23	-982.796	-1,360.543	-1,618.966	-1,630.102	-1,712.671	-789.364
(Include UGB)	change		-170.134	-268.623	-289.285	-190.622	155.330	-1,712.671	-789.364

UGB, the stock decreases and the rent increases. The total real estate value decreases when the UGB is not tight and it increases when the UGB is tight. Under the quasi-Pigouvian toll, the effect of reduced rent is larger and the total real estate value decreases.

Redistributing the revenue of the quasi-Pigouvian toll

The government gains revenue from the quasi-Pigouvian toll. By using this revenue in a variety of ways, the consumer's welfare should be improved. The government could invest the revenue in public goods, to improve public transport, to add road capacity or some other way. See, for example, Parry and Bento (2001) for revenue usage possibilities. I simply redistribute the revenue from the quasi-Pigouvian policy equally to all consumers.

The two columns from the left in table 6.4 (a), (b) and (c) show the impact of the quasi-Pigouvian toll on jobs, residents and vacant land, and selected variables when revenue is not distributed and distributed. The annual revenue of quasi-Pigouvian toll per RELU consumer is $1,173. If this revenue is distributed, the annual revenue per capita becomes $1,246. Thus the revenue increases when the revenue is redistributed due to the income effects of the redistributed revenue on traveling. If the revenue from the policy is distributed equally to all consumers, consumers spend this additional income on consumption goods, on housing, or on vehicle costs. When the goods consumption increases, non-work trips also increase. Since non-work travel increases, a part of the redistributed revenue is again paid for tolls.

As a result of the increased non-work travel, the congestion increases compared to the case when the revenue is not redistributed. The toll price would increase because of the higher congestion that prevails compared to the case of the non-distribution of revenue. Through consumers' reaction to the revenue distribution, other variables are changed. Because the amount of travel and the congestion increase, when the revenue is redistributed, total travel time increases from the 11.2% reduction (from the base case) to a 6.8% reduction (from the base case), and the total travel monetary cost increases from 74.8% to 82.7%, respectively. Similarly, since the housing demand increases the housing rent increases from an 8.4% and 6.2% reduction to a 3.5% and 2.4% reduction; since travel time increases, labor supply would decrease and wage increases from the ranging of the 15.7% and 15.8% reduction to the ranging of 8.6% and 8.8% reduction. In addition, when the revenue is distributed, since consumers demand more housing space, the land market become more competitive and the commercial rents also increase from a 8.3% and 8.6% reduction to a 3.8% and 4.0% reduction; since the demand for goods increases and due to the higher input prices the prices of goods increase from a 5.7% reduction to a 0.4% reduction. Because the rent increases, the annual gain from total value of stocks per capita increases from a $1,713 reduction to a $786 reduction.

The $f = 1$ and 2 types of unemployed consumers benefit and the $f = 3$ and 4 types of unemployed consumers get harmed by the equal redistribution of the aggregate quasi-Pigouvian toll revenue. For the high income groups of the unemployed consumers, the negative side effects of the revenue redistribution exceed the benefits from the revenue redistribution. The negative side effects are the higher travel monetary cost, consumption good prices, housing rent and congestion. Those groups, who get harmed from the revenue distribution, travel more often and their marginal utility of income is less than that of other unemployed lower income groups.

All income groups of employed consumers benefit from revenue redistribution. In their case, in addition to the similar effect for unemployed consumers, positive effect from the increased wage and negative effect from the increased work and non-work travel time play their roles.

When revenue is redistributed, jobs increase moderately in the city from a 17,596 increase to a 18,396 increase; and change very slightly in the suburbs. Similarly, the residents in the city decrease from a 44,228 increase to a 36,268 increase; and increase in the suburbs from a 44,228 reduction to a 36,268 reduction. Because consumers demand more housing space when income increases, vacant land decreases. Vacant land decreases in the city from a 4.0% increase to a 1.5% increase; and increase in suburbs from a 4.5% increase to a 1.9% increase. Since the amount of the vacant land in the city is limited, the amount that changes in the city is small. The demand for housing space could lead to the suburbanization of some residents, because there is not enough available vacant land in the city.

When the revenue is redistributed, the non-work travel increases by the income effect. VMT changes from a 13.6% reduction to a 11.6% reduction, and fuel consumption and CO_2 emissions change from a 17.1% reduction to a 14.8% reduction, respectively. Since the roads are more congested after the redistribution, the MPG decreases from a 4.2% to a 3.7% increase; and the speed decreases from a 10.8% increase to a 9.4% increase, respectively. When income increases, consumers prefer more inefficient vehicles because in the model, the more inefficient vehicles are larger and more comfortable to drive. Inefficiency increases from a 0.1% reduction when there is no redistribution to a 0.02% increase when there is redistribution.

Chapter 7. Conclusion

7.1 Extension and Conclusion

In this book, I improved and extended the RELU-TRAN model (Anas and Liu, 2007) by adding several features. I refer to this extended version as RELU-TRAN2. Three related developments were introduced in extending RELU-TRAN.

First, RELU-TRAN implicitly assumed that all drivers used the same car fuel economy in traveling. RELU-TRAN2 adds five car types differentiated by fuel economy in order to capture the trade-off between car fuel economy and other adjustments that consumer-workers can make when they are shocked by various exogenous changes. Thus, the discrete choice framework of the model is extended to include car-type choice under the assumption that the less fuel efficient cars have certain features such as comfort and safety that can be traded off against better fuel economy.

Second, in RELU-TRAN traffic congestion occurred only in travel between zones which are connected by major roads (corresponding to freeways and major arterials). But significant congestion also occurs on local roads. This was remedied by modeling congestion on such intra-zonal local roads in RELU-TRAN2.

Thirdly, in RELU-TRAN, the monetary cost of travel by car was the same for all drivers. But in RELU-TRAN2 the fuel use and speed relationship is introduced to make gasoline consumption an endogenous consequence of congestion. Thus, RELU-TRAN2 captures both the delay and fuel esternalities of traffic congestion.

In addition to the above major changes, it is also possible to introduce the value of time in travel not as a constant but as a vector of constants that are different for each income level, and to explicitly model the labor force participation decision of consumer-workers. And finally, RELU-TRAN2 calculates CO_2 emissions from car travel. Thus RELU-TRAN2 is a model that is appropriate to analyze the consumers' travel-related fuel consumption and CO_2 emissions.

The special contribution of this book is that it is the empirical study of how various anti-congestion policies affect urban sprawl, trip-making, vehicle miles traveled, fuel consumption and CO_2 emissions by cars in a general equilibrium setting for an urban area that takes into account housing markets, labor markets, the interconnection of industries and work trips as well as non-work trips related to consumption activities.

The most important findings of the book are summarized as follows with a brief overview of what was learned in each case.

1) **Responsiveness of travel behavior, fuel consumption and emissions to the price of gasoline and to vehicle fuel economy, and the rebound effect in vehicle miles traveled:**

   In a part of chapter 3, the short-run and long-run price elasticity of fuel consumption with respect to fuel price and with respect to vehicle fuel economy are tested using structured numerical simulations of the general equilibrium model representing short and long run adjustments. I find that the demand for fuel is not as elastic compared to econometric estimates of the corresponding elasticity in the literature, such as those of Small and Van Dender (2007a,b). But if I adjust the vehicle fuel economy levels by assuming that exogenous technological progress is occurring, the price elasticity becomes closer to that estimated in the econometric literature. This implies that technological progress is an important factor for mitigating fuel consumption and CO_2 emissions, more important perhaps than a gasoline tax would be. But this comes with an important caveat. In the case of the elasticity of fuel consumption with respect to vehicle fuel economy, the fuel consumption and the CO_2 emissions from cars are reduced more in the short-run than in the long-run. The reason for this is that there is a rebound effect that takes hold in the long run. That is when technological progress occurs in the long-run and cars become more fuel efficient, then the travel cost per mile decreases, and consumers drive more. Since in the long-run consumers can adjust more by increasing their travel miles, the fuel consumption and CO_2 emissions increase. Therefore, a rebound effect is observed in the long run that is not observed in the short run. To the author's knowledge such a rebound effect was not previously documented using a general equilibrium model. Also, because of the structured simulations in which various equilibration processes are added to the simulations one at a time, it is possible to trace empirically how each process affects the demand for fuel.

2) Effects of transportation improvements and other changes on suburbanization versus centralization of the population and of jobs:

In chapter 4 comparative statics exercises are reported. The convenience of car travel acts as an important suburbanization force for population. When the travel cost by auto becomes relatively cheaper, miles traveled increase and roads become more congested. Thus fuel consumption and CO_2 emissions increase. The accessibility to public transport is an important centralization force. When the travel cost of public transportation becomes relatively cheaper, the locations near the center which are more accessible to transit become more attractive and more densely populated, because they become easier to access from other zones by public transit. In this sense, that the travel cost by auto becomes lower and that the travel cost by public transit becomes higher are two different scenarios that have similar effects. When jobs and residents are suburbanized, the vacant land decreases in the suburbs. Thus no matter which criterion I use, job decentralization, residential decentralization or the diminution of suburban vacant land, I observe that there is more urban sprawl. But at the same time, the vacant land in the city also increases as this urban sprawl occurs, although the amount of this increase is limited.

An exception to the pattern of decentralization described above occurs when the monetary cost of public transport is changed. When it is increased, although both jobs and residents are suburbanized as mentioned above, the vacant land increases in the suburbs, and also in the city, which indicates less sprawl under the definition that sprawl is measured by land development.

The decrease in developed land (or increase in vacant land) is caused by the income effect of the higher public transit travel cost. This works to reduce the residential floor space per consumer.

When construction becomes more elastic with respect to the price of buildings, more construction occurs especially in the suburban zones where there is plenty of vacant land. This causes more suburbanization. In the suburbs, residents increase more than jobs and the difference between the number of jobs and residents increases, while in the city residents decrease more than jobs and the difference becomes smaller. The vacant land decreases in the suburbs and increases slightly in the city. Thus it is observed that more urban sprawl using either job decentralization, residential decentralization or suburban land development as the criterion. I find the intuitive result that the decentralization increases the fuel consumption and the CO_2 emissions.

3) The effects of anti-congestion pricing policies on suburbanization versus centralization:

In chapter 5, quasi-Pigouvian congestion tolls, a fuel tax on gasoline, a cordon toll around the downtown and a downtown parking fee are tested as alternative anti-congestion policies. The quasi-Pigouvian toll is designed to remove the externality due to the time delay and the externality due to fuel consumption. The fuel externality part of the quasi-Pigouvian toll is necessary because the congestion makes the driving speed slower and the slow driving speed is fuel inefficient. On the other hand, if the driving speed is too fast, it is also fuel inefficient. In such a case, by making the road more congested, the fuel consumption can become efficient. This part of the quasi-Pigouvian toll would be negative and it means that it is a subsidy for the drivers. If I watch closely the job and residence location choices and mode choices, the consumers' behavior becomes clear. As the congestion pricing becomes higher, the consumers who travel by auto decrease and those who travel by the other modes increase. In the jobs and residents location choices, this switching of modes is an important factor since the locations near CBD have advantages in terms of better access to public transit. Fuel consumption and CO_2 emissions are smoothly reduced as congestion tolls increase.

In the comparative statics, I had seen that increasing the travel cost of auto acted as a centralization force. But although the cordon toll increases the travel cost by auto, the MSA is suburbanized under the revenue neutral cordon toll or under the limited quasi-Pigouvian toll. Under the revenue neutral cordon toll, the jobs decrease by 7,648 in the CBD, increase by 1,247 in the city and increase 6,346 in the suburbs. The total number of jobs decreases because the increment of commuting cost discourages employment slightly. The residents decrease by 245 in the CBD, decrease by 1,321 in the city and increase by 1,566 in the suburbs. This suburbanization occurs because the cordon toll increases the travel cost by auto mostly locally, near the CBD. When the travel cost by auto increases, the locations near the center become more attractive because of good accesses to public transit. But the transportation cost by auto near the CBD becomes relatively higher than in the suburb, and the locations near the CBD become less preferred. This effect on auto costs for locations near the CBD is stronger than the effect of increased transit use, and the city becomes more suburbanized.

The parking fee also increases the travel cost by auto locally near the CBD. Thus while a uniformly higher travel cost by auto would work as a centralization force, an increase locally around the CBD works as suburbanization force. But this effect of the parking fee is relatively weaker than that of the cordon toll because through traffic does not pay the parking fee and neither do consumers who reside in the CBD but work outside the CBD. Jobs decrease by 449 but residents increase by 89 in the CBD. Jobs increase by 599 in the city excluding the CBD and decrease by 182 in the suburbs. Residents increase by 182 in the city excluding CBD and decrease by 271 in the suburbs.

The quasi-Pigouvian toll levied only on the major roads and the revenue neutral gasoline tax have opposite impacts on job location. The residents are centralized under both policies. As discussed when the comparative statics are exercised, when the travel cost by auto is increased the locations near the center become popular because there is advantage for using public transit. But under the quasi-Pigouvian toll, jobs decrease by 5,228 in the city and increase by 4,607 in the suburb. The increment of travel cost discourages potential labor to be employed. The residents increase by 6,455 and decrease by the same number in the suburbs. Thus jobs move to suburbs where it is easy to access labor, and residents move to the city where is easy to access jobs. Under the gasoline tax, all commuters by auto are taxed. Thus to reduce gasoline consumption, they are centralized. Jobs increase by 36,120 in the city and decreases by 37,570 in the suburb. The residents increase by 53,033 in the city and decrease the same number in the suburbs. The differences of jobs and residents in city and suburb decrease while both jobs and residents are centralized. The reductions in aggregate fuel consumption under the quasi-Pigouvian toll only on major roads and under the gasoline consumption are 7% and 12.3%, respectively.

When all major and minor roads are charged quasi-Pigouvian tolls, both jobs and residents become more centralized. Jobs increase by 17,596 in the city and decrease by 19,721 in the suburbs. Residents increase by 44,228 in the city and decrease by the same number in the suburbs. On the other hand under the revenue neutral gasoline tax, jobs increase by 50,469 in the city and decrease by 52,469 in the suburb. Residents increase by 78,466 in the city and decrease by the same population number in the suburbs. Thus the MSA is centralized more under the fuel tax than under the quasi-Pigouvian toll. This is because the quasi-Pigouvian toll is higher where there is more congestion and lower where there is less. In the case of the fuel tax the difference in the increase in monetary cost between congested roads and less congested roads does not become as large as it does under the quasi-Pigouvian tolls. Thus, near the center the congestion pricing is higher under the quasi-Pigouvian toll than under the fuel tax that is revenue neutral, and in suburb it is lower under the quasi-Pigouvian toll than under the fuel tax that is revenue neutral. Both jobs and residents are centralized because of increased travel cost by auto. At the same time, under the quasi-Pigouvian toll, it means that the jobs and residents are moving to the higher traveling cost locations, relative to under the fuel cost. Thus the centralization of MSA under the quasi-Pigouvian toll is less than under the fuel tax. The impacts of the two policies on the fuel consumption and CO_2 emissions are similar. These aggregates are reduced by 17.1% and 18.1% respectively.

4) The effects of the UGB and quasi-Pigouvian tolling compared:

In chapter 6, the urban growth boundary (UGB) as an alternative anti-congestion policy was tested. I compared the result of the UGB with the result of quasi-Pigouvian toll from chapter 5 and with the result of the quasi-Pigouvian toll when the aggregate revenue of the toll is redistributed equally among the consumers. It is found that both policies act as centralization forces and jobs and residences move to the city. When such pairs of residence-work locations are moved to the center, many trips also change their mode from auto to other modes. Thus fuel consumption and CO_2 emissions are decreased. I compare the result with quasi-Pigouvian tolling. Between UGB and quasi-Pigouvian toll, the difference of their impacts on fuel consumption and CO_2 emissions is larger than the difference of their impacts on jobs and residential location. The contribution of the UGB to reducing fuel consumption and CO_2 emissions is less than that of the quasi-Pigouvian toll. For example, when only 60% of the suburban vacant land is made available under the UGB, the jobs increase by 19,810 in the city and decrease by 19,515 in the suburbs. Residents increase by 32,665 in the city and decrease by 32,665 in the suburbs. Under the quasi-Pigouvian toll, jobs increase by 17,596 in the city and decrease by 19,721 in the suburbs. Residents increase by 44,228 in the city and decrease by 44,228 in the suburbs. On the other hand, the fuel consumption and CO_2 emissions decrease by only 0.7% under the same UGB while they decrease by 16.1% under the quasi-Pigouvian toll. When the toll revenue is redistributed, consumers gain income and thus make more non-work trips, and the fuel consumption and CO_2 emission reductions change from 17.1% to 14.8%.

7.2 Summary

Table 7.2 (a) shows the policies' results on the fuel consumption, CO_2 emission and VMT per person in a day. All policies succeed to reduce VMT and to mitigate the fuel consumption, CO_2 emission.

Table 7.2 (b) shows the policies' results on the commute travel time, the non-work travel time, the total travel time and the non-work travel per person in a day. Under all policies, the total travel time, the non-work travel time and the non-work trips per person are reduced. The commute travel time per

Table 7.2 (a) Policy results on fuel, CO_2, VMT per day.

Policy	Fuel (gallon) per consumer	CO_2 (gram) per consumer	VMT per consumer
Base	1.329	11,681	28.173
Quasi-Pigouvian congestion tolls on links	1.236	10,859	26.601
% change	-7.031	-7.031	-5.579
Gasoline tax (145.9%)	1.166	4,223	25.299
% change	-12.267	-12.267	-10.202
Quasi-Pigouvian congestion tolls	1.102	9,682	24.332
% change	-17.112	-17.112	-13.633
Gasoline tax (226.8%)	1.089	9,568	23.859
% change	-18.084	-18.084	-15.312
Limited quasi-Pigouvian congestion tolls	1.320	11,596	28.057
% change	-0.716	-0.716	-0.413
Cordon toll ($1.494)	1.320	11,596	28.056
% change	-0.722	-0.722	-0.416
Parking fee ($2.235)	1.318	11,580	28.023
% change	-0.863	-0.863	-0.534
UGB 1 (tightness 0.7)	1.322	11,620	28.000
% change	-0.523	-0.523	-0.615
UGB 2 (tightness 0.4)	1.314	11,548	27.785
% change	-1.137	-1.137	-1.378
UGB 3 (tightness 0.1)	1.303	11,453	27.477
% change	-1.952	-1.952	-2.471

employed consumer also decreases under the congestion pricing policies, but it increases under the UGB. Although the jobs and residents location move to the congested city under UGB, as is shown in Table 7.2 (b), the UGB does not charge the congestion pricing directly. Thus the commute travel time per employed consumer is increased by more congested road in the city.

Table 7.2 (c) shows the policies' results on the aggregate vacant land in suburb and the floor space per person. The suburban vacant land increases under all congestion pricing policies. Under the UGB, the vacant land increases in suburbs, because demolishing the buildings creates additional vacant land. Employed consumers reduce their floor space, except for the

Table 7.2 (b) Policy results on travel time and non-work travel per day.

Policy	Commute travel time (min) per employed consumer	Non-work travel time (min) per consumer	Total travel time (min) per consumer	Non-work travel per consumer
Base	64.104	91.808	142.990	1.461
Quasi-Pigouvian tolls on links	61.925	86.411	135.845	1.408
% change	-3.399	-5.879	-4.997	-3.631
Gasoline tax (145.9%)	61.586	82.129	131.282	1.366
% change	-3.928	-10.542	-8.188	-6.502
Quasi-Pigouvian congestion tolls	60.449	78.728	126.965	1.333
% change	-5.702	-14.247	-11.207	-8.763
Gasoline tax (226.8%)	60.596	78.442	126.797	1.355
% change	-5.472	-14.559	-11.324	-7.311
Limited quasi-Pigouvian congestion tolls	63.714	91.297	142.166	1.456
% change	-0.608	-0.557	-0.576	-0.347
Cordon toll ($1.494)	63.709	91.288	142.154	1.456
% change	-0.617	-0.566	-0.584	-0.356
Parking fee ($2.235)	63.656	91.447	142.271	1.460
% change	-0.699	-0.393	-0.503	-0.104
UGB 1 (tightness 0.7)	64.163	91.380	142.613	1.458
% change	0.092	-0.466	-0.264	-0.263
UGB 2 (tightness 0.4)	64.253	90.924	142.232	1.453
% change	0.232	-0.963	-0.530	-0.543
UGB 3 (tightness 0.1)	64.398	90.414	141.844	1.448835
% change	0.459	-1.518	-0.801	-0.860

Table 7.2 (c) Policy results on vacant land in suburb and floor space.

Policy	Sprawl (total suburban vacant land (acre))	Housing floor space (sq-ft) per consumer	
		Employed (k = 1) Employed (k = 2)	Unemployed (k = 1) Unemployed (k = 2)
base	1,178,888	988 1,092	429 474
QPT on links	1,194,329	959 1,051	441 485
% change	1.310	-2.932 -3.738	2.962 2.238
Gasoline tax (145.9%)	1,221,588	927 1,003	455 495
% change	3.622	-6.191 -8.153	6.279 4.300
Quasi-Pigouvian tolls	1,232,097	901 971	467 506
% change	4.514	-8.816 -11.105	8.903 6.738
Gasoline tax (226.8%)	1,236,121	906 971	466 503
% change	4.855	-8.344 -11.070	8.804 5.952
limited QPT	1,179,720	985 1,088	429 475
% change	0.071	-0.306 -0.341	0.204 0.210
Cordon toll ($1.494)	1,179,759	985 1,088	429 476
% change	0.074	-0.315 -0.353	0.218 0.221
Parking fee ($2.235)	1,179,788	986 1,090	429 475
% change	0.076	-0.207 -0.357	0.111 0.100
UGB 1 (tightness 0.7)	1,227,023	956 1,080	409 462
% change	3.923	-3.290 -1.108	-4.489 -2.609
UGB 2 (tightness 0.4)	1,279,361	920 1,069	387 447
% change	7.853	-6.910 -2.154	-9.693 -5.688
UGB 3 (tightness 0.1)	1,342,237	876 1,056	360 429
% change	12.170	-11.344 -3.280	-16.097 -9.528

highest income group under the parking fee, but unemployed consumers increase under the congestion pricing policies. Under the UGB that reduces the available land, both employed and unemployed consumers reduce floor space.

Table 7.2 (d) shows the policies' results on the jobs and residential locations. In general, the increase of travel cost by auto is a centralization force because the locations near the center are accessible to public transit. Under the quasi-Pigouvian toll and the revenue neutral gasoline tax, jobs and residents are centralized. Since the quasi-Pigoubian toll is higher near the center and lower in the suburbs than the gasoline tax, its effect on centralization is weaker than that of the gasoline tax. Under the quasi-

Table 7.2 (d) Policy results on jobs and residents location.

Policy	Jobs in the suburbs	Jobs in the city city ex CBD	Jobs in the CBD	Residents in the suburb	Residents in the city ex-CBD	Residents in the CBD
base	2,413,622	793,798	537,861	3,237,847	1,413,312	39,688
Quasi-Pigouvian on link	2,418,230	788,859	537,572	3,231,392	1,419,145	40,310
% change	0.191	-0.622	-0.054	-0.199	0.413	1.568
Gasoline tax (145.9%)	2,376,047	810,879	556,904	3,184,806	1,463,423	42,618
% change	-1.557	2.152	3.540	-1.638	3.546	7.384
Quasi-Pigouvian tolls	2,393,902	798,910	550,345	3,193,618	1,453,655	43,573
% change	-0.817	0.644	2.321	-1.366	2.854	9.789
Gasoline tax (226.8%)	2,361,154	817,186	564,932	3,159,381	1,487,189	44,278
% change	-2.174	2.946	5.033	-2.423	5.227	11.565
limited Quasi-Pigouvian tolls	2,419,840	794,865	530,524	3,239,405	1,411,983	39,459
% change	0.258	0.134	-1.364	0.048	-0.094	-0.578
Cordon toll ($1.494)	2,419,968	795,045	530,213	3,239,412	1,411,992	39,443
% change	0.263	0.157	-1.422	0.049	-0.094	-0.617
Parking fee ($2.235)	2,413,441	794,397	537,412	3,237,576	1,413,495	39,777
% change	-0.008	0.075	-0.083	-0.008	0.013	0.224
UGB 1 (tightness 0.7)	2,399,453	803,035	543,001	3,214,109	1,436,228	40,511
% change	-0.587	1.164	0.956	-0.733	1.621	2.073
UGB 2 (tightness 0.4)	2,382,075	814,396	549,309	3,184,976	1,464,361	41,510
% change	-1.307	2.595	2.128	-1.633	3.612	4.590
UGB 3 (tightness 0.1)	2,358,496	829,823	557,869	3,144,781	1,503,191	42,875
% change	-2.284	4.538	3.720	-2.874	6.359	8.030

Table 7.2 (e) Policy results on aggregate rents and consumer utility.

Policy	Aggregate rents in sub	Aggregate rents in city	Aggregate rents in CBD	Consumer expected Utility			
	Occupied floor space ($1000) (vacant land is not included)			Employed (f=1)	f=2	f=3	f=4
				Unemployed (f=1)	f=2	f=3	f=4
base	76,600,040	27,383,850	7,200,647	10.192	10.935	11.863	13.887
				9.640	10.351	11.224	13.180
QPT on link	73,081,750	26,035,365	6,924,847	10.145	10.892	11.824	13.855
				9.645	10.356	11.229	13.184
% change	-4.593	-4.924	-3.830	-0.457	-0.393	-0.333	-0.230
				0.054	0.049	0.042	0.031
Gasoline tax	68,155,263	25,358,434	6,874,073	10.092	10.848	11.784	13.822
(145.9%)				9.664	10.372	11.246	13.202
% change	-11.025	-7.397	-4.535	-0.983	-0.798	-0.671	-0.466
				0.244	0.206	0.194	0.167
QPT tolls	65,549,830	23,919,144	6,509,925	10.053	10.815	11.756	13.803
				9.683	10.390	11.265	13.221
% change	-14.426	-12.652	-9.593	-1.367	-1.099	-0.907	-0.599
				0.443	0.386	0.365	0.313
Gasoline tax	65,280,897	24,662,561	6,769,464	10.052	10.813	11.752	13.797
(226.8%)				9.672	10.379	11.253	13.209
% change	-14.777	-9.938	-5.988	-1.373	-1.114	-0.937	-0.644
				0.334	0.278	0.260	0.223
limited QPT	76,474,057	27,271,016	7,046,726	10.188	10.932	11.861	13.885
				9.641	10.351	11.225	13.181
% change	-0.164	-0.412	-2.138	-0.037	-0.030	-0.023	-0.012
				0.010	0.009	0.008	0.007
Cordon toll	76,460,388	27,269,126	7,040,449	10.188	10.932	11.861	13.885
($1.494)				9.641	10.352	11.225	13.181
% change	-0.182	-0.419	-2.225	-0.038	-0.031	-0.023	-0.012
				0.011	0.010	0.010	0.008
Parking fee	76,411,078	27,344,621	7,221,214	10.190	10.933	11.863	13.887
($2.235)				9.641	10.352	11.225	13.181
% change	-0.247	-0.143	0.285	-0.022	-0.014	-0.007	0.003
				0.011	0.012	0.011	0.009
UGB 1	77,251,914	28,157,106	7,393,823	10.186	10.929	11.857	13.880
(tightness 0.7)				9.618	10.329	11.202	13.158
% change	0.851	2.824	2.683	-0.062	-0.057	-0.055	-0.050
				-0.226	-0.209	-0.193	-0.166
UGB 2	78,254,047	29,189,491	7,656,418	10.179	10.922	11.850	13.872
(tightness 0.4)				9.590	10.301	11.174	13.129
% change	2.159	6.594	6.330	-0.128	-0.119	-0.114	-0.105
				-0.522	-0.482	-0.445	-0.384
UGB 3	79,711,759	30,668,099	8,029,535	10.170	10.913	11.841	13.862
(tightness 0.1)				9.551	10.262	11.135	13.090
% change	4.062	11.993	11.511	-0.211	-0.197	-0.190	-0.177
				-0.927	-0.857	-0.791	-0.682

Pigouvian toll only on the major links, residents are suburbanized, but the jobs are centralized. This is because auto commuters are not tolled if they reside and work in the same zone, jobs move to the zones where are more labors. Under the revenue neutral gasoline tax, both jobs and residents are centralized. The limited-quasi-Pigouvian tolls and the revenue neutral cordon toll that are charged to enter the CBD, and the revenue neutral CBD parking fee increase the travel cost by auto locally near the CBD. Thus consumers would prefer or avoid the location near the CBD. Jobs decrease under those three policies, while the residents increase under parking fee and decrease under the limited quasi-Pigouvian toll and the cordon toll. Under the parking fee, commuters who reside in CBD and work outside CBD does not pay the parking fee.

Table 7.2 (e) shows the policies' results on the aggregate rents from the occupied floor space and consumers' utility. The aggregate rents decrease under the congestion pricing policies, except the CBD under the parking fee, and increase under the UGB. The employed consumer's utility decrease under all policies but the utility of the employed highest income group increases under the parking fee. The unemployed consumers' utilities increase under all congestion pricing policies, but decrease under the UGB.

Reference

Alcott, Blake. 2005. "Jevon's Paradox," Ecological Economics, 54, 9–21.

Akiyama, Takamasa, Se-il Mun amd Masashi Okushima. 2004. "Second-Best Congestion Pricing in Urban Space: Cordon Pricing and Its Alternatives," Review of Network Economics, Vol.3, Issue 4, 401–414.

American Automobile Association. 2005. "Your Driving Costs"

Anas, Alex. 2007. "A unified theory of consumption, travel and trip chaining," Journal of Urban Economics, 62, 162–186.

Anas, Alex and Chaushie Chu. 1984. "Discrete Choice Models and the Housing Price and Travel to Work Elasticities of Location Demand," Journal of Urban Economics, 15, 107–123.

Anas, Alex and David Pines. 2008. "Anti-Sprawl Policies in a System of Congested Cities," Regional Science and Urban Economics, 38, 408–423.

Anas, Alex and Govinda R. Timilsina. 2009a. "Lock-in Effect of Road Expansion on CO_2 Emissions: Results from a Core-Periphery Model of Beijing," Working paper, SUNY at Buffalo.

Anas, Alex and Govinda R. Timilsina. 2009b. "Pricing Congestion to Curb CO_2 Emissions in São Paulo," Working paper, SUNY at Buffalo.

Anas, Alex, Govinda R. Timilsina and Siqi Zheng. 2008. "Effects of a Toll on Congestion versus a Tax on Gasoline on Car Travel, Fuel Consumption and CO_2 Emissions in Beijing," Working paper, SUNY at Buffalo.

Anas, Alex and Hyok-Joo Rhee. 2006. "Curbing Urban Sprawl with Congestion Tolls and Urban Boundaries," Regional Science and Urban Economics, 36, 510–541.

Anas, Alex and Hyok-Joo Rhee. 2007. "When are Urban Gtowht Boundaries Not Second-Best Policies to Congestion Tolls?," Journal of Urban Economics, 61, 263–286.

Anas, Alex and Ikki Kim. 1990. "Network Loading Versus Equilibrium Estimation of the Stochastic Route Choice Model: Maximu Likelihood and Least Squares Revisited," Journal of Regional Science, Vol. 30, No. 1, 89–103.

Anas, Alex and Ikki Kim. 1996. "General Equilibrium Models of Polycentric Urban Land Use with Endogenous Congestion and Job Agglomeration," Journal of Urban Economics, 40, 232–256.

Anas, Alex and Richard J. Arnott. 1991. "The Chicago Prototype Housing Market Model with Tenuer Choice and Its Policy Applications," Journal of Housing Research, Volume 5, Issue 1, 23–90.

Anas, Alex and Richard J. Arnott. 1997. "Taxes and allowances in a dynamic equilibrium model of urban housing with a size-quality hierarchy," Regional Science and Urban Economics, 27, 547–580.

Anas, Alex and Rong Xu. 1999. "Congestion, Land Use and Job Dispersion: A General Equilibrium Analysis," Journal of Urban Economics, 45(3), 451–473.

Anas, Alex and Yu Liu. 2007. "A Regional Economy, Land Use, and Transportation Model (RELU-TRAN©): Formulation, Algorithm Design, and Testing," Journal of Regional Science, Vol. 47, No. 3, 415–455.

Anas, Alex and Rong Xu. 1999. "Congestion, Land Use and Job Dispersion: A General Equilibrium Analysis," Journal of Urban Economics, 45(3), 451–473.

Armington, P. S. 1969. "Congestion, Land Use and Job Dispersion: A general Equilibrium Analysis," Journal of Urban Econimcs, 45, 3, 451–473.

Arnott, Richard. 1979. "Unpriced Transportation Congestion," Journal of Economic Theory, 21,

294–316.

Atherton, T. J., J. H. Suhrbier, and W. A. Jessiman. 1975. "The Use of Disaggregate Travel Demand Models to Analyze Carpooling Incentives," Report. Cambridge Systematics, Inc., Cambridge, Mass.

Backley, Dixie M. 1999. "The Long-Run Elasticity of New Housing Supply in the United States: Empirical Evidence for 1950 to 1994," Journal of Real Estate Finance and Economics, 18:1, 25–42.

Bar-Gera, Hillel. 2006. "Primal Method for Determining the Most Likely Route Flows in Large Road Networks," Transportation Science, Vol. 40, No. 3, 269–286.

Barth, Marth and Kanok Boriboonsomsin. 2008. "Real-World CO_2 Impacts of Traffic Congestion," Transportation Research Record, 2058, 163–171.

Beevers, Sean D. and David C. Carslaw. 2005 a. "The Impact of Congestion Charging on Vehicle Emissions in London," Atmospheric Environment, 39, 1–5.

Beevers, Sean D. and David C. Carslaw. 2005 b. "The impact of congestion charging on vehicle speed and its implications for assessing vehicle emissions," Atmospheric Environment, 39, 6875–6885.

Berkhout, Peter H.G., Jos C. Muskens and Jan W. Velthuijsen. 2000. "Defining the Rebound Effect," Energy Policy, 28, 425–432.

Bento, Antonio M., Sofia F. Franco and Daniel Kaffine. 2006. "The Efficiency and Distributional impacts of Alternative Anti-Sprawl Policies," Journal of Urban Economics, 59, 121–141.

Bhat, Chandra R. and Jessica U. Guo. 2007. "A Comprehensive Analysis of Built Environment Characteristics on Household Residential Choice and Auto Ownership Levels," Transportation Research Part B, 41, 506–526.

Bhat, Chandra R. and Sudeshna Sen. 2006. "Household Vehicle Type Holdings and Usage: An Application of the Multiple Discrete-Continuous Extreme Value (MDCEV) Model," Transportation Research Part B, 40, 35–53.

Bhat, Chandra R., Sudeshna Sen and Naveen Eluru. 2009. "The Impact of Demographics, Built Environment Attributes, Vehicle Characteristics, and Gasoline prices on Household Vehicle Holdings and Use," Transportation Research Part B, 43, 1–18.

Brookes, Leonard. 2000. "Energy Efficiency Fallacies Revisited," Energy Policy, 28, 355–366.

Brownstone, David and Thomas F. Golob. 2009. "The Impact of Residential Density on Vehicle Usage and Energy Consumption," Journal of Urban Economics, 65, 91–98.

Brueckner, Jan K.. 2000. "Urban Sprawl: Diagnosis and Remedies," International Regional Science Review, 23, 160–171.

Brueckner, Jan K.. 2007. "Urban Growth Boundaries: An Effective Second-Best Remedy for Unpriced Traffic Congestion?," Journal of Housing Economics, 16, 263–273.

Charles River Associates, Inc. 1972. "A Disaggregated Behavioral Model of Urban Travel Demand," Report to the U.S. Department of Transportation, Federal Highway Administration.

Daganzo, Carlos F. and Yoseff Sheffi. 1977. "On Stochastic Models of Trafic Assignments," Transportation Science, 11, 253–274.

Daniel, Joseph I. and Khalid Bekka. 2000. "The Environmental Impact of Highway Congestion Pricing," Journal of Urban Economics, 47, 180–215.

Davis, Stacy C. and Susan W. Diegel. 2004. "Transportation Energy Data Book: Edition 24," Oak Ridge National Laboratory.

De Salvo, Joseph S. and Mobinul Huq. 1996. "Income, Residential Location, and Mode Choice," Journal of Urban Economics, 40, 84–99.

DiPasquale, Denise and William C. Wheaton. 1994. "Housing Market Dynamics and the Future of Housing Prices," Journal of Urban Economics, 35, 1–27.

Dixit, A. 1973. "The Optimum Factory Town," Bell Journal of Economics and Management Science 4. 637–654.

Dixit, Avinash. And Joseph Stiglitz. 1977. "Monopolistic Competition and Optimum Product Diversity," American Economic Review, 67(3), 297–308.

Eliasson, Jonas and Lars-Göran Mattsson. 2006. "Equity Effects of Congestion Pricing Quantitative Methodology and a Case Study for Stockholm," Transportation Research Part A, 40, 602–620.

Espey, Molly. 1998. "Gasoline Demand Revisited: An International Meta-Analysis of Elasticities," Energy Economics, 20, 273–295.

Ethier, Wilfred J, 1982. "National and International Returns to Scale in the Modern Theory of International Trade," American Economic Review, American Economic Association, vol. 72(3), 389–405.

Fang, Hao Audrey. 2008. "A Discrete-Continuous Model of Households' Vehicle Choice and Usage, with an Application to the Effects of Residential Density," Transportation Research Part B, 42, 736–758.

Fujishima, Shota. 2007. "Second-Best Toll Policies in a Polycentric City," Working paper.

Glaeser, Edward L. and Matthew E. Kahn. 2008. "The Greenness of Cities: Carbon Dioxide Emissions and Urban Development," Working paper, Harvard Kennedy School, Taubman Center for State and Local Government.

Golob, Thomas F., Seyoung Kim and Weiping Ren. 1996. "How Households Use Different Types of Vehicles: A Structural Driver Allocation and Usage Model," Transpn. Res. A. Vol. 30, No. 2, 103–118.

Goodwin, Phil, Joyce Dargay and Mark Hanly. 2004. "Elasticities of Road Traffic and Fuel Consumption with Respect to Price and Income: A Review," Transport Reviews, Vol. 24, No. 3, 275–292.

Graham, Daniel J. and Stephan Galister. 2002. "The demand for automobile fuel: a survey of elasticities," Journal of Transport Economics and Policy, Volume 36, 1, 1–26.

Green, Richard K., Stephan Malpezzi and Stephan K. Mayo. 2005. "Metropolitan-Specific Estimates of the Price Elasticity of Supply of Housing, and Their Sources," The American Economic Review, Vol. 95, No. 2, 334–339.

Greene, David L., James R. Kahn and Robert C. Gibson. 1999. "Fuel Economy Rebound Effect for U.S. Household Vehicles," The Energy Journal, Vol. 20, No. 3, 1–31.

Greening, Lorna A., David L. Greene and Carmen Difiglio. 2000. "Energy Efficiency and Consumption – The Rebound Effect – A Survey," Energy Policy, 28, 389–401.

Harrington, Winston, Alan J. Krupnick and Anna Alberini. 2001. "Overcoming Public Aversion to Congestion Pricing," Transportation Research Part A, 35, 87–105.

Hausman, Jerry A. and Whitney K. Newey. 1995. "Nonparametric Estimation of Exact Consumers Surplus and Deadweight Loss," Econometrica, Vol. 63, No. 6, 1445–1476.

Hughes, Jonathan E., Christopher R. Knittel, and Daniel Sperling. 2006. "Evidence of a Shift in the Short-Run Price Elasticity of Gasoline Demand," Center for the Study of Energy Markets, University of California Energy Institute, UC Berkeley.

Ihara, Tomohiko, Yukihiro Kikegawa, Kazutake Asahi, Yutaka Genchi and Hiroaki Kondo. 2008. "Changes in Year-Round Air Temperature and Annual Energy Consumption in Office Building Areas by Urban Heat-Island Countermeasures and Energy-Saving Measures," Applied Energy, 85, 12–25.

Illinois Department of Transportation Office of Planning and Programming. 2000. "The Illinois Travel Statistics."

Kanemoto, Yoshitsugu. 1977. "Cost-Benefit Analysis and the Second Best Land Use for

Transportation," Journal of Urban Economics, 4, 483–503.
Kayser, Hilke A.. 2000. "Gasoline Demand and Car Choice: Estimating Gasoline Demand Using Household Information," Energy Economics, 22, 331–348.
Kikegawa, Yukihiro, Yutaka Genchi, Hiroaki Kondo, Keisuke Hanaki. 2006. "Impacts of City-Block-Scale Countermeasures Against Urban Heat-Island Phenomena Upon A Building's Energy-Consumption For Air-Conditioning," Applied Energy, 83, 649–668.
Kimmel, Jean and Thomas J. Kniesner. 1998. "New Evidence on Labor Supply: Employment VersusHours Elasticities by Sex and Marital Status," Journal of Monetary Economics, 42, 289–301.
Lerman S. R. 1977. " Location, housing and automobile ownership and mode choice to work: A joint choice model," Trans. Res. Rec., 610, 6–11.
Leape, Jonathan. 2006. "The London Congestion Charge," Journal of Economic Perspectives, Vol. 20, 4, 157–176.
Madlener, Reinhard and Blake Alcott. 2009. "Energy Rebound and Economic Growth: A Review of the Main Issues and Research Needs," Energy, 34, 370–376.
Mills, E.S., 1972. Studies in the Structure of the Urban Economy. Johns Hopkins University Press, Baltimore and London.
Ng, Cheng Feng. 2007. "Analyzing Anti-Sprawl Policies in a Location Model with Congestion, Agglomeration Economics, and Open Space," Working paper.
Nicol, C.J.. 2003. "Elasticities of demand for gasoline in Canada and the United States," Energy Economics, 25, 201–214.
Sullivan, A.M., 1983. The general equilibrium effects of congestion externalities. Journal of Urban Economics 14, 80–104.
Parry, Ian W. H. and Antonio Bento. 2001. "Revenue Recycling and the Welfare Effects of Road Pricing," The Scandinavian Journal of Economics, Vol. 103, No. 4., 645–671.
Parry, Ian W. H. and Kenneth A. Small. 2005. "Does Britain or the United States Have the Right Gasoline Tax?," The American Economic Review, Vol. 95, No. 4, 1276–1289.
Pines, David and Efraim Sadka. 1985. "Zoning, First-Best, Second-Best and Third-Best Criteria fro Allocating Land for Roads," Journal of Urban Economics, 17, 167–183.
Proost, Stef and Kurt Van Dender. 2001. "The welfare impacts of alternative policies to address atmospheric pollution in urban road transport," Regional Science and Urban Economics, 31, 383–411.
Puller, Steven L. and Lorna A. Greening. 1999. "Household adjustment to gasoline price change: an analysis using 9 years of US survey data," Energy Economics, 21, 37–52.
The Regional Transportation Assets Management System (RTAMS) websites; http://www.rtams.org/ui/homepage.asp
Saitoh, T. S., T. Shimada and H. Hoshi. 1996. "Modeling and Simulation of The Tokyo Urban Heat Island," Atmospheric Environment, Vol. 30, No. 20, 3431–3442.
Saitoh, Takeo S., Noboru Yamada, Daigo Ando and Kazuyoshi Kurata. 2005. "A Grand Design of Future Electric Vehicle to Reduce Urban Warming and CO_2 Emissions in Urban Area," Renewable Energy, 30, 1847–1860.
Santos, Georgina and Laurent Rojey. 2004. "Distributional Impacts of Road Pricing: The Truth Behind the Myth," Transportation, 31, 21–42.
Schmalensee, Richard and Thomas M. Stoker. 1999. "Household Gasoline Demand in The United States," Econometrica, Vol. 67, No. 3, 645–662.
Small, Kenneth and Kurt Van Dender. 2007 a. "Fuel Efficiency and Motor Vehicle Travel: The Declining Rebound Effect," Energy Journal, vol. 28, no. 1, 25–51.

Small, Kenneth and Kurt Van Dender. 2007 b. "If Cars Were More Efficient, Would We Use Less Fuel?," Access 31, Transportation Research at the Univercity of California, 8–13.

Smith, Barton A.. 1976. "The Supply of Urban Housing," The Quarterly Journal of Economics, Vol. 90, No. 3, 389–405.

Train K. E. 1976. "A post-BART model of mode choice: Some specification tests," WP No. 7620. Urban Travel Demand Forecasting Project, University of California at Berkeley.

Verhoef, Erik T.. 2005, "Second-Best Congestion Pricing Schemes in the Monocentric City," Journal of Urban Economics, 58, 367–388.

Wellisch, Dietmar. 1995. "Locational Choices of Firms and Decentralized Environmental Policy with Various Instruments," Journal of Urban Economics, 37, 290–310.

Wheaton, W. C.. 1974. "A Comparative Statics Analysis of Urban spatial Structure," Journal of Economic Theory, 9, 223–237.

World Resources Institute. 2007. "Addendum 1 to the Illinois Greenhouse Gas Emissions Inventory and Projections, Overview Report: Detailed Greenhouse Gase Emissions, Illinois Sectors," Prepared for the Illinois Climate Change Advisory Group.

Yatchew, Adonis and Joungyeo Angela No. 2001. "Household Gasoline Demand in Canada," Econometrica, Vol. 69, No. 6, 1697–1709.

U.S. Energy Information Administration.
http://www.eia.doe.gov/oiaf/1605/flash/flash.html

Zhu, Shanjiang, David Levinson and Lei Zhang. 2007. "An Agent-based Route Choice Model," Working paper.

著者略歴

平松　燈（ひらまつ・ともる）

1976 年：大阪府に生まれる。
2000 年：関西学院大学　総合政策学部　卒業
在学中、サティヤ・ワチャナ・キリスト教大学（インドネシア）へ交換留学
2003 年：大阪大学大学院　国際公共政策研究科　博士前期課程　修了　修士
2006 年：ニューヨーク州立大学バッファロー校　経済学部　M.A.
2010 年：ニューヨーク州立大学バッファロー校　経済学部　Ph.D
2012 年 2 月現在：ニューヨーク州立大学バッファロー校経済学部　博士研究員、
　　　　　　　　　カリフォルニア大学リバーサイド校 Edward J. Blakely CSSD
　　　　　　　　　（持続可能郊外開発センター）博士研究員

1976: Born in Osaka, Japan.
2000: B.A. in Policy Studies, Kwansei Gakuin University, Japan.
2000: Exchange Program, Satya Wacana Christian University, Indonesia.
2003: M.A. in International Public Policy, Osaka University, Japan.
2006: M.A. in Economics, State University of New York at Buffalo, USA.
2010: Ph.D. in Economics, State University of New York at Buffalo, USA.
As of February 2012: Post-Doctoral fellow, Edward J. Blakely Center for Sustainable
　　　　　　Suburban Development, University of California Riverside, USA.
　　　　　　Research Associate, Department of Economics, State University of
　　　　　　New York at Buffalo, USA.

Simulation Analysis of Urban Economy

2012 年 10 月 10 日初版第一刷発行

著　者　平松　燈

発行者　田中きく代
発行所　関西学院大学出版会
所在地　〒662-0891
　　　　兵庫県西宮市上ケ原一番町 1-155
電　話　0798-53-7002

印　刷　協和印刷株式会社

©2012 Tomoru Hiramatsu
Printed in Japan by Kwansei Gakuin University Press
ISBN 978-4-86283-122-4
乱丁・落丁本はお取り替えいたします。
本書の全部または一部を無断で複写・複製することを禁じます。
http://www.kwansei.ac.jp/press